# THE PRINCESS WHO CHANGED THE WORLD

### Nicholas Davies

**BLAKE**

B DIANA

Published by Blake Publishing Ltd,
3 Bramber Court, 2 Bramber Road,
London W14 9PB, England

First published in hardback in Great Britain 1997
Published in paperback 1998

ISBN 1 85782 380-X

British Library Cataloguing-in-Publication Data:
A catalogue record for this book is available
from the British Library.

Typeset by BCP

Printed in Great Britain by Creative Print and Design
(Wales), Ebbw Vale, Gwent

1 3 5 7 9 10 8 6 4 2

# Contents

# Chapter One

## Angel of Hope

Every so often during the last few years, the postman who delivered to Emma May's home in Copthorne, West Sussex, knew that her special friend had written young Emma another letter. He recognised those letters from Kensington Palace — he knew they were personal letters from Diana, Princess of Wales.

The postman knew that young Emma May was a girl of quite exceptional courage. She had been born with a rare chromosome disorder called Turner's Syndrome, which not only caused heart and kidney problems in young children but also stunted their growth. As a result, Emma had to make regular visits to Great Ormond Street Hospital for Children in London, staying there while she underwent difficult and painful stretching surgery. Doctors and nurses see many brave youngsters, but Emma May was exceptional.

Bright, blue-eyed Emma would lie in hospital for months at a time, wondering what the future held for

1

her. She had always been a sickly child, unable to enjoy the normal rigours and rough-and-tumble of childhood. Whenever she went into hospital, she knew it would mean pain, sometimes extreme pain, and always physical discomfort. When Emma was ten years old, the doctors and nurses at Great Ormond Street who cared for and nursed her had become so overwhelmed by her courage that in 1992 she was awarded the annual bravery prize for children who had triumphed over adversity.

The hospital's patron, Diana, Princess of Wales, came, as always, to present the award and it was then that she first met Emma.

After that meeting, Diana would tell staff, 'Her eyes are wonderful; she seems a remarkable child. How can she take such pain and still smile? She makes me feel ashamed.'

Diana never forgot young Emma. Indeed, the last letter Emma, now 16, received from Diana arrived at her home in July, only five weeks before Diana's fatal car crash.

Shortly after Diana presented her with the bravery award, Emma said, 'Diana has told me that I am her special friend. She is wonderful. She comes and sits on my bed and talks to me. I don't call her "Princess" any more, I just call her Diana, and she calls me Emma. That's because we're friends.'

Emma says of her relationship with Diana, 'So much of what has happened to me is down to Princess Diana. She has been an inspiration to me. Her support was invaluable to me when I felt down and rotten, but knowing she was thinking of me really helped me through some hard times.

'During that first meeting when I was ten, Diana

told me that I had to keep in touch with her, to write to her, telling her how I was getting on. I felt a bit silly writing to her and I never expected to receive a letter back. But she wrote back immediately, telling me how lovely it was hearing from me and asking me to keep writing, telling her how I was progressing. She really seemed interested.

'Some time later, I wrote to Diana again telling her that I was doing some fundraising for Great Ormond Street. The hospital had been so wonderful to me I wanted to do something in return. Once again, she immediately wrote back, with a wonderful big cheque for the fund. But she told me never to reveal how much she had sent so I won't, not even now. But I can say it was a big, big help.'

Emma May's last major surgery took place at the hospital in April 1995. But after that, Diana continued to keep in touch, writing to her parents, asking how she was getting on and then checking to see how she was progressing at school.

Emma commented, 'Diana never seemed to lose interest in me or in the hospital. She gave me the strength to face the future, to believe that one day everything would be fine and, because she told me, I believed her. She was such an extraordinary person that when she said something you believed her.'

Emma May was not the only child to have faith in Princess Diana. All over the world there are children who have met Diana in similar, disturbing situations and, somehow, she would encourage them to believe in themselves and have faith in the future. She gave them hope which they never forgot. And these are the children who will remember her all their lives.

On many occasions when Diana carried out her charity work, it had to be high profile so that the photographers and television crews could get their pictures and the journalists could write their pieces, encouraging those people who saw the good works the charities were carrying out to contribute, swelling the coffers with desperately needed funds. As patron of these charities, Diana was only too happy to pose for such activities. But some journalists would carp, exclaiming that she only appeared at such charitable functions when she knew the cameras would be present.

That was a slur on Diana's good name and totally untrue.

In fact, Diana saw far, far more ill, sick and dying patients, particularly children, when there were no cameras present to record the scene. And Diana preferred it that way because she discovered that on a one-to-one basis, particularly with children, they would relax more easily and become more confident.

The case of Bonnie Hendel was typical. Diana had met Bonnie at St Mary's Hospital, Paddington, in London, where she was lying in her sick bed, suffering from AIDS. She was just 12 years old. She had been diagnosed HIV-positive some years earlier, but no one knew how she had contracted the life-threatening disease.

During a tour of the AIDS ward where a number of children lay suffering, Diana met Bonnie who was desperately ill, lethargic and looking miserable. The doctors had warned Diana that they had no idea how long Bonnie had left to live. Diana noticed that Bonnie had not even touched her food that day and she sat and began talking to her, quietly encouraging her to try some of her dinner, trying also to kindle some spark and some hope into her life. After patiently chatting to Diana for ten minutes, Bonnie agreed to eat some food and Diana stayed with her until she had finished the entire meal. Afterwards, Diana met Bonnie's parents and although they all knew at that moment that Bonnie's future was indeed bleak, Diana asked them to keep in touch.

When Diana had left, Bonnie told the doctors, 'I don't need any more medicine, just lunch with Diana every day. She makes me feel better.'

Within days, Diana had written to Bonnie, wishing her well and enclosing a photograph of herself which Bonnie would keep by her bed and kiss every morning and every night. Within a matter of weeks, doctors at St Mary's phoned Kensington Palace asking that Diana be informed that Bonnie was only hours away from death. Diana was out, but as soon as she returned to the palace and received the urgent note, she immediately got into her car and was driven straight to the hospital, a 15-minute ride away.

As she walked into the hospital, Diana was told that Bonnie had died two hours earlier. Upstairs, her parents were in a private room, grieving. Diana went to join them, apologising for not having arrived in time. For 15 minutes, the three of them remained together in that room, their arms around each other's shoulders as the tears ran down their faces. Afterwards, Bonnie's mother told Diana, 'You were a heroine to Bonnie; she loved you.'

When Diana left the hospital some time later, she was holding a handkerchief to her eyes, trying to stem the tears. But there was not a photographer nor a journalist in sight. Diana had not taken the trouble to rush to Bonnie's bedside because she thought it might provide a photo for the next day's papers, but simply out of her love and concern for a helpless child dying of AIDS.

That was the real Diana, the person many will remember from similar meetings in circumstances which hospital patients will never forget. Few people ever knew of the afternoons and evenings Diana would drive to various hospitals and slip in unnoticed to make, and more importantly, to maintain, friendships which had often been forged when the patient was seriously ill. But the nation understood Diana's remarkable qualities of compassion and understanding. And that was the reason why hundreds of thousands of people came to say 'goodbye' to Diana at the moment of her death, bringing flowers, cards and mementoes to London's royal palaces, and why people who had never met her cried tears of dismay, shock and sorrow at her death. They believed in Diana because she showed tenderness for others, tried to help the homeless, the disadvantaged, the ill and the dying, supporting unfashionable charities which fight diseases such as AIDS and leprosy, and bringing hope and friendship where before there had been only despair and isolation.

In particular, it was Diana's remarkable relationship with children that people loved and admired. As Anne Houston, director of ChildLine Scotland, said, 'We were all struck by Diana's understanding of children's problems when she visited us in Glasgow. She had an amazing empathy with children and showed great interest in the training our volunteer counsellors receive.'

Danielle Stephenson was eight years old when she first met Diana. She had been admitted to Rose Ward at the Royal Brompton Hospital in Chelsea with an irregular heartbeat that doctors had to monitor.

'One day, we were told that someone very famous was coming to see us,' Danielle said, 'and we had no idea who it was. We thought it might have been a famous footballer. We had such a shock when we realised it was Diana. The first time we met, my friend Sophie, who was also on the ward, shook her hand. Then she told Diana that she had just been to the loo and had forgotten to wash her hands. Princess Di really laughed.'

Danielle met Diana on about 12 separate occasions. Whenever Danielle was admitted to the Royal Brompton, it seemed that Diana was on one of her visits, only two of which were covered by journalists.

'She would sit and talk to me and we talked about everything,' Danielle recalls. 'I told her about my guinea pigs and she would tell me that she used to keep guinea pigs and hamsters when she was a little girl. We even talked about Ricky and Bianca's wedding in *EastEnders*; she knew all about it. I would ask her about her boys, Prince William and Prince Harry, and she would tell me how they were getting on at school.'

Fortunately, Danielle was able to leave hospital in May 1996 but they met shortly afterwards when she and Diana attended a book launch to raise funds for the Royal Brompton's heart unit. 'As soon as she saw me, Diana came over and gave me a big hug and a kiss. That day, Diana insisted that Mum and me should call and see her at Kensington Palace the next time we were visiting the hospital.

'I called Diana one day in April this year and told her I had to visit the hospital as an outpatient that day and could she come and see me. She said she had a lunch appointment but said that Mum and me should go to the Palace afterwards to see her. We were late getting to London and had to rush to get to the Palace on time. It was a very hot day and we felt funny going up to the Palace and asking for the Princess. But as soon as she heard we were there, she came rushing downstairs. She gave me a big cuddle and took us upstairs. She gave us cold drinks and we stayed for a chat. There were presents, too ... a pair of initialled necklaces for me and my sister Natasha.'

Danielle's mother, Denise Stephenson, said, 'The Princess seemed to love giving presents. Once she brought Danielle a beautiful cake and she seemed more excited about it than Danielle. Some time later, Danielle had to go back into hospital at short notice and I was caught unprepared. That evening, my husband brought me an overnight bag but forgot to pack any underwear for me. Later, Diana came to see how Danielle was and, as we chatted, I mentioned that I had no change of underwear.

'Straight away, Diana said that I should have told her sooner as she would have brought something of hers to lend me. Then, to my astonishment, she insisted that I bring my laundry round to Kensington Palace rather than take it home to Southend, so that she could arrange for someone to wash and iron it for us. It was a remarkable, spontaneous kindness. That's the sort of person she was. And she always made Danielle feel wonderful ... you could see the spark in her eyes when she knew Diana was coming to visit.'

Such visits to hospitals throughout London and south-east England took place on a weekly basis during the last ten years of Diana's life. The great majority of them were private visits, never open to the Press and always gauged so that Diana could spend time chatting to some of the seriously ill patients. She would never walk into a ward, nod a few times at the patients, smile and then disappear. She wanted to meet people, particularly children or those the doctors felt her visits would help. And she would say to the doctors, 'Just tell me if I can be of particular help and I will do whatever you think is best.'

Victoria Hemphill, 14, from 'Derry in Northern Ireland, was a patient at Harefield Hospital in Middlesex before Christmas 1996, recovering from a transplant operation after her body had rejected a new heart.

'I was feeling pretty down about everything when I heard that Princess Diana was coming to visit,' Victoria said. 'At first, I couldn't believe it. I was so excited I forgot to ask for her autograph, but the second time she visited me I remembered. Someone took a photo of us together and she signed that for me, too. It was fabulous.'

Speaking after Diana's death, Victoria said, 'Quite often when Diana came to visit I was feeling pretty low, but when I heard she would be coming to see me, I would chirp up and feel much better. I always wondered what she would be wearing and what she would say. She was always bright and chirpy and she made me feel better. Sometimes she used to talk to me about how annoying the Press were towards her, never giving her a chance. When the newspapers teased her for wearing black nail polish, I told her that

I was on her side because I thought it was nice. It was amazing. A few weeks later, she came to see me again and she remembered the nail polish. She brought me the black nail polish as a present and then sat down and painted my nails for me. She was just wonderful.'

For a few months, Diana would visit Victoria at the hospital every week. Diana sent her presents, including a signed photograph of her, William and Harry, a bouquet of flowers and fashion magazines.

Victoria commented, 'We would discuss everything. During the summer of 1997 we talked about landmines and the need to get rid of them ... we discussed the new Prime Minister, Tony Blair. She told me they got on pretty well together. Diana even gave me her home phone number and told me I could call her at any time just for a chat. But I never did.

'I think Diana grew to trust me. Some people seemed to be nervous talking to Diana because she was a Princess, but I got to know her really well. We always got on well. She was like a big sister to me rather than a mother, but we talked a lot about William and Harry.

'She told me once that she had to take William to Great Ormond Street Hospital when he got hit on the head with a golf ball. She told me that she used to do little extra things for Harry because he would never be King like William, and she felt sorry for him. She talked about them so often I felt as though I knew them. She told me that when I got better I could go to Kensington Palace and meet them.

'I am so sad that she has died and that I'll never meet her again. She was a real friend to me, my best friend. I am lucky to have met her and been cheered up so often by her and I will always remember the happiness she brought me.'

Princess Diana became involved with three-year-old Darius Wyke-Little when she made one of her impromptu visits to Great Ormond Street Hospital. The first day she saw him, Darius was critically ill with a chromosome disorder and serious heart defects. His parents were so fearful for his life that they lived in the hospital day and night, willing him to stay alive.

His mother, Jane Wyke-Little from Leatherhead in Surrey, recalled, 'At that time, Darius was so ill we didn't know whether he would ever leave the hospital. When Diana came in to see him, there was a feeling of excitement in the ward among the parents and children and I always wondered whether he somehow sensed that excitement. That first time we met, our lives were a constant grind of doom and gloom but, somehow, she was able to lift our spirits and gave us hope that all would eventually be well.

'Although he was so young, he began to remember who she was whenever she came to see him. We would pick her out if he saw her on television or in a newspaper. Every time she came to the hospital, she would make a point of coming to the ward, talking to us and the nurses and doctors, checking on his condition. Then she would talk to us. I could tell she was genuinely concerned for him. Once she came in and he was sound asleep. She didn't want to wake him but she went up to his cot and gently laid her hand on him, a wonderful touch that made me realise what a remarkably compassionate woman she was.

'We always counted ourselves lucky that Diana came into our lives. She meant a lot to Darius, though he had no real idea who she was. But she gave us hope and confidence and that rubbed off on Darius.'

And there were others who will never forget Diana's generosity of spirit.

Alan and Janette Murray, from Clapton in East London, had been told that their two-year-old daughter, Mary-Jan, had only a 50-50 chance of survival after she underwent two major operations to repair a hole in her heart. The couple were sitting at their baby's bedside at Great Ormond Street when Diana arrived.

Janette said, 'No one had any idea the Princess was coming until 30 minutes before she arrived. We will never forget the moment she walked into Mary-Jan's room. She just lit up the room. She radiated a kind of calm, warm feeling. Diana stood beside Mary-Jan who was sleeping and asked about her treatment, the operation, what we were expecting. That week was the worst we had ever had to face. We were desperate, fearing she would die, fearing we would never see her at home again.

'We told her the truth ... we told her we thought Mary-Jan was going to die. Diana was wonderful, calm and purposeful. She told us that she felt, having talked to the doctors, that Mary-Jan would probably pull through. She seemed convinced she would survive and her positive attitude gave us strength and courage. Meeting Diana that day was something special, something that we will never forget for the rest of our lives. When we were at our lowest point, Diana gave us hope. Mary-Jan is alive and getting stronger every month and we are now looking at a bright future with her. But Diana is gone.'

Eleven-year-old Joy Bradbury woke up in the

Royal Brompton Hospital having undergone open-heart surgery. She was still critically ill, hovering between life and death, and doctors weren't sure whether she would survive the trauma of the operation. She was still on a ventilator and unable to speak. She had drifted in and out of consciousness, watched by doctors and nurses who kept her under constant supervision. Then she awoke again and standing by her bedside was a woman with blonde hair smiling down at her, a woman in jeans and a sweater whom Joy instantly recognised. It was Diana. Until that moment, Joy had not even had the strength to smile and her eyes had appeared listless to the nurses who were caring for her. Suddenly, a smile crept across her face and her eyes lit up.

'It was a wonderful, magical moment,' said her mother, Doreen, who was there at her bedside. Diana gave her the will to live because she showed she cared for Joy. By her presence, Diana had made Joy and the family feel special. And she never lost contact. Thank God, Joy made a wonderful recovery and, last Christmas, she received a card from Diana wishing her well. That's the sort of person she was, always thinking of other people, putting ordinary people first, caring for them. That's why everyone was so distraught at her death.'

Diana also became involved in helping the parents of tiny, vulnerable babies who were seriously ill, giving her support and encouragement. The first time Paul and Jo Thompson from Oxhey, Hertfordshire, met Diana was when she came to visit the Paediatric Intensive Care Unit at St Mary's Hospital, Paddington in West London. Their son, Harry, only 12 months old, was suffering from a rare disease which destroys the lungs.

'Diana came to comfort us and give us support shortly after Harry's first birthday. We were there sitting by his cot when she came to visit. She held his hand and chatted to us as though she was part of our family. She was so sincere, you could just tell she was genuine ... she had this compassionate aura about her. She was wonderful. She said she would keep in touch and that somehow gave us hope.

'A month after her visit, however, we were told by doctors that Harry would never recover from the bronchiolitis. Somehow, Diana heard that Harry would die and she sent us a handwritten note expressing her concern and sympathy. She wished us all the best. It meant a lot to us. At that moment, our lives were falling apart and it was so lovely to know that someone like her cared for us and for Harry. There was no reason for Diana to write that letter — no one knew about it — and yet she took the trouble to do so, to show she cared.'

In fact, shortly after receiving the letter from Diana, baby Harry began to improve. Jo said, 'It is a miracle that Harry is still here. They thought he only had weeks to live but somehow he has pulled through and he's getting stronger and stronger. I wish Diana could see him now.'

Dr Parviz Habibi, director of the Paediatric Intensive Care Unit, said, 'When Harry deteriorated so seriously we notified Diana because she had asked us to keep her informed of his progress. Once Diana pledged her support to a patient, she did so in style. We knew she was a genuine and honest person — she proved it time and again. Harry's parents had gone through hell with worry and she gave them moral support when they desperately needed it. That was why she was such a remarkable person.'

However, there were very few who realised the stress, the extraordinary toll those secret hospital visits took on Diana. She would arrive back at Kensington Palace, walk up to her bedroom on the second floor and collapse on the bed, lying there crying and distraught at the suffering of the children she had seen that day. She felt their pain and wretchedness. Throughout her visits, she would always be the smiling, upbeat, happy Princess, but the distress she witnessed, week in, week out, took its toll, draining her and leaving her physically exhausted.

And yet, it wasn't only children who benefited from Diana's warmth and compassion. When Prince Charles fell from his pony while playing polo during the summer of 1991, breaking his arm, Diana rushed to the Nottingham hospital that evening to be with him. Lying in a coma in the hospital's Intensive Care Unit was Dean Woodward, a local Nottingham man, who had been involved that day in a serious car crash. Diana noticed an old woman waiting nearby in some distress and went to see if she was all right. The woman, Dean Woodward's mother, explained to her that her son was dangerously ill and she was worried that he might not recover.

Later, Dean said, 'I was told that Diana immediately came to see me lying in Intensive Care and put her hand on my leg and gently rubbed it, as though giving some comfort to me. She told my wife that she hoped and prayed that I would pull through. She also told her that she thought I would.

'Some time later, I was recuperating in hospital and, out of the blue, Diana phoned and asked me if I wanted anything. I told her that it would be great to see her. To my astonishment, she came to visit me one day when I was recovering at my uncle's house in Nottingham. She came the following January. A few hours before she arrived, a car drew up outside and four or five bodyguards came in to check the house to see if it was safe for the Princess. She stayed and chatted for two hours. It was great. We talked about everything under the sun, just as you would with any friend.'

Dean's wife, Jane, commented, 'When she said she would come and see us I thought it was a prank, especially when these men came in to check out the house. When I saw her get out of the car, I just wanted to run away. But within minutes of her walking in, everything was fine and I felt really relaxed. When she talked to us, it seemed we were all on the same level. She wasn't posh or anything, just normal like one of us. She always seemed natural and so charming. We spent some of the time talking about her boys and she talked about ours, just like you would with anyone. I shall never forget her.

'Even after that visit, Diana would keep in touch, phoning once a week and chatting to Dean's uncle who would tell her how his nephew was progressing because Dean had not fully recovered from his head injury. Even two years later when he was fully fit, Diana would write once or twice a year, asking how we were all coping and wishing us well. We received the last letter in June, ten weeks before she died. It seems extraordinary that a Princess should still keep in touch with us after such a long time. It shows what a wonderful person she was.'

To one or two people, whom Diana came to

know very well, relationships born out of anguish and sorrow became almost permanent friendships from which it seemed Diana, too, gained strength to face the future after the break-up of her marriage. It was the incurable illness of their daughter Louise that brought Philip and Judy Woolcock to Diana's attention.

Diana befriended the family, helping them to cope first with the nightmare of Louise's terminal cancer and, later, with the struggle to continue their lives without their beloved daughter. Gradually, Diana began to confide in them as well, talking about the failure of her marriage, her love for her sons and, during August, the new happiness she had found with Dodi Fayed.

The Woolcocks, both teachers from Poulton-le-Fylde, Lancashire, never spoke of their friendship with Diana because they felt she wouldn't have wanted any publicity over a matter so private.

Philip Woolcock, 45 and a former social worker, talked of the tragic death of his daughter and the friendship that arose as a result.

'Louise was 18 and looking forward to university when she was diagnosed as having a virulent form of cancer. We took the decision to protect her from the knowledge that she was dying, trying instead to help her through a traumatic course of chemotherapy.

'But Louise was so wonderfully brave that she began raising money for a cancer charity to help others. Diana heard of her efforts and came to see her in the summer of 1991. That first meeting was magic. They had lunch together, talking for an hour and both giggling like schoolgirls. Louise was always incredibly loquacious and bubbly and I think Diana was moved because she felt Louise should have had her whole life ahead of her.'

At the end of that first meeting, Philip Woolcock asked Diana if she would open the local day hospice being established in honour of his daughter and Diana told him to write to her but, 'she could promise nothing'. On 28 July 1992, Diana came to open the hospice but Louise had come out of remission and was close to death.

Philip continued the story. 'By any normal scale Louise should not have been alive for that visit, but the thought of meeting the Princess again seemed to instil in her a new-found strength and determination. Even though she was full of morphine, she forced herself into a wheelchair and out into the reception area. When Diana arrived, she almost bounded up to Louise and they were soon giggling again as they had done during that first meeting. It was wonderful to see. But one week later, Louise was dead.'

Diana was informed by the hospital of her death and the Woolcocks received a telegram of condolence from Diana. Shortly afterwards, Diana phoned and asked if she could come and see them.

'We spent a long time just sitting talking with her in a small room,' said Philip. 'It was about this time that the newspapers were full of Diana's marriage problems and she looked tired and distraught. Her knuckles were white, her eyes full of tears.

'Eventually, I asked her how she was and suddenly it all came spilling out ... about her marriage, her distress ... her loneliness. She said, "I've had 11 years of this and I'm getting out."

'Judy and I were amazed that the future Queen of England was sitting in our living room confiding in us. She spoke with an honesty and an understanding that we had never experienced with anybody else. But that visit from Diana made us both realise that life was worth living despite our terrible loss.'

From 1992 until a few days before her death, Diana kept in touch with the Woolcocks, primarily through long phonecalls.

Judy recalled one famous conversation. 'My son Sam had had his navel pierced and his hair bleached and I told Diana about it and she laughed, saying, "Gosh, I don't know what my mother-in-law would do if William did that!"

'She also told me that she didn't know how she would cope with the situation when William found his first girlfriend. She said, "I don't think there's anyone on the scene at the moment ... I hope!"'

During her last phonecall to the Woolcocks in August 1997, Diana had sounded bubbly and happy.

'She spent 15 minutes chatting away to us about everything — children, holidays, work,' said Philip. 'She sounded so happy and we both felt happy for her. We expected the relationship between Dodi and Diana to continue and then we woke on the Sunday to the terrible news. We were devastated. We feel we have been privileged knowing Diana so well but now she is gone we will miss her terribly. I just want people to know what a wonderful difference she made to so many people's lives.'

The general public never realised that Diana spent so much of her time, both during the day and in the evening, secretly visiting any number of seriously ill patients in hospitals in and around London. She was often criticised by the media for spending too much of her time keeping fit in London's smart health clubs or visiting alternative therapy centres, which many people found strange. It appeared that she had little time for anything else in her life. They didn't realise that Diana would spend time each day writing letters, often by hand, to hospital patients young and old, whom she had met throughout the past year or more, comforting and lifting their spirits, working wonders by giving them hope for the future when all seemed bleak.

In the great majority of her private visits to hospitals, Diana would arrive alone, often having driven herself. She would telephone before leaving Kensington Palace, asking if it was 'OK' for her to visit. Unlike any other member of the Royal Family, she preferred to arrive without a bodyguard, a lady-in-waiting or a secretary. She always preferred to chat to patients face to face, especially children, with no one else around, so that the atmosphere would be more personal and less formal.

Diana also appreciated the work the teams of doctors, surgeons, consultants and nurses put in, day-in, day-out, never sparing themselves when patients needed their expertise. Robert Creighton, Chief Executive of the Great Ormond Street Hospital, explained, 'For 18 months we cared for a poor little Bosnian girl, Irma, aged eight, who had been seriously injured when a bomb exploded near her during the fighting in 1993. Irma was paralysed from the head down and we tried to make her life easier. Diana came to visit her once or twice. She would sit with her and stroke her forehead and would encourage the little girl to smile, trying to give some encouragement to the child who for so long hovered between life and death. And then, sadly, on 31 March

1995, Irma died. The following day, Diana was phoned and told that Irma had died and she asked if she could come and meet all the staff who had been involved with caring for the little girl. There was probably a core of about a dozen doctors and nurses who had been closely involved with Irma, and she came and met each and every one of them. It was a sad, moving experience for all those people and Diana. But the staff really appreciated that she wanted to come and say "thank you" to them for all their care and nursing of the little Bosnian girl that no one in England knew anything about.

'There were no cameras, no journalists present. There was only Diana. It was typical of her. She felt for people, understood them like no one ever had before. I often witnessed her meeting parents and sick children, and I must tell you it was always a remarkably moving experience. Both the parents and children seemed to trust her instantly, to gravitate towards her as though they had known her for ages. Usually, in hospitals, children take time to adapt to a stranger, but not to Diana. She had an instant rapport with them that was warm and natural, and children responded to her. It was wonderful to see. I can honestly say that Diana's presence will be impossible to replace. She was unique.'

Diana, however, would also gain strength and a warm feeling of well-being, that she was giving something of herself to other people far less fortunate than her. She understood that she was living a privileged existence and she felt that visiting the very sick and the disadvantaged was a personal duty which she grew to love. She had begun her private visits after years of feeling sorry for herself, often indulging in her own misery because of what she saw was a painful existence, being trapped in a loveless marriage. Diana came to recognise that she had an extraordinary capacity for unhappiness which is one reason why she wanted to encourage others to overcome their sadness. Diana genuinely felt the pain of others and responded to it out of a sincere concern for those who were suffering both mentally and physically.

When she began to visit hospitals as a form of therapy, and saw children suffering, often fighting for their very lives, it hit her hard and made her feel that her own troubles were as nothing compared to theirs. It became her own personal therapy and the more she visited hospitals privately, the more she realised that her own misery was of little or no consequence. It also stopped her from returning to those dark days of her life when she was unable to control her eating habits, when she became so wrapped up in her own wretchedness. The sick children gave Diana a feeling that her life could be useful, that she was carrying out a mission that she was good at, by giving of herself and focussing her compassion on others.

And there was, of course, all the other charity work — the public, high-profile visits in front of photographers and television crews and throngs of journalists, which she didn't enjoy half as much. But she knew that that work was all very necessary, for it encouraged people to put their hands into their purses and pockets and contribute to worthy causes. The charities needed the money to carry on their wonderful work and Diana understood that her presence gave their coffers a boost of much-needed income. For that reason alone, she was happy to help.

Perhaps one of Diana's most courageous and remarkable public coups was her decision to become involved with AIDS patients when the disease was almost a taboo subject in many circles in Britain. She felt that AIDS victims were being unfairly treated, even shunned by society, particularly by 'the great and the good' of many who worked for charity organisations. She also realised that many members of the general public had become fearful of AIDS victims, believing that if they came too close, or kissed or touched an AIDS sufferer, they, too, would be immediately infected, and very possibly die.

It was in April 1987 that Diana agreed to open Britain's first purpose-built ward for AIDS patients at London's Middlesex Hospital. The newspapers were amazed that a royal such as Princess Diana, the mother of two young sons, would take such an enormous risk as meeting AIDS patients 'without wearing protective clothing'. Shocked and dismayed, many people thought that Diana's decision to shake the hand of a man who was dying of AIDS was foolhardy at best and stupid at worst.

Diana's determination to break down the prejudice that surrounded AIDS and her personal commitment to that task were primarily responsible for ordinary people, charities and the Government adopting a more relaxed and understanding attitude to the disease.

As Pamela, Lady Harlech, an AIDS fund-raiser, said, 'One cannot overestimate the importance of what Diana did the day she touched an AIDS patient with her bare hand. At a stroke, it changed people's conception of the disease. And when in New York, Diana picked up a baby with AIDS and cuddled her, completely taking all the stigma out of the disease.'

Nick Partridge, Director of the Terence Higgins Trust, a charity that cares for AIDS patients, revealed that Diana's interest in helping to de-stigmatise AIDS didn't end there.

'She wanted to keep abreast of the scientific and medical advances being made in the search for a cure for AIDS. Every two or three months, I would brief her, informing her of the medical advances and the up-to-the-minute treatments for sufferers. She never lost interest.'

And there was leprosy, the highly infectious bacterial disease which results in severe physical deformities. Diana realised that, like AIDS sufferers, lepers were being shunned across the world, rejected by people frightened of coming into contact with them or even touching them.

Baptist Minister Tony Lloyd, executive director of the Leprosy Mission based in Peterborough, spoke of Diana's personal involvement in the charity.

'Our first trip together was to Harare in Zimbabwe in 1993 and I noticed that Diana was looking at a woman with no fingers. After a short while, Diana went behind a partition in the hospital and I saw she was crying. A little while later, after she had composed herself, Diana told me that she hadn't been crying for the woman but because of the thankfulness that she was finally getting proper help and treatment.

'Diana was completely without racial prejudice. She would talk to blacks and whites in the same way and was completely fearless for herself. We flew to a refugee camp near the Mozambique border and she was happily shaking hands with all of them and talking and joking with them as if she had known them for ages. Once, I heard someone in Africa say that Diana was like sunshine coming to visit them, for she had this incredible charisma and, I have to say, I was in awe of it.

'I believe she sympathised with lepers because she realised they had been both rejected and cast out from society, forced to live like outsiders for ever, until they eventually died. It seemed to me that, in her care of lepers, Diana was searching for a spiritual dimension. The more I came to know her and work with her, the more I felt, in the last couple of years, that she had found a sort of peace in her life and seemed much clearer in her purpose.'

Tony Lloyd added, 'Princess Diana brought three things to the leprosy cause. First, a high profile; second, money, personal money from her own bank account to the tune of thousands of pounds which no one ever knew about; and third, she helped to overcome the stigma of leprosy as she had with AIDS. She touched lepers, she held children dying of leprosy in her arms, nursing and caring for them. No one in her position had ever done anything like that before and we thank God for her.'

Caring for people in secret had become Diana's personal therapy but, because the Press and the public had little knowledge of that part of her life, there were also very few who knew of another side of Diana's complex character.

# Chapter Two

# The Party Girl

The handful of close personal friends who knew Diana really well will miss a side of her personality that few were privileged to know — her fun.

Everyone remembered the newspaper stories of 'Shy Di', the blushing, youthful bride with little or no confidence who was too nervous to make a speech in public. And so she was.

At school and in her teens, Diana was, however, always a giggler, one of those girls who, if she began to giggle, had trouble stopping, so she would not only go on and on but her laugh would become infectious, encouraging other girls and schoolfriends until a whole dormitory or class were giggling uncontrollably.

And yet, despite her natural reserve, Diana did earn a reputation at school for getting into mischief, though her teachers recalled it was generally not of a serious nature. She would, however, try to make classmates smile or giggle, she encouraged others to be naughty in class and she loved to tickle her friends until some of them were screaming for her to stop. But, apparently, Diana did nothing that landed her in serious trouble.

There were two examples of Diana's sense of fun that she first enjoyed during her schooldays and never forgot. She loved practical jokes. It was at school that she first experienced them and was renowned for being the joker in her class. If there was trouble in the classroom or the dormitory, Diana was often discovered to be the perpetrator. She would invariably be the girl making apple-pie beds for her friends and was usually the first to throw flour-filled bombs, made with socks and handkerchiefs, around the room.

And then there was mimicry. Once again, she learned to imitate others while at school and it was an art form she would practise for the rest of her life whenever the opportunity arose. One of the reasons she got into trouble at school was because she would study the voices and mannerisms of the teachers, reducing the class to giggles and laughter before the teacher walked into the room to take the lesson. Nearly always, Diana was the culprit.

A year or so after her marriage and while staying at Balmoral with Prince Charles and the rest of the Royals, the family and guests were waiting for the Queen to walk into the drawing room, as they waited every evening of the week except Sunday. Diana suddenly began to impersonate the Queen and everyone turned to listen to her. She began with the Queen's famous phrase 'My husband and I'. Diana's take-off was brilliant but unfortunately rather ill-timed. She hadn't noticed the Queen walk into the room until it was too late. The polite laughter ceased abruptly and Diana blushed to the roots of her hair. No one said a word but Diana realised that her mother-in-law was not amused. She never repeated the joke.

Throughout her life, Diana used her powers as a mimic but always for what she saw as innocent fun. She would impersonate waiters and servants, prime ministers and presidents, senior clergymen as well as those in high places who worked around the royal palaces. She was particularly adept at imitating Scottish accents, as well as those from India and the sub-continent. She was not so strong on American accents, but foreigners trying to speak English was her party piece, reducing friends to tears as they roared with laughter.

And yet, when Diana first moved to London as a teenager, she was painfully shy. She had led a sheltered life at home in Northamptonshire and at her boarding schools far removed from the hurly-burly of a city day-school. As a result, her first tentative steps into the great social whirl of London's youth scene was somewhat traumatic. At parties, Diana would stand with a drink in her hand and hope to find a friend to chat to because she hadn't the confidence of some of the girls who would happily start conversations with other girls or the object of their attentions, the young men. Diana was awfully shy of boys, never daring to make the first move. She would, however, see a group of teenagers or twenty-something girls chatting together and walk up to join them but, even then, she would usually remain silent, preferring simply to listen to the conversation, laugh at the right places but always being careful not to draw attention to herself by saying something controversial or silly. On the occasions she did pluck up the courage to speak out, she would usually blush and then smile nervously, not daring to look to see if people were staring at her.

It took some years for Diana to gain the confidence to laugh out loud, chat happily to strangers and become the centre of attention. But during the last ten years of her life, a new Diana emerged like a butterfly, her nerves conquered, her confidence riding high.

There appeared to be three main reasons for Diana's new-found confidence. Undeniably, William and Harry meant that Diana could meet and chat to other mothers about their children on an equal basis, sharing experiences, discussing the responsibilities, the tedium and the fun of motherhood as well as the antics of their respective sons. As soon as William began attending school in London, Diana was keen to become involved with other parents, inviting their young sons and daughters to Kensington Palace so that William would have friends his own age to play with. From the beginning, Diana was determined that her children would grow up in as natural and normal an environment as possible, which meant having friends from different social backgrounds.

Diana loved to take William, and later Harry, to other people's homes so they would grow up experiencing other, less restrictive ways of life. These acquaintances didn't live in palaces, waited on hand and foot by servants, footmen and maids. And she would also invite parents back to Kensington Palace where everyone would sit around tucking in to children's tea, eating biscuits, jelly, ice cream and crisps. From the age of five it would be beefburgers, or chicken nuggets, and usually with chips, tomato sauce and Coke.

Diana adored playing the role of mother. As far as she was concerned, she loved inviting four or five children to the Palace, and hearing the noise of screaming, chattering youngsters echoing along the usually quiet, sombre corridors. The young friends would usually all sit in the kitchen and Diana would feed them, often other children as well as her own, picking things off the floor, clearing up the spilt food and drink, wiping the children's clothes with damp cloths and finally wiping and drying hands and faces. She revelled in the domesticity and the fun of having other children to tea. These weren't parties — these were simply afternoon teas for a few children so that William and Harry could play with them, learning to understand the hurly-burly of squabbles and the lessons of give and take.

But such innocent pleasures gave Diana confidence. Later, that confidence would be reflected in the way she dealt with total strangers, the hundreds of people she met through her charities, many on a one-to-one basis. She was never shy with dealing with those who felt as she had done in her dark days, rejected and lonely with no hope for the future. With all these people, young and old, she exuded such confidence that those with whom she was talking felt an immediate understanding, even a bond, with this total stranger, feeling little or no discomfort at chatting casually with a real, live Princess.

And at adult parties thrown by friends after her split from Prince Charles, Diana became far more outgoing. Gone was the blushing young woman who hid behind others or sat alone. The new Diana, born in the early 1990s, would walk into a party thrown by one of her friends with a big smile on her face and usually some flowers for the hostess. These were intimate dinner parties or occasional cocktail evenings where Diana knew most of the guests and where she felt among friends. These were the occasions when Diana felt relaxed and under no pressure whatsoever, where no one bothered about what she was wearing or what the latest gossip about her in the newspapers had been.

And she would laugh and enjoy the evening, pass remarks, some of them unflattering, about mutual friends, but she would shy away from being vicious or cutting. She had endured too many such experiences herself and she knew how hurtful such remarks could be. She enjoyed those nights probably more than anyone else present. And those who attended would recall the pleasure Diana derived from such gatherings, spending much of the evening laughing and giggling, sometimes hardly able to control herself, gripping her sides as the laughter started to hurt.

Only in public did Diana approach things more seriously. When she was on duty, particularly anything concerning her charity work, whether visiting patients or chatting with charity directors at Kensington Palace, Diana was always sensitive to the particular demands of the job. In private, however, she was always prepared to enjoy the lighter side of life. She saw a divide, a distinction between her public and her private responsibilities. She would crack jokes about herself, put herself down, talk in an unflattering way about her intelligence, her body, her sporting achievements, always self-deprecatingly, not to draw attention to herself but simply because she didn't take herself that seriously. One of the reasons she so detested the protocol of the Royal Family was because of the sober regard everyone had for themselves. No one was ever prepared to crack a joke at their own expense, particularly some of the senior courtiers, many of whom she believed never smiled!

She would deliberately make pretty appalling jokes at dinner parties at Kensington Palace when Prince Charles was entertaining, purely in an effort to break the ice. She hated the fact that everyone sat around the table poker-faced, speaking in the most stilted and stultifying way because they were dining with members of the Royal Family.

Diana would often try to inject some fun into proceedings, often to the amazement of her fellow diners.

On one occasion, she and Charles were having dinner with Prince Andrew and Sarah, as well as other guests. Sarah butted in saying that she had a new joke, and began, 'What smells worse than an anchovy?'

Before anyone else dared guess, Diana quipped, 'An anchovy's bottom.'

Sarah and Diana fell about laughing, but Charles found the joke distasteful and ill-mannered. The two young women had only been having fun. It was another case of Diana not taking herself terribly seriously and misjudging the general attitudes of the group.

Annabel Goldsmith, a friend of Diana's for many years, will never forget her sense of humour and, more especially, her smile.

'She loved to be in situations where there was no protocol,' said Annabel, 'where everyone was natural and cared nothing for tradition, and that was why she loved being in people's homes with their families.

'I will miss her radiant smile as she would arrive at our house bursting through the door — it was always a burst — and hugged us all, so full of life and happiness at the thought of a few hours' escape from what I knew to have been a lonely existence.

'My home in the country was simply the rock or the haven that she could turn to for escape, where she knew she would never be betrayed. Everyone liked her and she seemed to like everyone, especially all the children. She would tease everyone in the family and we would all tease her back as though she was a part of our family. She had an incredibly wicked sense of humour.

'Sunday lunch at our country house is often chaotic with lots of people sitting around a large table. She would come down to Richmond from Kensington Palace with the boys and would help to prepare the meal, doing whatever was necessary as she kept an eye on the youngsters. Everyone helps themselves and lunch is eaten so fast that Diana eventually started to time us. 'Right,' she would say, 'today was an all-time record ... fifteen minutes.' Laughter would ring round the table and everyone would speak and shout and talk at the same time. There was no ceremony during those Sunday lunches and Diana loved it.'

Annabel Goldsmith would recall those lunches with affection and warmth, happy that at her home Diana could be the natural, happy person the world never knew. Diana would be totally involved in the repartee that shot round the dining room table, showing people who didn't know her that well just how different she was in the flesh to the person they read about in the newspapers. Quick-witted, smiling and vivacious, Diana would enthrall and surprise guests at such lunches and teas.

And after lunch, Diana would never leave the work for other people. Annabel Goldsmith recalled, 'After coffee, she would often offer to take the cups out to the kitchen — and just as often, I would find her wearing the bright yellow rubber gloves and doing the washing up. If I tried to stop her, she would tell me to go away.'

And Annabel Goldsmith spoke of their last meeting. 'One of my most enduring memories is of her last visit this summer when she came to lunch with the boys after their holiday in St Tropez with the Fayeds. I can still picture her, sitting on the sofa cuddling Harry — she was always cuddling him — and exchanging quips with William as mothers usually do with their teenage sons.'

There was nothing Diana enjoyed more than spending time at other people's houses with William and Harry, showing them how other people lived, how other families responded and interacted with each other. They saw how ordinary people cracked jokes, teased each other, ran around, made mistakes, indulged in fights and arguments and, above all, had fun and enjoyed themselves. She was always concerned that William and Harry, bought up in the tradition of the Royals, would never learn how to enjoy their lives and would become victims of their background and their destiny, their lives for ever to be dictated by protocol.

Receiving visitors and going to other people's homes were some of the most important occasions in Diana's life, but only when she took the boys with her. Some weekends, when the boys were home from boarding school, Diana would encourage them to visit other children or have school friends pop round to Kensington Palace. Somewhat timidly, Diana would phone mothers of children whom she knew were friendly with William and Harry.

'Are you doing anything with the boys this weekend?' she would ask.

Her friends would know that Diana was, in her inimitable way, either looking for an invitation or asking whether the family would want to visit the Palace.

'Would you like to come over?' was usually the answer and Diana's voice would change, happy in the knowledge that she and the boys were going out to a private house where there would be no Press, no photographers and no one who would dream of betraying the fact that she was visiting friends. There seemed to be an unwritten understanding that those with whom she mixed socially, or who knew her children, never discussed her private life or any of the nonsense that was written about her in the tabloids. Those that did raise such a matter were quietly dropped from Diana's list of confidants because she believed her private life was nothing whatsoever to do with others who could never know all the issues at stake.

Diana's smile and radiance as soon as she walked in  at the door would show how happy such an invitation made her.

Lady Cosima Somerset became a close confidante of Diana's only in the last 18 months of her life, but she would recall that, as a result, they spent a great deal of time seeing each other and chatting on the phone. They went on holidays together, spent weekends together, attended dinner parties together, took tea together and laughed and joked. They had fun in the way that Diana thoroughly enjoyed, the way she had learned as a girl at boarding school.

Cosima recalled a flight that she took with Diana to Lahore, Pakistan, to visit Imran Khan's cancer hospital.

'From the moment we boarded the plane we started laughing. We had planned our beauty sleep but realised that we were not going to sleep a wink. The pull-out beds were inadequately designed and mine was worst of all. Diana all but fell out of her bed and we began giggling like schoolgirls. It rapidly became a dormitory farce. But Diana loved it. She was relaxing, enjoying herself and laughing.

'We finally arrived at Lahore and, in desperation, after a night without sleep, Diana asked the pilot if he could go into a holding pattern. She disappeared into one of the bathrooms, emerging 15 minutes later looking breathtaking.'

On another occasion, Lady Cosima, who became almost another sister to Diana in the last months, spent a weekend with Diana in Majorca at the famous La Residencia Hotel. They even shared a suite together and, because the rain never stopped throughout the 48 hours they were in Majorca, the two women spent most of the time closeted together, chatting about all sorts of things and making the most of the enjoyable facilities on offer.

She recalled, 'We made use of every hotel facility that weekend. We would bump into each other going into and coming out of more and more outlandish treatments, seaweed on our eyebrows or covered in the debris of a clay bath. In fact, we became confused about which treatments we had had. At Sunday lunch we became, once again, helpless with laughter. The guests were quite elderly and it was very quiet in the dining room. But one of the staff had put "Je t'aime" on the music system and it was relayed into the dining room with all the moans and groans at full volume. It seemed louder and more comic because of the genteel tranquillity. We also seemed to be the only two who noticed it, and we couldn't stop laughing.'

At a dinner party thrown by Taki, the Greek playboy and *Spectator* columnist, before Christmas 1996, Diana was once more seen at her best — happy, up-beat and fun, the way her friends will always remember her. Afterwards, a group of Taki's friends came round to his house and a major party, typical of the high-living Greek millionaire, developed. Diana was seen by friends happily sitting cross-legged on the floor with a drink between her legs.

As a guest commented, 'I looked down to see two or three young woman sitting on the floor chatting away and thought how relaxed they were. They seemed to be laughing and giggling and having fun so I decided to join them. It was only then that I realised that one of them was Diana. I must say I had the shock of my life for no one had told me that the Princess of Wales would be present. I thought about the matter afterwards and realised how great it was that Diana could behave in such a natural way. I had never met her before and from that moment my view of her changed. She was fun, easy-going and ready to collapse with laughter along with the rest of us.'

After her separation in December 1992, Diana began throwing her own intimate dinner parties, often at weekends when William and Harry were away at boarding school. She started making phonecalls at some time during the week, fearing that she would be spending yet another Saturday night alone and despondent. Invitations for Diana to attend weekend house parties or simply Saturday night dinners had been legion but the moment that those aristocratic houses and their hostesses heard of Diana's marriage problems, the number of invitations slumped.

Unperturbed by what she saw as her fair-weather friends, Diana also invited couples to Kensington Palace.

Her dinner parties would always be informal, fun, light-hearted affairs, so unlike the more formal dinner parties she had attended with Prince Charles where many of the guests felt bound by protocol in the presence of the Prince and Princess of Wales. Diana was determined that her Saturday evening soirées would be nothing like that. Invariably, the evening would start with champagne and the meal itself would be organised relatively informally, often with people helping themselves to dishes laid out on the table while everyone sat around eating, drinking and chatting. There would always be music — Diana's type of music — reflecting her love of the more popular artists such as Elton John and Luciano Pavarotti.

There would also inevitably be laughter.

Diana also threw 'girls' evenings', when married and single women were invited to the Palace, encouraged to let their hair down and chatter about everyone and everything, drinking bottles of wine and having light, snacky food rather than formal dining.

As one of her former ladies-in-waiting who attended many of these gatherings recalled, 'There would usually be seven or eight of us sitting around the table gossiping and laughing and sometimes all talking at the same time, wanting to get a word in edgeways above the babble of voices. We were all thirty-somethings and yet it sounded as though we were all under twenty, desperate to have our say and make our point. But it was always such fun and Diana would be roaring with laughter.

'Quite often, some of the women, including Diana, would be wiping their tears from so much laughter. And that's how I will always remember her.'

# CHAPTER THREE

## IN THE BEGINNING

Diana Frances Spencer was born on Saturday, 1 July 1961, when Prince Charles was nearly 13 years old. Her arrival, unusually, only merited a nine-word announcement in *The Times*: 'Viscountess Althorp gave birth to a daughter on Saturday.'

The baby girl, born to be a Lady but destined to become a Princess, was the fourth child of Viscount Johnny Althorp, whose father was Earl Spencer and whose mother was Frances Roche, the daughter of the fourth Baron Fermoy and close friend of King George VI.

Their eldest child was Sarah, born in 1955, with whom Charles had an ongoing love affair before becoming involved with Diana. Jane, born in 1957, was their second daughter, and their third child, John, born in 1960, survived only ten hours. It was not until 1964 — three years after Diana was born — that Charles, the son and heir they had always wanted, arrived.

Diana was born at home, in the lovely ten-bedroom Victorian country home, Park House, on the Sandringham estate next door to the royal residence in a beautiful part of Norfolk. The Spencers were so unprepared for another girl that they hadn't even chosen a girl's name. And for the baby Diana, all was happiness. She immediately took to Joy Hearn, the midwife, and then her nanny as surrogate mothers and for the first month of her life slept in a cot in Joy Hearn's room.

Twenty years later, Joy Hearn would recall, 'Diana was breast-fed from the very beginning and I think that helped her be a perfectly happy and contented child. And she was wonderful ... I don't remember her ever waking me through the night.'

Diana's childhood years were happy. She followed her elder sisters wherever they went and learned to take the rough-and-tumble of being the youngest of three active girls. They would play around the estate, climbing trees, riding scooters and tricycles and tea trays were used as makeshift sleds to slide down the stone steps at the front of the house. Many people suspect that this carefree, rumbustious start in life was the reason behind Diana often being considered as something of a tomboy.

Some felt that Diana grew up being ignored, left to fend for herself when her two elder sisters wanted to play on their own, leaving Diana to fend for herself. She was certainly not made to feel special, which probably accounted for her strength of character. Early in Diana's life, she had to be self-reliant and no one was going to make life easy for her. And yet it wasn't that her parents ignored their youngest daughter, it was only that the Spencers' time and energies were split between all their children.

Although Diana was probably totally unaware of what was happening, the Spencers' marriage was going through rough times. Frances was bored with life in Norfolk and missed the social whirl of London's rich and famous.

One of Diana's nannies was Gertrude Allen, then a woman in her sixties with a wonderful reputation for bringing up the young sons and daughters of the aristocracy. She recalled, 'When Diana was born, her elder sisters treated Diana rather like a doll but they became tired of that as Diana began to walk and run and join in their games. Understandably, Diana wanted to be part of her elder sisters' fun, and that led to resentment at first, for Sarah and Jane simply didn't want a young child trying to take part in their games.'

But Diana would not give up and she tried to keep up with her elder sisters even though she was not quite old enough. Eventually, Sarah and Jane accepted their baby sister and she would join in many of their activities. But their nanny — 'Ally', as she was called by the children — also remembered Diana's reaction to the arrival of baby Charles.

'She adored Charles and treated him just like a doll in the same way as her sisters had treated her. She would dress him in clothes, undress him and then start again but the sweet boy didn't seem to mind too much. She was very kind to him and very sweet.'

Johnny Althorp's new-found confidence after finally producing an heir made him a happy man. He loved his quiet, peaceful life as a gentleman farmer. He had managers to help him work the farm. He enjoyed being one of the most important people in Norfolk's small society scene. And his children saw a great deal of their father, especially at night before bedtime when he would play their favourite game — 'bears' — in which the broad-backed Johnny would prowl on hands and knees like a grizzly bear, while the children would leap, screaming with excitement, on to his back as he tried to catch them.

But the storm clouds were gathering. While Johnny Althorp happily sat on local committees, played cricket with the village team and worked with the local opera group, Frances, 14 years his junior, felt that the marriage had become stale and stifling. She left the upbringing of the children more and more to the highly competent Ally and began visiting London again. As soon as Sarah and Jane were old enough to attend boarding school, Frances, still a good-looking young woman and only 30 years old, threw herself into London society life, enjoying parties, dinners, cocktail evenings, the theatre and ballet. Before long, Frances fell in love. The man was Peter Shand Kydd, a wallpaper millionaire, graduate of Edinburgh University, and a former Royal Navy Officer, who was then married to a talented artist.

After taking a small apartment in Cadogan Place where she lived most of the week, Frances issued a statement to the British Press in 1967, saying, 'I am living apart from my husband now. It is very unfortunate. I don't know if there will be a reconciliation.'

To Johnny Althorp at their farm in Norfolk, the announcement came as a thunderbolt. He would say later, 'How many of those 14 years were happy? I thought all of them, until the moment we parted. I was wrong. We hadn't fallen apart. We had drifted apart.'

In London, Frances's surprise announcement set

the tongues of upper-crust socialites wagging, producing a mountain of speculation. No one could believe that this beautiful young woman, with such aristocratic connections, could simply walk away from her family and embark on a single life in London.

Back home at Park House, however, Frances's decision to break with her husband devastated Sarah and Jane though Diana, then aged six, was hardly aware of it. Indeed, Diana rather enjoyed the excitement of visiting London by train to stay in her mother's apartment, though most of the time she stayed at home with her beloved father. However, the excitement would soon turned to sorrow and confusion in Diana's young mind. A year later, after a prolonged and bitter legal battle, Johnny Althorp was granted a divorce on the grounds of his wife's adultery, and, quite extraordinarily in Britain at that time, custody of all the children was granted to him.

Lawyers believed that one reason why the judge harshly deprived Frances of her children was that her own mother not only supported Johnny Althorp, but also told the court that she did not believe her own daughter to be a suitable mother. She described Frances's actions as 'monstrous' and 'unthinkable'. To this day, Frances remains acutely sensitive to the charge that she deserted her four children. She claimed that she was a victim of cruelty in the marriage and insists that she was a responsible mother who became caught up in a love affair with a married man.

Diana and young Charles were enrolled in Silfield School, seven miles from Sandringham, and Diana saw little of her mother. She grew increasingly close to her father as he anxiously sought to fill the vacuum, playing both parental roles as best he could. Diana assumed the mother's role with young Charles, dressing him every morning, escorting him to and from school and bathing him at night.

Save for her rock of a father, however, Diana's life became more insecure as a succession of nannies came and went after Ally left Park House. About this time, her favourite cat, Marmalade, died. Nannies found life difficult at Park House because the girls refused to accept discipline from anyone but their father.

One nanny who stayed two years, Mrs Thompson, would later say of Diana, 'She was simply obstinate. She just would not co-operate. I think Diana may have seen how her elder sister Sarah behaved and copied her. So, I did the only thing I could in the circumstances. I'd send her to her room until I felt she had been punished long enough ... then she was allowed out. But it didn't alter her obstinacy.'

Mrs Thompson described the twice-weekly battle to wash Diana's long, blonde hair. 'I remember that she didn't like having her hair washed. I would lie her down in the bath, with her head on one arm, and start to wash her hair. That was always a fight. She would sulk and struggle to start with. But, as her nanny, I had to win ... and, in the end, after much struggling, and often a few tears, she would have her hair washed.'

As a little girl, of course, Diana loved going to parties, partly because she had few friends and wasn't invited to many. Nanny Thompson remembered one at Sandringham. 'Wearing a new frock, and having allowed me to wash her hair, Diana, then seven, and her brother Charles went to the "big house" next door for tea with Prince Andrew and Prince Edward. After tea, I went to see what was happening. I found Diana and Andrew screaming around the house, playing hide-and-seek with the Queen!'

Like many young aristocratic children, Diana was encouraged to take up horse riding and a pony was bought for her. She loved the little pony and would happily groom him and clean out his box at weekends. Soon, Diana became too daring when riding him, taking too many fences and too many risks at speed. One day, the pony stopped at a fence and Diana went flying over his head, breaking her arm. It took three months to heal and the fall shattered her confidence, ending Diana's interest in horse riding. Indeed, from that time on she never enjoyed riding again, although she would later be encouraged to do so by Prince Charles, the Queen and other members of the Royal Family.

Diana later told one of her flatmates, 'I even prayed to God to give me the courage to ride once again. I desperately wanted to please Charles, to be able to ride out with him because I realised it was so important for him ... for us. And yet I just couldn't relax. I don't know why, heaven knows I tried hard enough, but I just couldn't. Sometimes I would cry alone at night about it.'

Diana enjoyed her two years at Silfield School, evidently the only school she ever truly liked. It seemed that she found emotional security at the school despite the shattered home life. Her father tried everything possible to fill the gap left by her mother. He offered affection and tried hard to fulfil the maternal role as well, but with little success.

Wrought with a sense of guilt over his broken marriage, Johnny spoiled his daughters as he sought to compensate for Frances's absence. Johnny Althorp was a man's man, brought up in the army, in the stuffy, rigid world of the 1930s, when men of his class would have thought it improper, indeed incomprehensible, that a father should concern himself with the upbringing of children, especially three young daughters. In his experience, all those matters were quite alien, to be left to the mother, nanny or governess. The unfortunate Johnny Althorp was barely capable of understanding what his responsibilities should be to his four motherless offspring.

Johnny did invite his own mother and his mother-in-law, Lady Fermoy, to spend some time in Norfolk, to care for and help out with the children, especially during school holidays, but neither grandmother was ever around long enough to play a decisive role in their upbringing.

Johnny did not seem to realise that his children needed outside interests, for he thought they could happily play together. As a result, there was little encouragement for the children to become involved with any activities outside the close confines of their country home and no real encouragement to read books, take piano lessons or engage in any other musical activity. Diana even missed out on the companionship of the local Girl Guides troop and, later, the young farmers' club.

Brought up in the heart of the country, Diana might have been introduced to such pastimes as bird watching or fishing, shooting, stalking or rabbiting, but she wasn't. She had virtually no interests outside the family home and no mother to direct her life, or to encourage her to widen her horizons and so broaden her education and interest in life. Inevitably, Diana found time weighing heavily on her hands and she would spend hours alone with her childish thoughts.

As a woman from Sandringham commented later, 'In a way, she was a sad little kid. Not morose, but lost and certainly deprived. What Diana lacked and so deeply missed was a real family life. She may have been the daughter of an heir to an earldom, but any little girl with an ordinary father, and, if you like, a back-street home in the East End of London was richer by far.'

During her lifetime, Diana only once spoke of the pain of her early life, telling a ten-year-old handicapped boy in 1987 that she had never been to the zoo, or visited a circus or a theatre during her own childhood. But she never once spoke about the break with her mother. It seemed that Diana had set up a mental barrier to those derelict years, the years she lived apart from her mother with whom she would never become close. It appeared that she had simply wiped the heartbreak and the loss from her memory — a normal enough psychological reaction for a young child in those circumstances. To the end of her life and beyond, biographers have tried to assess the effect of the parental break-up on Diana and, undeniably, Diana did miss the maternal affection, stability and everyday discipline of a loving, nurturing home which all children need.

The imposed discipline from nannies or surrogate parents was less than satisfactory, and Diana's father could not always be there for her when she most needed love and attention. No one will know just how much of an effect those early years had on the development of Diana's character and personality.

Eventually the prim, diligent little Diana earned herself the nickname 'Duchess' at Silfield School for her bearing and quiet determination. But at the age of nine she left the emotional security of Silfield to attend Riddlesworth School, the boarding school Sarah and Jane had attended before. The school was only two hours away from Park House and prided itself on being a 'home away from home' for its 120 girls. Johnny Althorp hoped so.

During her years at Riddlesworth Diana was outstanding in no area except her affection for younger girls. Years later, Elizabeth Risdale, Diana's Headmistress, would say, 'Diana was an average child but she could read well and her writing was clear. One thing I do remember is that all her pictures and drawings were dedicated to "Mummy and Daddy".'

It was at Riddlesworth, that the shy young Diana cared for Peanuts, her guinea pig, with which she was besotted, proving to be a doting 'mother', feeding the animal religiously, cleaning his cage daily and, when at home, playing with him on the kitchen table during school holidays.

But Diana and her two sisters were in for a shock when their father introduced them to the new woman in his life, Raine, the Countess of Dartmouth, then 45, the dynamic, forceful daughter of novelist Barbara Cartland. She began visiting Park House in the early 1970s and, before long, she had not only become a regular visitor but, to the dismay of Sarah, Jane and Diana, she began to take over the place, running the house. More importantly, Raine saw herself as the surrogate mother to the three girls and decided to take them under her wing. The girls, however, objected to Raine taking the place of their mother and they became so off-hand and objectionable to Raine that Johnny Althorp began restricting her visits to Park House to the months the girls were away at boarding school.

In 1975, the seventh Earl Spencer died at the age of 83 and Johnny Althorp became the eighth Earl. As a result, Diana became known as Lady Diana Spencer and her brother Charles, being the heir, became Viscount Althorp. The new title meant another upheaval, with the family taking over the Spencer ancestral home, Althorp House, set among 8,500 acres of pasture and park land in Northamptonshire. The move also meant that Diana, then a shy and reserved 14-year-old, moved to an area where she knew absolutely no one. And being at boarding school for most of the year, she would have little opportunity of meeting girls of her own age.

Diana had moved school once more, following in the footsteps of her mother and her elder sisters by attending West Heath, near Sevenoaks in Kent. Later, Ruth Rudge, the Headmistress, recalled, 'Of course, I came to know all three Spencer girls very well, and they were all totally different personalities. Diana was not as brainy as the other two girls, but she did have the most endearing qualities. Diana seemed to love children and had an easy, engaging manner with them. I remember she spent many hours caring for the handicapped children at a centre near the school. She was a girl who noticed what needed to be done, then did it willingly and happily.

'But,' Ruth Rudge continued, 'Diana was no goody-goody. She could be naughty — talking when lights were out, hiding her tuck, and making other girls giggle in assembly or class with some timely remarks.'

Later, Diana herself would recall being 'quite naughty' at West Heath. She once smeared blue eye shadow on her knees and pretended it was a painful bruise that prevented her doing some sporting activity on a cold winter's day; she remembered pillow fights and romps with the other girls in the dormitory; midnight feasts at the end of term, and even occasional custard pie throwing. When caught, the usual punishment was running six times around the assembly hall or the lacrosse pitch, or weeding the garden. Diana would confess later, with a smile, 'I became a great expert at weeding.'

When Diana was 15, her father proposed to Raine, the woman who by then dominated his life. They were married in a quiet civil ceremony in London in July 1976. None of Johnny's children attended the wedding nor did they receive an invitation.

The relationship between Raine and the three girls grew worse, and when Raine decided to renovate the entire house, she raised the money by selling some of the art treasures and the furniture which had adorned the ancestral home for decades. The sale generated a great deal of interest and raised £4 million. Diana would confide later how hurt she had been by the sale of so many family treasures, leaving blank spaces on the drawing room walls.

Before the arrival of Raine, life had been relatively uncomplicated at Althorp House, with the maids and old retainers enjoying the peace and tranquillity of the estate, even though it was in need of total renovation. Raine changed all that. To make

Althorp a going concern she pruned the family budget, firing faithful servants, reducing the number of cleaning ladies and cutting back on the number of gardeners and casual staff who maintained the beautiful, decaying old mansion. And Raine then set about redecorating and refurbishing Althorp House to her own taste, one which shocked the three sisters as it was was seen to be too gaudy, too lavish for one of Britain's principal stately homes.

For Diana, her teenage years were lonely ones. Her two elder sisters were growing up fast and Diana spent her holidays at home, locked in her room, wandering around the villages near her home or writing letters to her school pals, recounting the latest awful 'horror' undertaken by Raine. To keep out of her stepmother's way, Diana made friends, or rather acquaintances, with local shopkeepers and the housewives she met in the villages. She was always friendly, offering a smile and stopping to chat. But teenage parties, barbecues and village dances were a rarity for Diana and Northamptonshire was never known as an area where the aristocracy entertained.

At school, Diana was on good terms with most of her classmates, although she never worked hard at her education, fearing she could never emulate the excellent exam results her sisters recorded. Diana found it increasingly difficult to cope, to concentrate and study at West Heath, and she became convinced that she was the dunce of the family. She failed her first set of 'O'-level examinations and, five months later, she sat the exams again. She failed them again. All of them.

Johnny Spencer urged Diana to return to school and sit the exams once more in the following summer.

But, aware that Diana would be embarrassed at returning as a failure to West Heath, her sister Sarah persuaded her father to send Diana to a finishing school in Switzerland, the Chateau d'Oex near Gstaad, the Institut Alpin Vidamenette. Diana was 17 but her experiences of life were seemingly non-existent. She had never had a boyfriend, she'd hardly ever attended a dance and was now to go to Switzerland. Her life had been so sheltered that the woman who would eventually fly around the world as a roving ambassador had never had a holiday abroad, and had not even experienced a trip on a ship or a plane. It is a graphic illustration of the kind of limited life young Diana had led.

So it was with some excitement that Diana set off for Switzerland, but the thrill of being on her own in a foreign country soon waned. Almost immediately, she became homesick and confessed to crying herself to sleep for the first week. Unable to settle, she decided that the only option was to run away. Six weeks later, she returned home in tears.

When Diana set about finding work, she joined her sisters in London but had no idea what to do. She had left school with no qualifications and no knowledge of such basic skills as shorthand and typing, cooking or working as a personal assistant. Given those limitations, she did the only thing she liked — looking after children. Many well-to-do parents in London employ young women to 'nanny', to help care for their children while they work, socialise or go shopping. For class-conscious young mothers, Diana was a perfect au pair. She spoke well, dressed like a 'Sloane Ranger' and appeared to have an impeccable family background, yet she never revealed that she was in fact Lady Diana Spencer, daughter of Earl Spencer. Her work, however, hardly earned her enough to feed herself and, to earn extra money, she would occasionally work as a home help, cleaning people's homes, dusting, polishing, ironing and sometimes babysitting in the evenings.

At first, she moved in with her mother but then shared a flat with some other girls she got to know. In 1978, however, with money from a family trust, Diana, on the advice of her mother, bought a London flat for £100,000 in Coleherne Court, Fulham, West London. On buying a three-bedroom apartment, Diana was able to invite other girls to stay and pay rent, providing Diana with an income to run the flat and feed and clothe herself. Diana loved the idea of sharing — eventually having four flatmates — because it was an instant way of meeting other young people, including young men.

Still amazingly shy and reserved, Diana, now a home-owner and landlord earned herself a certain cachet among her peers. She bought herself an old 'sit-up-and-beg' bicycle with a basket on the handlebars and used that to travel around London, thereby avoiding the 'horrid' bus and Underground.

The first person to move into Diana's flat was a friend from West Heath, Carolyn Pride, who was training as a soprano at the Royal College of Music. She would say later, 'We were really fluffy-haired Sloanes but we did have a great time together and we all got on well. It was fun, with lots of laughter and silliness ... we were all young and learning to enjoy life. But there was nothing wild about us.'

But Diana and Carolyn would keep in touch and Diana became godmother to Carolyn's son, Jack. In turn, she is godmother to Prince Harry. Carolyn was one of the young women Diana turned to during the traumatic years of her marriage break-up.

Fed up with cleaning other people's homes and caring for other people's children, Diana applied for what she described as her first 'proper' job, as a helper at the Young England Kindergarten in St George's Square, Pimlico, a few miles from Buckingham Palace. The children were small and Diana was responsible for groups of five youngsters. She loved the work, and the children, in turn, seemed to adore her, responding to her natural, warm, open approach.

In retrospect, it was ironic that during 1977 and 1978, Prince Charles dated Diana's elder sister, the lovely Titian-haired Sarah, and there were many who believed that Lady Sarah Spencer would indeed become the Princess of Wales. For more than a year, Charles and the ebullient Sarah, who had always been considered the most rebellious of the Spencer girls, were lovers and Charles's close friends believed that he would soon pop the question. Charles wooed her as though they were already engaged, sending her flowers, writing her intimate letters, arranging candle-lit dinners and treating her with respectful deference. In February 1978, Charles took Sarah on holiday, skiing at Klosters, the same Swiss resort where Charles and Diana would spend many great holidays together.

Charles, too, thought he had found his future Queen in Sarah, but he wasn't entirely sure, particularly when she began to boss him about, taking command of situations. Though in her own way Sarah loved him dearly, she was never *in love* with him. Sarah wanted a passionate love affair with a man she truly loved and she knew in her heart that, however flattering it would be to marry the Prince of Wales and become a member of the Royal Family, she was not prepared to make that commitment if she didn't love the man. And she didn't. But arguments developed and Charles thought Sarah too headstrong.

Some weeks after their Klosters holiday together, Sarah commented to the Press, 'If he asked me to marry him, I would turn him down. I'm not in love with him. I wouldn't marry anyone I didn't love, whether he was the dustman or the King of England!'

In the summer of 1979, Charles met Sarah's younger sister, Diana, an immature, shy and reserved teenager, seemingly younger than her 18 years. Charles had known Diana, as he had known all the Spencer family, from the occasions when the Royal Family stayed at Sandringham, so they weren't strangers to each other. Sarah was thrilled when Diana told her that Charles had invited her out on a date. But Sarah warned her younger sister that Charles was really an incurable romantic.

But within months of meeting, a tragedy occurred which would have the most extraordinary effect on the lives of three people, the repercussions of which would rock the monarchy and the House of Windsor to its foundations. The tragedy would also cause pain and heartache, not only to the British nation as a whole but, more particularly, to the three people at its epicentre, Diana, Prince Charles — and a woman Diana had never met or even heard of — Camilla Parker Bowles.

Earl Mountbatten, the man whom Charles trusted,

respected and regarded as a surrogate father, was murdered by the IRA while on a fishing holiday in Ireland in August 1979. His assassination would lead to Charles marrying Diana, though not before an angry, and distraught Prince Charles had recovered his senses and his equilibrium in the arms of his former lover, Camilla.

Grieving, sometimes raving with fury, Charles turned to the only person whom he believed could save his sanity.

Camilla and Charles had first known each other in 1970, before Charles left London to serve at sea with the Royal Navy. They had enjoyed a brief platonic affair when Charles took Camilla to stay at Earl Mountbatten's country home, Broadlands in Hampshire. But a few months after Charles went to sea, Camilla had become engaged to Andrew Parker Bowles, a dashing cavalry officer, man-about-town and some ten years older than Camilla. But Charles never forgot Camilla and they would write to each other. He became godfather to her first child, Tom, and they would see each other on a purely platonic basis from time to time.

But during the following six months, Charles and Camilla's love and passion for each other knew no bounds. Her husband Andrew was posted to Rhodesia in September 1979 to accompany Lord Soames, who had been appointed to preside over the elections which were to bring black majority rule to Rhodesia, one of Britain's last territories in Africa.

Charles had never known such trauma in his life and Camilla tried to assume Mountbatten's role in advising him what he should do. Charles begged Camilla to divorce her husband and marry him but she refused point-blank, reminding him that it was the love of King Edward VII for his beloved Wallis Simpson, a divorced woman, which had ended with Edward's abdication in 1936. She told him that another such royal crisis over a divorced woman might herald the end of the monarchy. Reluctantly, he agreed to follow the advice that his great-uncle 'Dickie' Mountbatten had given him some years earlier: 'A young man in your position should go out, sow his wild oats, and then find a young virgin ... marry her, and then train her to be the next Queen of England.'

At the back of Charles's mind, however, lurked another reason why he should earnestly search for a bride. For the first time in his life, he realised that death could be only a bomb away and he knew that as the heir to the British throne it was his duty to produce an heir to carry on the Windsor line of accession.

In May 1980, Charles once again invited Diana on a date and he found the young Spencer girl more mature and more fun than he had remembered from the previous year. Diana was a virgin, 19 years old and someone who had loved Charles from afar for years since seeing him at Sandringham one Christmas when she was 16 years old. Within nine months they were engaged and the love story which the world followed with extraordinary interest began to unfold.

# CHAPTER FOUR

## LOVE AND MARRIAGE

There was no question in Diana's mind that she wanted to marry Prince Charles, though outwardly she remained remarkably cool and calm, even to the friends who shared her Fulham apartment. She still climbed past the bicycles that clogged the entrance to the block of flats; she still enjoyed eating spaghetti on her knees as they all watched the small television in their living room; and she still took her turn cleaning the flat and doing the washing up.

That life seemed natural and normal to Diana and she enjoyed the camaraderie of being surrounded by up to four other girls all fighting for the bathroom; searching for her tights hanging on the communal clothes horse and keeping her part of the fridge they all shared neat and tidy. Indeed, at times Diana felt as though she was back at boarding school enjoying the fun and laughter and listening to the stories of their various love lives.

Diana was teased by the other girls as soon as the

newspapers were full of her relationship with Prince Charles. But she didn't mind, taking it all in her stride but never revealing anything to them that she didn't want them to know. And, in turn, they pulled her leg and cracked jokes about her life as the future Queen of England. If one or two had drunk a glass of wine too many they would sometimes curtsey to Diana and she would push them over, making them lose their balance. Then they would all shriek with laughter as they had done years before at school.

Diana's first passionate kiss with Charles apparently took place on *HMS Britannia* during the summer of 1980 when Prince Charles asked her to join him for the party on board the Royal Yacht during Cowes Week, to which Prince Philip invited the owners and other guests aboard for the evening. There was champagne, food, dancing and fun because with Prince Philip as the host everyone could let their hair down and enjoy themselves. Indeed, some of the evening was spent around the piano singing sea shanties as well as some rather dubious and *risqué* Royal Navy songs.

Back in London, Charles began to date Diana seriously and together they would devise plans to smuggle her into Buckingham Palace for quiet, intimate dinners without the photographers cottoning on. At that time, the tabloids were chasing Prince Charles as eagerly as they would later hound Diana. Charles was now over 30 and stories appeared regularly in the Press suggesting that Prince Philip was urging his son to marry, settle down and produce an heir to the throne.

Every young woman whom Charles saw or even talked to became the object of media interest, some of the girls finding it difficult to cope with the attentions of the Press who never seemed to take 'no' for an answer. Charles was determined that Diana should not have to run that same gauntlet because he wasn't sure that she would be able to handle the non-stop questioning, the harrassment and the attentions of a pack of determined *paparazzi*. Ironically, Diana became quite adept at dealing with them, never stopping to talk to them when asked a question, but always smiling in her charming, inimitable way, which seemed to disconcert many of the royal hacks. At other times, Diana would totally ignore the assembled throng, and yet the journalists and photographers soon appeared to rather like and trust her.

Charles and Diana were wonderful together, enjoying each other's company whenever they met and keen to see each other as much as possible. Charles was convinced that he had met someone who could make him forget the other great love of his life, Camilla Parker Bowles, for here was a young woman who took his breath away, the perfect aristocratic girl from the country who, one day, would make the most beautiful Queen of England.

But there was one test he wanted Diana to undergo and she gladly did so. Whenever Charles met someone with whom he hoped there might be a lasting relationship, he would always take them to Scotland for a long weekend and submit them to the 'Craigowan Test', the house on the Balmoral estate at which Charles and the girl would stay, cared for, of course, by staff. This test involved the poor girl sitting around Craigowan House all day reading books and magazines while he would be out stalking, shooting or fishing in the River Dee. He much preferred it if the girl donned her green wellies, trousers and Barbour coat and accompanied him, though this would entail loading guns, trudging across moors for hours or standing on the river bank watching Charles trying to catch fish from dawn until dusk.

Charles would subject any potential girlfriends to this test because, to him, Balmoral was an important part of his life, a place which he cherished and to which he loved to escape from the demanding routine of his royal duties. Indeed, Charles would often visit Balmoral alone so that he could spend time on his own, solely with his thoughts, enjoying the idyll of country life. He realised that at Balmoral any potential wife could not be a person in her own right but would have to conform, to be a silent, supportive, decorative appendage. The test was important for any prospective, long-term girlfriend, for if she failed that hurdle, Charles knew that there was no point in continuing the relationship.

With some trepidation, Charles took Diana to Balmoral in September 1980, just a few weeks after they had danced and kissed aboard *Brittania*. Charles knew that Diana was no outdoor, horsey girl, for she had told him as much during their long conversations over innumerable intimate dinners in his suite of rooms at Buckingham Palace. And yet he had known Diana in her early formative years, had seen her from time to time at Sandringham and believed that, because of her background and upbringing, she would be bound to understand and appreciate Charles's love of the country.

Diana, now 19, took her needlepoint and two Mills and Boon books which she had started to read at school and still enjoyed as escapist frothy fiction. Each day Charles and his friends went out shooting and each day Diana, along with other married and unmarried young women, dutifully trooped across the moors to join the men for a picnic lunch, served on china plates with crystal wine glasses and the most excellent food, waited on, as ever, by the footmen who brought the traditional wicker hampers to wherever the royal party were enjoying themselves.

At dinner at Balmoral each night, Diana would find herself placed anywhere other than next to Charles for it was also a tradition that couples, even married couples, did not sit together to make the conversation more open. Afterwards there was dancing and, once again, Diana did not see much of Charles because it was his duty to dance with every other woman, in turn, as any host in royal circles would be expected to do. But Diana always managed to have the last waltz.

Three weeks later, Diana was once again invited to Scotland, this time to a smaller and more intimate gathering at Birkhall, the Scottish home of the Queen Mother and the home where Charles used to escape during the unbearable years he spent at Gordonstoun, the school his father insisted that he attend.

In October, Charles took Diana to visit Highgrove, the country house in Gloucestershire that Charles had purchased earlier that year for £800,000. At the time Diana and Charles visited, the house was still being renovated and was only partly furnished. The house had only had three bedrooms completed but Charles didn't seem to mind the mess. Indeed, for a fastidiously organised person, he appeared rather to enjoy the informality and jumble of the place after his years in the stiff, orderly atmosphere of Buckingham Palace. Diana was surprised at how enthusiastic Charles could be about Highgrove, excitedly taking her from room to room, explaining his plans for the lay-out and the decoration, insisting that they inspect the gardens so that he could show her what he planned to grow where and why. Then she realised that Charles had never had a place he could call his own. He was 32 years of age and this was his first home. She liked him for that youthful enthusiasm.

During the autumn of 1980, Diana visited Highgrove frequently at weekends, but Charles would never let her stay the night for fear that the good villagers of Tetbury might hear of it and spread the word. He was determined that no one would be able to say anything that could sully the good name and reputation of the person he was fast believing would be his wife. Diana would drive down to Gloucestershire and Charles might return from his official duties at around tea-time. They would walk through the grounds, talk about the latest plans for the house and, after a light supper, Charles would drive Diana back to London.

It was during one of those weekend visits that Diana met Camilla Parker Bowles, the woman who would cast such a shadow over the subsequent years. She would become, as Diana put it so succinctly, the third unofficial member of their marriage. Charles wanted Camilla's opinion of the girl he hoped would marry him. Diana knew that Camilla had been an old friend, and that they had known each other briefly in their young days before Charles went off to sea. But Diana was totally unaware that, only a few months before, Charles and Camilla had been the most ardent and passionate lovers. Nor did she know that Charles had asked, indeed begged, Camilla to divorce her husband and marry him. Nor did Diana know that it had been Camilla who had forced Charles to leave her, move out of her life, forget she ever existed, and go instead and find a suitable young woman to marry, raise a family and who would, eventually, sit next to him on the throne as his Queen.

As the world now knows, it was in the cabbage patch at Camilla's house in Gloucestershire that Charles first discussed marriage with Diana but only after Camilla had given Charles her opinion that Diana would make a wonderful wife for him, a good mother to his children and an ideal woman to support him when he became King.

As the winter nights drew closer, Press speculation mounted that the lovely, virginal, sweet Diana would become his bride and, as a result, Charles and Diana had to play a never-ending game of cat and mouse to keep one jump ahead of the photographers and reporters who followed them everywhere. The crucial moment came when journalists discovered that Diana had celebrated Charles's thirty-second birthday with him privately at a small house on the Sandringham estate, next door to the house where Diana had been born and brought up.

From that moment, the public took Diana to their hearts, and hoped that she would make Charles a good wife and a wonderful future Queen. Their misgivings centred first on the age difference, for Charles was 32 and Diana only 19, a gap of 13 years; and second, on the fact that Diana was simply too young. But the consensus was that Charles had done the right thing in falling for a lovely, genuine English girl rather than a European nonentity from some little-known Royal family.

Charles, in fact, officially proposed to Diana in January 1981 during an afternoon together at Highgrove which still resembled what Diana called 'the building site'. Charles's faithful valet, Stephen Barry, drove down from Buckingham Palace with a lovely picnic and a bottle of champagne. He left them together in one of the drawing rooms. It was then, over a glass of champagne, that Charles asked Diana to be his wife, adding that he did not want an immediate reply. He told her that she must think of his proposal because of the life it would entail for her if she accepted. Diana agreed to think about the proposal but her mind was already made up.

Charles was someone who always liked to put a proposition to someone first and ask them to go away and think about it before reaching a decision. He explained to Diana that becoming the Princess of Wales might sound irresistible to many young women, but it was no easy task. He explained that living in the public eye could be a gruelling experience, always having to keep up appearances, never letting her emotions show in public and, no matter how tired and exhausted one felt, a Princess always had to appear smiling, interested and on top form.

Charles explained that never again could she remain anonymous, and that she would never be able to enjoy the simple pleasure of being alone when shopping, eating in a restaurant or having a coffee, for she would be instantly recognised. There was also her personal security to be considered. He knew that Diana was aware of some of the problems that lay ahead but, in his heart, he knew from experience that living the life of a Royal was very, very difficult for someone not born into a royal family.

Diana told Charles only days later that she had made up her mind and that her answer was 'yes'. Charles, however, wanted her to be absolutely sure and suggested she accompany her mother to Australia for a three-week break, where she could stay with her sister and think and talk over with her mother the enormous implications of the decision and the life she would face in the years to come.

Hours after the official announcement of the engagement on 24 February 1981, and the photographs in the gardens of Buckingham Palace, Diana moved her belongings into Clarence House, the royal residence in The Mall, a few hundred yards from Buckingham Palace. There to take care and instruct the young Diana was Ruth, Lady Fermoy, Diana's grandmother, who was also a close friend and lady-in-waiting to the Queen Mother. Lady Fermoy was to instruct Diana on protocol, tradition, behaviour and dress and the way she should address members of the family, staff and advisers.

Forty-eight hours later, however, and known only to a very few people, Diana had moved her things from Clarence House down the road to the Palace. She was installed in a suite of rooms next to those occupied by Charles and there she remained, undetected by the media, until after their wedding five months later. It seemed quite remarkable that the Queen and the Queen Mother should have given their consent. Charles and Diana spent every night together in Charles's apartment and were only separated whenever Charles had to attend to royal duties which necessitated staying away overnight. Those who saw both of them at that time recall that both Diana and Charles were very, very happy and obviously in love.

It was during those few months that Diana began to lose her 'shy Di' image. And in July of that year, she emerged for her wedding looking slimmer, more graceful, more assured and more beautiful. The metamorphosis was due not only to Diana's determination to slim and appear more sophisticated, but also to the staff of Vogue, the fashion magazine, where her sister Jane had worked. Diana would call in at their offices once or twice a week for consultations and the staff would give her ideas about everything from make-up to dress sense, from how to sit properly and curtsy to learning how to hold her head and never, never look bored.

It was during those months when Charles was attending to royal duties that Diana began to read the newspapers, all of them. At first, she would be upset by the slightest criticism or a picture of herself she didn't like, but within a few weeks she was learning to understand what the papers wanted, how they treated a story and how the tabloids could unashamedly distort the truth. For most of the time, however, in those early weeks the stories about Diana were supportive and some even adulatory for the public had already taken 'Lady Di' to their hearts.

It was the beginning of a remarkable relationship between Diana and the British public. Her appalling death in Paris only helped to cement their love, respect and admiration for the young woman the people believed was one of them. When Diana rejoiced, as she did at her wedding and the births of William and Harry, so did the nation; but when Diana was pained and wronged, they, too, felt her pain and her anguish and they shared her grief. When Diana tried to put her life together by engaging in heart-rending charity work, the people applauded her love for others; and when it seemed that the entire Royal Family shunned Diana, the innocent victim of a broken marriage, the people took her side. It was the most amazing relationship between a people and a Princess which would reach its crescendo at the moment of her death.

As the first grey light dawned over London on Wednesday, 29 July 1981, the city, usually bare and lifeless at such an inhospitable hour, was thronged with tens of thousands of happy, noisy people determined to enjoy the wedding of the century. For three days, people had camped out in order to secure a good view of the pageantry and splendour and to catch a glimpse of Lady Di.

The early part of the day was an ordeal for Diana; her nerves were on edge, she had hardly slept a wink that night and she wasn't sure that she could go through with the ceremony. When she put on her magnificent wedding dress, Diana looked in the mirror and burst into tears, ruining her make-up and causing panic among those waiting to help in their particular way. It was her sister Jane who took control, talking quietly to Diana as she mopped her tear-stained face, organised fresh make-up and persuaded her young sister that everything would be fine. It was, in fact, magnificent and Diana became a star across the world.

The Prince and Princess spent their wedding night at Broadlands, Earl Mountbatten's former home in the beautiful Hampshire countryside. Since Mountbatten's murder it had been the home of his grandson and Charles's friend, Lord Romsey. Broadlands was also the house where Elizabeth and Philip spent the first week of their honeymoon in 1947. Charles and Diana honeymooned on *Britannia*, cruising the Mediterranean, evading the *paparazzi* who unsuccessfully searched the area for the young couple.

Stephen Barry, Charles's valet who accompanied them on their cruise, recalled, 'They were 14 days of bliss. For the first time in years, I didn't have to wake Charles in the mornings. They slept as long as they wanted and we merely had to send in a cold breakfast of fresh fruit and tea when he rang for breakfast.

'He and the Princess spent most of their evenings alone on the royal deck. They would take dinner at about eight and then relax alone, chatting and watching the coastline as we steamed slowly along. We had no idea when they went to bed. Their quarters were very simple but comfortable and charming. Everything on the royal deck is white with red upholstery and grey carpets. They spent most of the day alone on the veranda of the royal deck and took their meals in the sitting room below.

'Most days, we steamed along the North African coast where we would try to find a deserted beach where the couple could be alone. First, a small tender would go out to make sure the beach was deserted, that there were no journalists about. Then another boat would take the couple ashore and most days they would picnic on the beach. The Prince loves to sunbathe and the Princess loves to swim, so they were both content. The Princess spent a lot of time snapping away, mostly views and pictures of Charles.'

Later, Barry commented, 'Diana was wonderfully happy on honeymoon. She was in seventh heaven. She spent the entire time with Charles. She didn't even want to be separated from him for a moment. She never wanted to stop kissing him ... there was a look of absolute adoration in her eyes the entire time. I don't think I ever saw her so happy ever again. Not that degree of radiance. She was blissfully happy.

'And Charles, too, seemed to be enjoying himself immensely. But he was more sober, more relaxed about the whole honeymoon and he didn't appear so ecstatic. But then I would never have imagined Charles behaving in the way Diana did.'

Although most of the time the couple were alone, Charles and Diana joined in with the crew, officers and staff whenever there were parties on board or barbecues ashore. Diana tried to make the honeymoon fun for everyone.

Within days of returning to England, the royal couple held an informal press conference at Balmoral on the understanding that, afterwards, the Press would leave them alone. Everyone who attended reported that the couple were 'simply in love', unable to take their eyes or their hands off each other. Diana described the honeymoon as 'fabulous' and said she 'could highly recommend marriage'.

But the honeymoon was over and the grey, rainy days at Balmoral with protocol and tradition became the order of the day, so completely different from their lazy, carefree days together in the sun Diana had enjoyed so much with her Prince all to herself. Now it seemed that her husband was public property, and she discovered that the most important person in his life was no longer his bride of two weeks, but his mother.

An inkling of what tortures lay ahead came on her first night at Balmoral as she and Charles dressed for dinner, their first formal meal together with the rest of the family. As usual, a number of distinguished guests were staying with the Queen and Prince Philip. First, Diana discovered that she could not take as long as she wished to bathe, dress and make-up. She now had to conform to the rigid discipline of a royal household.

Charles and Diana were expected downstairs for pre-dinner drinks at precisely 7.30pm, and, of course, Charles was ready and waiting at 7.25pm. He knew the routine, the unwritten decree that at no time and under no circumstances did one ever keep the Queen waiting. Charles, who had always respected his mother, accepted without question the rigid lifestyle of Balmoral. He had learned it at a very young age. And Diana would say later that it was Charles's utter devotion and acquiescence to the Queen, her mother-in-law, on all matters that began to annoy and, later, infuriate Diana. She realised very early on that no matter what views she expounded in a discussion or an argument with the Queen, even if Charles thought differently in private, he would always agree with his mother.

On one occasion, Diana told friends later, Charles had told her how ravishing she looked in an evening dress with a plunging neck-line, but when the Queen pointed out to her at dinner that she felt the dress was a little revealing for a member of the Royal Family, Charles immediately took his mother's side, making Diana feel embarrassed and awkward.

During those first weeks of married life at

Balmoral, the realisation of what lay ahead hit Diana hard. Throughout her life she had never had to do anything she didn't want, and even when her father had endeavoured to discipline her, she had always managed to win him round. Now, things were dramatically different and she didn't like it. Suddenly she was expected to stand and talk to total strangers, hardly ever aware of who they were, not knowing if she was talking to a Government Minister, a visiting Ambassador or a senior civil servant. And these conversations with strangers would continue for 30 minutes whilst she was offered one drink, sometimes two but never more. She would recall later that what kept her sane on such occasions was thinking of her life with her pals at their Fulham flat, drinking bottles of cheap plonk from the kitchen table without a care in the world.

And that was just the start of the exacting protocol. At precisely 8.00pm, when dinner was announced, Diana had to take Charles's hand and walk by his side to their seats at table. Like every other guest, Diana would be obliged to remain standing behind her chair until the Queen was seated. Only then was she permitted to sit down. What made matters worse was that usually on such occasions she was not permitted to sit next to Charles but would be placed between two men with whom she had nothing whatsoever in common and whom she considered far too old or intellectual to engage in conversation which wouldn't bore her or them.

Diana would confess later, 'All I talked about with them was the bloody weather!'

She also told one of Charles's equerries, 'I am petrified of the Queen. I shake all over when I'm in her presence. I can't look her in the eye, and just go to pieces whenever she enters the room. She tries to be nice and put me at my ease but I feel so embarrassed, so awkward when I'm with her, I blush and my mind goes blank.'

In those first weeks at Balmoral, and even throughout the following year, Diana would usually sit at table during mealtimes and say absolutely nothing, looking towards Charles for help. When the family was alone, with no guests, there would be witty, sophisticated talk, in-jokes which only the Royal Family understood, innuendo and suggestion, all of which went over Diana's head. She wrote to one of her flatmates, 'I feel totally out of place here. I sometimes wonder what on earth I've got myself into. I feel so small, so lonely, so out of my depth.'

And that was just the start of the evening. Dinner could sometimes last for two hours or more depending on the guests and the whim of the Queen. No one was permitted to leave the table until the Queen rose to leave. Charles, of course, was accustomed to such form — Diana was used to having a quick snack and running off to wherever she wanted afterwards. This rigid adherence to stuffy protocol stifled and bored Diana.

And what horrified Diana was the realisation that this ordeal was not just a one-off affair. This ghastly ritual would take place every single night they stayed at Balmoral or Windsor Castle with the Queen. This was going to be her life for the rest of her days. Despite the reassuring and patient counselling she had received before the wedding from experts like Charles's office boss, former naval Chief Petty Officer Michael Colborne, and the Prince's Private

Secretary, the lawyer-courtier Edward Adeane, Diana hadn't fully grasped just how excruciatingly formal it was all going to be.

During that first four-week holiday at Balmoral, Diana pleaded with Charles to allow her to escape to London on some pretext because she was finding it difficult coping with the starchy ritual, the little insignificant fixed routines that by tradition had to be followed to the letter. The highly disciplined Charles would not countenance the idea, knowing it would upset his mother. The longer the couple stayed at Balmoral that autumn, the more lonely, upset and depressed Diana became. And she had been married just two months.

Diana was also bored. The wonderful time she had enjoyed on honeymoon when she and Charles lazed together in the sun with no interruptions and no formal rituals seemed like another age compared to the life she was now experiencing in the cold, damp of Scotland where she never knew from one moment to the next whether she was doing right or wrong. It rained almost incessantly that autumn in the Highlands and Diana had to endure eight weeks cooped up in the castle, summoned to meals and meetings, her only freedom being the walks through the mist and rain accompanying Charles and the family on their country pursuits.

Diana would never forget the Queen extolling the virtues of the place. 'It's rather like hibernating when you come and stay at Balmoral,' she told Diana. 'It's lovely here. You can walk for miles without meeting another person.'

Diana at this time was a youthful, vibrant 20-year-old, who loved the excitement of living in

London, the camaraderie of friends, shopping in the King's Road, dining out in Italian bistros and wine bars, laughing and joking with girlfriends. The Queen's affirmation of the solitary life at Balmoral was like a death knell to Diana. She vowed during that first holiday that she would do her utmost to persuade Charles never to stay longer than a weekend at Balmoral ... ever!

Diana tried to make friends with the staff in the same way as she had always made friends with the staff and villagers at home when she was growing up in the Northamptonshire countryside. But even they remained aloof, upsetting her even more and making Diana feel that she was destined for a lonely and miserable life.

In an effort to make friends with someone with whom she could hold ordinary, everyday conversations, Diana began to visit the servants' quarters as she had always done at home. There, she would always be welcomed in the kitchens, chatting to the cook and the daily maid, the odd job man and whoever was around. She would sit at the kitchen table and enjoy a cake and a cup of coffee and sometimes she would help the cook to prepare meals.

One day, after Diana visited her new friends in the kitchen she returned for a further chat and company. The Yeoman of the Glass and China, a responsible position at Balmoral, approached her as she walked through the door with a smile and a cheery 'hello'. Pointing at the door, the Yeoman told her politely but bluntly, 'Through there, Ma'am, is your side of the house; through here is our side of the house.'

Diana was taken aback, unsure how to respond.

The Yeoman stood still, not saying another word, effectively barring her way into the kitchen. The Princess had no option. She blushed madly, turned and fled through the door, never to return to the kitchens. It had been an awful, eye-opening lesson for the young Diana. Now she had nowhere to go for company and a pleasant chat. She had not understood that there was a difference between the life of the aristocracy and royalty. In royal circles, there still exists the most strict relationship between the royals and those who work for them. Below stairs, comprising all kitchen staff, household maids, butlers, footmen, drivers, grooms and gardeners, the relationship is never permitted to be anything other than servant and master. Above stairs are the personal staff of the royals, such as senior advisers, ladies-in-waiting, valets, private secretaries, managers and office staff. The Royals do form closer relationships with these people; they will listen to them, chat with them and, on occasions, defer to them. But members of the personal staff are never permitted to believe for one moment that they are ever the equals of the Royal Family.

As a result of her *débâcle* below stairs, Diana's misery deepened and on two or three occasions during that eight-week sojourn in Scotland, she broke down in tears. One minute she would burst into tears, sometimes at table, in full view of the entire family and that would cause her more embarrassment. On other occasions, in the privacy of the suite of rooms she shared with Charles, servants would hear Diana in a rage shouting at her predicament, exploding with frustration. Charles, brought up to avoid public displays of any emotion whatsoever, was embarrassed and unhappy at Diana's moods.

Charles cared greatly for Diana at this time and he only wanted her to be happy. He had no idea what to do or how to cope with an emotional woman. He invited friends to Balmoral to stay for the weekend. One such visitor was Lady Romsey, who, through Charles, had met Diana occasionally in the months before her wedding. She would go out walking with Diana, trying to calm her and find out what was causing her such misery.

In desperation, Diana even turned to Charles's valet, Stephen Barry, who had witnessed a number of her emotional outbursts.

'I don't know what to do,' she would tell him. 'I am so unhappy here. Charles doesn't seem to understand me. He prefers to be out shooting, stalking, fishing or even chatting to his mother than spending time with me. I feel he's abandoned me. Just because I don't want to go out, he leaves me here alone all day. I hate it.'

Back in London, Diana calmed down and tried to relax as she began once more to see her old girlfriends, inviting them over for coffee, lunch or tea and chatting to them. She slipped out shopping with friends on a few occasions and began to enjoy life once more. Charles, too, attempted to please her by going out of his way to entertain more young people whom, he hoped, she would like.

One early attempt misfired badly. Charles arranged a dinner party at Kensington Palace for some of his polo pals, among them the Vestey brothers and their wives, the two Hipwood brothers and their partners and the Canadian stores billionaire Galen Weston. Young, rich, boisterous and fun,

Charles believed Diana would love the evening. It was a disaster. On the whole, Diana found his polo friends somewhat loud, juvenile and boring. She would complain that all they wanted to talk about was polo matches and their ponies.

And that was not all.

It seemed to Diana that everyone had more claim to Charles's attention than she did — throughout the entire day. She simply wanted to spend time with her husband, the man she still adored and whom she thought could do no wrong and would never wrong her. She became jealous of the hours Charles spent discussing whatever it was with his advisers, officials and managers of his various affairs. Charles would be away for two or three nights, as he had been before, perhaps visiting Scotland and the North of England. He would often be away all day opening a factory somewhere, attending meetings of his Prince's Trust, meeting Ambassadors and overseas visitors, as well as spending time running the Duchy of Cornwall, a multi-million pound business.

Diana would argue with Charles that now he was a married man his life, too, would have to change, as hers had done. She told him that she wasn't content to sit around the Palace all day twiddling her thumbs, waiting for him to return. She wanted to share her life with him, have time with him alone, not share him with assorted flunkies.

Within weeks of returning to Kensington Palace, a very unhappy Diana told Charles that she could not go on with their life together as it was — something had to change. So she decided that if Charles wasn't going to change his lifestyle, then she wouldn't change hers. She told him that she would stop accompanying him on official engagements.

To say that her statement shocked Charles is an understatement. The idea that a member of the Royal Family should refuse to carry out any official duties had never entered his head — it was unthinkable. But Diana was determined. It was not to be the last time that the young, wilful Diana would carry out threats in her effort to change the thinking and the traditions of the House of Windsor.

# CHAPTER FIVE

## BETRAYAL

It was twelve months after the birth of Prince Harry in September 1984 that Diana began to suspect that Charles had found another woman. And she was right. The affair between Charles and his former lover, Camilla Parker Bowles, had started innocently enough in the spring of 1985 when Charles went to see Camilla for advice.

He had turned to her frequently ever since the early days of his marriage. He had been worried about Diana, — her moods, her tantrums and her demands — since shortly after the honeymoon, but when Camilla heard that Diana was pregnant, she told Charles that many women suffered from feelings of desolation and loneliness during the first months of pregnancy when their bodies were undergoing enormous hormonal changes. Camilla advised Charles to be patient and do all in his power to make her feel loved and wanted.

After William's birth in July 1982, when Diana suffered slight post-natal depression, Charles turned to Camilla again and she suggested that he would have to be understanding, considerate, kind and loving and help her to get over the trauma. In turn, Charles told Camilla that he had tried everything, that he felt desperately sorry for his beloved Diana but that she didn't seem to want to listen or take note of any of his attempts to placate her.

Back at Kensington Palace, Charles was at his wit's end. He talked to his advisers and to doctors and all told him he had to be patient and understanding and that, in the end, all would be well. But Diana's mood swings seemed to become gradually more acute. Charles decided to give Diana everything she demanded, attend to her every whim and hope and pray that she would once again become the wonderful person he loved and adored during their blissfully happy courtship.

As a result, Charles had to ask 40 of his closest aides, some of them people he had known since his Royal Navy days in the mid-1970s, to leave royal service and find other jobs. In reality, Diana dismissed all but one of those 40 people, among them senior advisers and menial household staff, whom Diana feared might be siding with Charles, their former employer, rather than showing allegiance to both of them equally. Charles fought to retain some of them and did so for a matter of months. But in the end, they all left and Charles, with Diana's help, hired almost an entirely new team of aides and staff.

It was the sacking of so many people that alerted the newspapers to the fact that, no matter what was said publicly, something serious had to be going on at Kensington Palace. And the finger began to point towards Diana. The servants who quit, or were fired, spoke of Diana's mood swings, of violent arguments, and of Diana's penchant for throwing things at her husband.

After the birth of Harry in September 1984, rumours of strife within the family began to circulate. Once again, stories about Diana suffering from post-natal depression were leaked.

But as the months passed, newspaper pictures of Diana showed her looking thin and pale, as though suffering from some ailment. And she looked miserable, too. The laughter and sparkling eyes with which the world had fallen in love only a few years earlier had disappeared. Before long, stories of Diana's eating disorders became public knowledge and the newspapers were full of 'insider' information saying that Diana was, in turn, suffering from *'anorexia nervosa'* and bouts of *'bulimia'*.

Doctors and psychologists were of the opinion that Diana's eating disorders must be the result of deep trauma and unhappiness. But they had no idea why she should be feeling so desperate. They argued that she was the Princess of Wales, a young woman married to Prince Charles, the heir to the throne, the mother of two beautiful, healthy boys and that she had a Palace full of servants to care for her every need. Newspaper reports examined her lifestyle, her enormous bills for designer clothes, her frequent visits to beauty salons and hairdressers, and her visits to psychics and fortune tellers. They could not understand why a young mother, who had seemed so happy and full of life, should have become only a pale shadow of her former self. Some wondered whether she was suffering from a serious life-threatening illness, like cancer.

But no reassuring statements came from Buckingham Palace or Kensington Palace and though the tabloids watched her every move, photographed her incessantly and wrote columns of allegedly 'reliable' information from palace insiders, the nation was left to argue and discuss what was *really* wrong with the Princess.

Inside Kensington Palace, however, life for those who lived and worked there was becoming more difficult, if not intolerable. Those who worked alongside Charles and Diana knew that all was not well with their relationship but they did not know why the fairytale marriage that seemed to have been made in heaven had gone so disastrously wrong. In fact, from the spring of 1985, six months after the birth of Prince Harry, Charles had lost patience with his beautiful wife.

He no longer knew what, if anything, he could do to cheer her up, to re-invigorate their relationship and to get their marriage back on the rails. He believed he had tried everything, including giving Diana anything she wanted, in deference to her every wish; he had fired all the staff she had no longer wanted and supported her in whatever venture or charity with which she wished to become involved. She had wanted children and she now had two lovely boys, yet they appeared to give her little pleasure. All Diana seemed to want to do was see friends for lunch and watch television at night. She didn't want guests to visit and she no longer wanted to visit others or spend weekends in the country as house guests.

But Diana felt that Charles no longer loved her, cared for her or wanted anything to do with her. He seemingly didn't want to sleep in the same bed and would often stay the night in the spare bedroom on the top floor of Kensington Palace. She felt that Charles was slowly but inexorably pushing her out of his life and the more she thought this was his intention, the more panicky she became. She seemed unable to control her emotions or her eating habits and, on occasions, she would go to Charles, imploring him to hold her to make her feel wanted and secure, but he would push her away as though wanting nothing to do with her. Those actions broke Diana's heart.

For his part, Prince Charles asked everyone he could trust what he was doing wrong and what he could do to solve what he saw was Diana's inability to lead a normal life without trauma, rage or rows. When no advice appeared to work, he turned in desperation to Camilla. Charles found Camilla a woman he could talk to no matter how delicate those discussions were. He told her everything, every aspect of his and Diana's life together, and about their violent arguments and what he saw as Diana's intolerable demands which he could no longer accommodate.

Within weeks, Charles and Camilla had become lovers again and Charles told Diana that because their marriage seemed to be in such dire straits, he had decided to move his office to Highgrove. He told Diana that he would be spending many days and nights at his country estate and he hoped that, on her own, she would get over the problems that seemed to be tormenting her. But Charles never mentioned Camilla.

It was not long before Diana reached the conclusion that Charles, the man she had adored above all others, the man she had all but worshipped in those early days together, the man she saw as her prince and her guardian angel, had left her for his old friend, Camilla. She could not comprehend why Charles would have done this, for Diana had no idea at that time that Charles's relationship with Camilla had ever been more than one of friendship. Never for one moment did Diana realise that they had been lovers only a matter of months before she and Charles had started going out together.

Diana turned to marriage guidance counsellors to console herself. Indeed, she went further and became patron of Relate, the counselling charity. She would sit in on case studies and would then take part in discussions of various cases she had listened to. In most cases, Relate counsellors would work to patch up a marriage if at all possible, and Diana could see that in some cases the counselling worked. She hoped that Charles might return to her and the boys so that once again they could enjoy being a family unit. She did all this because she hoped to learn what had gone wrong with her marriage and what she could do to put it right.

She would confess later, 'Attending those sessions made me realise my mistakes. I wasn't the perfect wife ... I can see that now.'

Helping her cope with the trauma of losing her husband was the bubbly, high-spirited Sarah Ferguson who would later marry Prince Andrew. Diana found Sarah a breath of fresh air, a welcome relief from the stuffy people she had to deal with every day at the Palace. Through the summer of 1985, Sarah introduced Diana to a younger, more vibrant set and Diana began to enjoy herself once more. She enjoyed chatting away about trivia, laughing and giggling, sharing jokes and simply having fun, all the things that had gone out of her life shortly after her marriage to Charles.

By the spring of 1986, Diana found herself still enjoying life, despite the pain her marriage brought. Overnight, so it seemed to Diana, she found that she no longer loved Charles and wondered how on earth she had been so swept off her feet only a few years before. She looked at him in a detached, cold way and realised that the love had evaporated. She also realised that she didn't want him as her husband any more, that she was happy for him to be living at Highgrove in Gloucestershire so that she could get on with her life and enjoy herself in London on her own.

She started to go out more frequently with Sarah and other friends who would invite her to cocktail parties and private dinners. She gradually returned to eating properly and drinking more champagne than she had ever done before; she started to take a pride once more in her appearance, spend more time at the gym and spoil herself shopping for designer clothes using Prince Charles's American Express card. She loved taking lunches with girlfriends in London's small, intimate restaurants. And, for the first time in her life, she found herself flirting!

It was as though Diana had finally matured from the teenager who found it difficult talking to young men, the shy young girl who would blush with embarrassment at a moment's indiscretion, the girl who found it all but impossible to stand up and make a speech without feeling nervous, agitated and apprehensive. Throughout 1986 and 1987, Diana became increasingly confident and discovered, somewhat to her amazement, that she was actually enjoying life. Egged on by Sarah and others, Diana became more daring.

She had a fling with a handsome, 28-year-old City banker and Old Etonian, Philip Dunne. Diana invited Dunne on the royal party's skiing holiday at Klosters in early 1987 and also to Royal Ascot. The young couple were seen lunching together in sophisticated intimate restaurants. After attending the wedding of Lord Worcester and TV star Tracy Ward, Diana and Dunne danced together until dawn, seemingly oblivious to the other people on the dance floor. Tongues began to wag and the tabloids began to sniff trouble in the royal marriage.

Later the same year, Diana shared the royal box at a David Bowie concert with another handsome, young aristocratic Englishman, Major David Waterhouse, 31, a nephew of the Duke of Marlborough and a cavalry officer in the élite Life Guards. Seemingly unconcerned at the conclusions people might draw, Diana rested her head on his shoulder during the concert and danced with him afterwards. Diana was seen enjoying herself immensely, laughing and joking with the Guards officer and caring little that it would become the subject of intense speculation.

Diana didn't care a damn and laughed at the tabloids which were 'tut-tutting' at her apparently irresponsible behaviour. But they had no idea at that time that she knew in her heart that Charles was having an affair with another woman, giving her *carte blanche* to do as she wished. Indeed, it seemed that one of the reasons Diana acted in such an outrageous way was to show Charles that two could play at his game.

Throughout the summer of 1987, however, Diana had been taking riding lessons with Captain James Hewitt. He had offered to teach William and Harry to ride and when Diana spoke of her fear of horse riding he agreed to teach her as well. The more time Diana spent with Hewitt, the more she realised she enjoyed his company. Within a matter of months they were lovers. Diana spoiled Hewitt, buying the impoverished cavalry officer Saville Row suits costing £1,500 each, made-to-measure Jermyn Street shirts at £75 each, and shoes costing £700 a pair. In return, Hewitt gave Diana one of his old cricket sweaters and a £30 padded jacket to keep her warm in winter.

But Hewitt also gave Diana the attention she craved. She loved his kind and gentle manner and the way he seemed to anticipate not only her moods but her every need. They would spend nights together at Kensington Palace, Althorp House and at Hewitt's mother's cottage in Devon. There, they would push two single beds together and spend the night in each other's arms while Diana's personal detective slept in the adjoining room. Diana discovered a passion she had never experienced before and she loved it.

Just as importantly, Diana rediscovered her sense of fun with Hewitt. She believed that one of the reasons the affair lasted so long was that they used to enjoy themselves together, laugh at ridiculous things, and have the sort of fun she had last enjoyed with her flatmates as a single girl. Hewitt made Diana laugh, cracking silly jokes, fooling around, teasing each other. He made her feel young again and she needed that sense of freedom after her painful years of boredom and frustration. And that's what she loved. But those happy times would not last.

Hewitt was posted to Germany with his Regiment and Diana wouldn't see him for weeks at a time. And before the Gulf War against Iraq's Saddam Hussein, Hewitt was posted to Saudi Arabia for two months. When he returned, Diana cooled, fearing he had not the strength of character she wanted in a man. She also wondered whether his protestations of love had been genuine, as hers had. She would admit in her famous *Panorama* interview that at one time she was 'very much in love' with him.

What worried Diana was the thought that Hewitt was, in fact, rather a shallow character who might have become involved with her because of the cachet of having bedded the Princess of Wales, the wife of the heir to the throne, rather than solely enjoying a truly loving relationship as she had done. She recalled that on one occasion during the Gulf War, a desperate Hewitt had asked a tabloid reporter if he could use his mobile phone because he needed to talk to the Princess of Wales back home at Kensington Palace. And Hewitt then carried on a three-minute conversation with her while reporters stood around listening. When she read of the incident in a tabloid, she wondered how the man could have been so stupid.

She also remembered that her beloved Hewitt had cracked jokes about making love with the future Queen of England as they lay in bed together. She didn't really think that was terribly amusing.

From the very beginning of the affair with Hewitt, the Queen and Prince Philip had been kept informed of Diana's adultery. Her personal bodyguards at that time, Inspector Ken Wharfe and Sergeant Alan Peters, had a duty to pass on such information to their senior officers who, in turn, informed the Queen's Private Secretary, Sir Robert Fellowes. He then would tell the Queen what had been going on. Yet nothing whatsoever was said to Diana and no action was taken.

The Queen knew, of course, that Charles and Diana's relationship was in deep trouble and that, to all intents and purposes, their marriage was over. She also knew that Charles was carrying on an adulterous relationship with Camilla Parker Bowles. But the Queen knew from experience that marriages often survive, despite many rocky periods. The Queen's own marriage had suffered from time to time over the years and she hoped that Diana would simply lead her own life and continue the sham that all was well between her and Charles for the sake of the children, the House of Windsor and the nation.

Diana, however, was mortified when she heard that Hewitt, with the help of a ghost writer, was to tell all in a sensational book which would reveal everything of their affair. She also feared that Hewitt might publish photographs or the contents of the love letters she had written to him during their three-year-long affair. When the book, *Princess in Love*, appeared in the shops, Diana breathed a sigh of relief that all the intimate details of their sexual relationship had not been included, for at least Hewitt's examination of events stopped at the bedroom door. But her secret love affair, her grand passion, was now in the public domain, with 75,000 books selling in the first 24 hours.

Diana adored the fact that the critics tore the book to shreds describing it as 'a squirm-inducing embarrassment' and that the gallant Guards officer was variously described as 'a cad', 'a bounder' and 'vermin'. Senior public officials suggested various punishments, ranging from public execution to walking the plank! Diana was called on to sue Hewitt for libel. She did not do so but she believed that Hewitt had received what he had richly deserved, the public's condemnation for betraying the woman he professed to have loved.

From the moment Diana had first heard that Hewitt planned to write a book, Diana had been worried at how the public would react to her adultery. She didn't care that the Royal Family would have been shaken by the revelations, nor the fact that the great mass of the public would know that she was not the saintly figure they all believed her to be. She hoped that the public would realise that she was driven into another man's arms because of the callous way she had been treated by Prince Charles.

WE DON'T BLAME YOU, DIANA screamed the *Daily Mirror* and went on to report that in a poll, 73 per cent of *Mirror* readers backed Diana, believing that she had been driven into the arms of another by a cold and unfeeling husband. All that made her feel so much better, boosting her confidence, but she still feared that she should never have allowed herself to become so involved with a man like Hewitt.

Unbeknown to Diana and the British public, the despicable Hewitt betrayed Diana further. Hewitt boasted to journalists and the few friends that he had left of Diana's sexual secrets. He would tell of her demands, her sexual appetite, her sexual relationship with Charles and of her pleasure when making love to him.

In late October 1994, when Diana finally summoned up the courage to make her first public appearance following the Hewitt scandal, Diana found the crowds cheering and shouting for her as if nothing had happened. When she returned home that evening, she told her faithful butler, Harold Brown, 37, who had been with her for ten years, 'Well, no one threw any rotten eggs.'

'I didn't think they would, Ma'am,' he replied. Diana had survived another disastrous love affair with her reputation barely dented. But it had been close.

Meanwhile, the nation continued to lay the blame for the end of the marriage firmly at Charles's door. They were convinced that he had returned to his mistress in the early years of the marriage, leaving Diana to fend for herself as best she could. The nation believed that Diana had been mistreated and abandoned by a callous man, just as millions of women have been treated by their wayward partners. They saw Diana as being left to bring up William and Harry on her own. All they could see was that Charles was living 100 miles away from home at Highgrove, with his mistress living only 15 minutes away, while Diana had been abandoned, miserable and unhappy, and suffering from eating disorders caused directly by her husband's unfeeling behaviour towards her. That view of the royal marriage would never change.

Despite the fact that their marriage was over in all but name, Diana still did not want a legal separation or a divorce from Charles. She knew that William and Harry had accepted the situation that their parents led separate lives, lived in different parts of the country and hardly ever met, and she believed that they preferred to know that their parents were still married in the vague hope that perhaps, one day, they might get back together again. Diana had not spent many hours listening to marriage guidance counsellors without appreciating that children often wanted their parents to remain married even if they didn't get on together.

Despite her wishes, however, she was left in no doubt that she had no choice in the matter. Prince Charles would have happily continued the relationship as it was. He was content to stay married to Diana, primarily for the sake of William and Harry. Whenever the subject was broached with Prince William, he said he wanted his parents to remain married. Charles was happy with Camilla, buried in the Gloucestershire countryside, riding and going on long walks together with their dogs. He was perfectly happy that Diana should get on with her life and enjoy other relationships with other men, just as long as she didn't bring the Royal Family into disrepute or, worse still, bring embarrassment to him or the children.

But certain members of the Royal Family thought differently. They believed that the obvious breakdown in the Wales's marriage was causing problems for the House of Windsor, due primarily to Diana's undoubted popularity. They feared that Diana and her charity work would continue to attract the majority of the Press attention to the detriment of every other member of the Royal Family. And that wasn't good news for the House of Windsor. They believed that separation and divorce was the only answer.

In the end, Charles was virtually ordered to go ahead and seek a separation. Behind the scenes, lawyers were briefed to thrash out the separation and, furthermore, prepare for the possibility of a divorce.

In December 1992, Prime Minister John Major told a packed House of Commons that 'with regret' he had to announce that the Prince and Princess of Wales were to separate.

A few days later, Diana said to one of her close friends; 'I was not surprised that I was made to separate from Charles, and yet I was still taken aback by what I was being told. It's not very nice simply to be informed that you are to be separated from your husband, that you have no say, no rights, that your opinions are not sought on any matter. I just said "thank you" and walked out. In a matter of minutes, my whole life had been shattered, but it was none of my doing. I had been cast aside, thrown out like an old coat. I felt sick.'

But her treatment at the hands of the Royal Family made Diana a more determined woman than she had ever been before. Now she was convinced that she would never let the Royals dominate and ruin the lives of either William or Harry. She knew that William would come under the most enormous pressure to conform as Charles had done in his young days. Diana knew that they would endeavour to 'educate' William to carry out his duty, to obey every bit of rigid protocol as Charles had done and risk the possibility of becoming a psychological wreck. The separation made Diana realise that she was now outside the Royal Family, facing life on her own. But the Royals had given Diana a mission in life — to fight for her boys, and to make sure they were brought up as normal, ordinary teenagers.

That was the reason she began to give them a broader education than she had before. That is why she took them on visits to the homeless and the disadvantaged, visited cancer patients in hospital and showed them how the underprivileged, poor and most vulnerable people in society coped with their different lifestyles. Occasionally, the tabloids criticised her for such actions, but she didn't care about their opinions because she believed that she had a mission to educate her sons through as broad a range of experiences as possible.

That was the prime reason, from the moment of their separation, for Diana taking control of her life and flying the nest, putting space between her and Charles and the rest of the House of Windsor. If the Royals didn't want her as part of their family, then she was going to make sure that she did whatever she wanted, with no restrictions. Now, her only commitment was to William and Harry and it was as their mother that she engineered the situation that she should be permitted to continue living at Kensington Palace. Other Royals believed that she should have been gently persuaded — forced if necessary — to quit Kensington Palace and live outside London. They believed that such an exile would have meant keeping her out of the limelight, allowing more column inches for other members of the family and the good charitable works they did week in, week out, year in, year out, which, for the greater part, went totally unnoticed by the Press, television or the general public.

The Royals knew that the tabloids, the quality papers and the TV stations were primarily interested in Princess Diana and the work she did for charity. They recalled that on one occasion in 1992, Charles had been travelling overseas to Germany on an official three-day royal visit while Diana was travelling to the Far East as part of her charity work. One photographer and one reporter accompanied Prince Charles; more than 300 reporters, photographers and TV crews travelled with Diana.

It was during 1992 and 1993 that reports began to circulate that Diana was a somewhat unstable character. No one knew the source of those reports, but word circulated around newspaper and TV pundits, a few politicians and it reached influential dinner parties. Gossip did the rest. In a matter of weeks, people were watching Diana more closely, remarking on some of her activities, doubting the quality of some of her friends.

The innuendos and the attacks grew more fierce, often leaving people wondering if the media knew things about Diana that had not been divulged to the general public. Even the tabloids joined in the attack. At the time of the Hewitt book, Richard Littlejohn, a columnist in the *Sun*, wrote: 'Diana is the scheming little shrew who had no qualms about betraying her husband, so she can hardly bleat when her ex-lover dishes the dirt ... At least the Hewitt revelations have exposed Diana's carefully-honed Mother Teresa act as a complete sham ... And if Diana thinks Hewitt shouldn't make money out of his relationship with her, then it's about time she stopped living off a man whom she quite clearly despises.'

She read of all those attacks in the newspapers and some upset her. And that was one of the main reasons she set out to seduce the editors of the tabloids and the broadsheets, the radio and TV executives, inviting them to private lunch parties at Kensington Palace and talking to them, putting her point of view and letting them judge whether she was indeed 'a little unstable'. Sometimes she would invite six or seven at a time, sometimes just two or three. Diana fluttered her eyelids and flattered them, fixed them with her most engaging look, made them feel special and made them feel she believed they were special, too — special and important. They loved that. Their egos massaged, their vanity and pride burnished, her guests would leave the Palace, sit back in their chauffeur-driven limousines, and feel privileged and proud as they were driven back to their offices.

It was a brilliant ploy and it worked. Once again, Diana began reading more flattering pieces about her, her lifestyle, her charity work and her ambitions. The criticism had been muted.

And then Diana would get on with her life. She would have other affairs and other romantic involvements throughout the 1990s, but the great majority of the nation believed that she had every right to try to find another man for herself. They wanted Diana to find someone who would care for her, love her and perhaps to marry her in the fullness of time.

For a while, Diana was madly in love with a millionaire art dealer who, unfortunately, was already married with a grown-up family. She had met him at Windsor Castle in the summer of 1985 at a reception for those who had been invited to join the royal party attending Royal Ascot that afternoon. The debonair, young-looking man with rather long, dark, wavy hair, immaculately dressed in his morning suit, caught Diana's eye. She also noticed how handsome, relaxed and friendly he seemed. By his side stood a young woman, a few years older than Diana, whom she noted was slim, attractive and dressed in a beautiful silk, printed summer dress. She wondered whether they were married for they seemed ideally suited. She also wondered if they were happy together.

The man was Oliver Hoare, a 39-year-old antique dealer specialising in Iranian art; the woman was his wife, Diane, then 37; the daughter of a French heiress, the Baroness Louise de Waldner, one of the Queen Mother's closest friends. Charles joined Diana and together they walked over to chat to Oliver and Diane.

The two women began talking and found they had much in common. Oliver and Diane had three children, two sons and a little girl, Olivia, then two, and just a few months older than Harry. The two women talked often that day, preferring to chat rather than follow the racing which neither found compelling. Both women had a considerable interest in fashion. Prince Charles and Oliver had always got on well together, because of Oliver's interest in art and antiques. The relationship between Charles and Diana and the Hoares developed. Within a matter of weeks, the Hoares came to dinner at Kensington Palace and Diana found both of them fascinating and far more fun than Charles's usual dinner guests, many of whom Diana would describe in private as 'boring old farts'.

The Hoares understood that Charles and Diana were having marriage problems and Diane would listen to Diana's concerns and sympathise. Occasionally, Diana would phone Diane in tears. Oliver offered to act as a go-between and Charles readily agreed. During the protracted drama of the following few years, Oliver and his wife would try to help, but to no avail. When Charles and Diana stopped speaking to each other, Diana turned to Oliver and poured out her heart. He would visit Kensington Palace when Charles was away and Diana would pace up and down, venting her anger and her frustration, her eyes often filled with tears.

In part, Diana favoured Oliver Hoare as an intermediary because one of his great friends had been Camilla. Hoare and Camilla had met earlier in the 1970s when they were both young, and she, too, had enjoyed his company, his wit and his sophistication. Later, Charles and Camilla dined with the Hoares at their London mansion, but Diana was not told of that.

Diana wanted to know every tiny piece of information about the woman she believed had stolen her husband, the woman she would, more often than not, refer to as 'that bitch'. Diana would often fire questions at Oliver Hoare, wanting to learn as much as possible about her rival. Hoare found himself in an impossible situation. He was close to both Charles and Diana and did not wish to be seen taking sides in a marital disagreement.

Diana found that she needed Oliver's presence and understanding more and more, until the need for his undivided attention verged on desperation. She would cry on his shoulder, throw herself into his arms and could hardly survive 24 hours without seeing him or, at the very least, talking to him on the phone. Diana, however, had no idea that during 1992 she had become a burden to Oliver, putting a tremendous strain on his marriage. Eventually, Diane accused her husband of having an affair with Diana, as he spent one or two evenings a week with the Princess, either dining out, going for long drives in the country, accompanying her to cocktail and dinner parties or spending time alone with her at Kensington Palace, sometimes not returning home until the early hours. At weekends, Diana would spend 30 minutes or more on the phone talking to Oliver, much to the annoyance of his wife.

Some time during 1992, Diana realised that she had fallen hopelessly and completely in love with Oliver Hoare, someone whom she believed had all the attributes any woman would want in a man — strength, honour, charm, wit, sophistication and a gut-wrenching sexual attraction. Diana later revealed that she considered Oliver Hoare 'drop-dead gorgeous'. Diana came to the conclusion that Oliver was the man she wanted.

But she was not sure that the attraction was reciprocal. She also wondered whether Oliver wanted the burden of an involvement with her, the estranged wife of his friend, the Prince of Wales. Overnight, he would become the focus of every photographer and royal reporter in Fleet Street. There was also the matter of his wife and children. Oliver Hoare had never enjoyed the limelight. A quiet man, he preferred to lead a more sheltered, less ostentatious existence, shunning rather than seeking the glare of publicity. Even his car was ordinary, a standard Volvo Estate.

During the summer of 1993, Diane Hoare reached the end of her patience with the Princess of Wales. Now, whenever Diane answered the phone to the Princess, Diana would no longer want to chat for a while, but would rather brusquely ask to speak immediately to Oliver. He, in turn, would still see Diana once or twice a week, and over the weekends the phonecalls would never stop. But Oliver Hoare began to tire of his role as the demands on his time and his life were becoming unbearable. His wife, too, was insisting that he should end his association with the Princess so that their life together could return to normal.

After Oliver asked Diana to stop phoning him, calls would still come to the house. When he or his wife answered, there would be silence and the phone would go dead. During a 16-month period, Diane Hoare estimated that there must have been 300 'silent' calls! Finally, in desperation, Oliver Hoare called British Telecom and sophisticated tracker equipment was installed. The Hoares were given a code to tap into their handset as the nuisance caller came on the line. For two months there was nothing. Early in 1994, however, the calls resumed in earnest.

Some days later, Oliver Hoare was given a list showing where the calls had come from. One number was Diana's personal number inside Kensington Palace. Later, police informed him that the calls were traced to two phones inside Kensington Palace, Diana's mobile phone, two phone boxes near the Palace and a phone at the home of her sister, Lady Sarah McCorquodale. The information was passed to Commander Robert Marsh, head of the Royal Protection Squad, who discussed the matter at the most senior level at the Home Office before passing the information to Sir Robert Fellowes, the Queen's Private Secretary and Diana's brother-in-law. He contacted Diana. Nothing is known of that conversation but the calls stopped abruptly. The police elected not to prosecute and the extraordinary affair was allowed to drop after Oliver and Diane

Hoare said that they did not wish to press charges.

Weeks later, the *News of the World* reported the story of the malicious phonecalls and the fact that suspicion had fallen on Diana. The headline DI'S CRANKY PHONE CALLS TO MARRIED TYCOON caused her great embarrassment.

But her reaction to the tabloid furore showed her new confidence. That Sunday morning, Diana was besieged by newsmen and photographers as she went to play tennis at The Chelsea Harbour Club. She smiled happily for the cameras. She wore her favourite American flag sweatshirt, revealing light-blue shorts and trainers. Diana appeared not to have a care in the world. She was also wearing dark glasses. Questions were flung at her by the waiting reporters, but she didn't say a word. Every question was met with a confident smile. As she reached her car, she gave the photographers a one-fingered salute with her middle finger, the ultimate insult, and left her hand lingering in the air for a full five seconds!

Britain's agony aunts wrote open letters to the Princess, advising her to seek help, talk to a counsellor or call the Samaritans to guide her through her difficulties. And they reminded her, as if she needed reminding, that isolation and loneliness was the price she would have to pay for her freedom from a loveless marriage. Psychiatrists suggested that Diana had made the calls to the Hoares' house because she was desperately lonely or had been rebuffed by Oliver Hoare and simply wanted to hear the voice of the person she loved and trusted. Some marriage guidance counsellors insisted Diana must now be a 'lonely and frightened person', a woman who felt 'abandoned' and who was 'panicking', unable to find comfort in anyone save the person she wanted to talk to. Diana knew, however, that she had blown her relationship with Oliver. So she went back to the gym and a stricter routine of fitness and swimming. It was her therapy, and she was determined to put her last love affair out of her mind by relaxing, enjoying life again and deciding on her future.

Her good intentions, however, would end in more turmoil and trouble.

After training at The Chelsea Harbour Club most mornings, she would take her seat at the back of the restaurant, on table number eight, while she drank orange juice and, occasionally, a cappuccino. She liked sitting at her vantage point, which gave her a view of everyone else as well as all the comings and goings, while remaining discreetly in the background. Of course, Diana was being more than a little naïve if she believed she could ever remain unnoticed in a café or shop or anywhere else. Over a drink, she would chat to her fitness advisers and sometimes to friends she met at the club.

It was during one of these mornings in the late Spring of 1994 that she saw a young man who looked vaguely familiar. She was introduced to him. He was Will Carling, the Captain of the England rugby team and one of Britain's best known and most popular sportsmen. She had, in fact, met him before when she had been the guest of honour at rugby internationals. During the following few weeks, the two would meet every so often at the club and they struck up a friendship.

Three months after Diana and Carling met, however, Carling married Julia Smith, a willowy, bubbly, good-looking woman who ran her own PR firm. A month after their first meeting, Carling asked her to marry him. But Carling and Diana continued to meet at the club and Carling would tease Diana about her lack of hard muscle, telling her that her biceps were like sparrow's legs. Carling offered to take Diana to his specialist gymnasium, BiMAL, a medical sports and rehabilitation clinic, a centre for Britain's top sportsmen. Diana became a regular visitor.

Diana invited Carling to Kensington Palace, primarily to meet her two sons who were becoming rugby enthusiasts — and Will Carling was their hero. Diana won many Brownie points for bringing Carling back to the Palace and the boys talked and chatted to him non-stop whenever he called round.

Someone who took some interest in the relationship between Diana and Carling was his former personal assistant, Hilary Ryan. She said, 'In late 1994, Diana and Will Carling had a spat because Will had asked one of her staff to come and work for him without seeking her permission. For a while, Diana and Will didn't even speak when they met at the Harbour Club, but Will would go at the same time just to see her. During those weeks, he seemed awfully downcast. But by February 1995, everything seemed to be back on track and Will and Diana would meet regularly three times a week for a light breakfast after working out. He would tell me that he would be away from the office for several hours and they often went back to Kensington Palace together.

'Carling ordered a special "hot" phone line to be installed which I was instructed must not be used or answered by anyone in the office, not even me, his PA. I knew the line had been installed for Diana so she never had to go through the switchboard. They would occasionally chat on the phone for an hour or more, laughing and giggling ... at other times, they seemed to be having quiet, intimate conversations.'

Diana and Carling gave each other pet names, Diana calling him 'Captain' while he called her 'The Boss'.

In March 1995, Carling arranged for the young Princes to attend an England get-together before the Rugby Union World Cup finals were to be played in South Africa. The boys were thrilled and so was Diana. They thoroughly approved of the new man in their mother's life but they didn't know just how intimately close Carling and Diana had become. When news of their relationship reached the newspapers, Julia Carling was understandably very annoyed, attacking the Princess.

'This has happened to her before,' she said, 'and you would hope she won't do those things again, but she obviously does.'

Unfortunately, Julia added, 'She picked the wrong couple to do it with this time because we can only get stronger from it. It's horrible to go through. But it does make you stronger no matter how much someone is trying to destroy what you have. Our relationship is very strong anyway — and thank God for that.'

The British public were spellbound, following every detail of the struggle over the English rugby hero, one of the nation's best known and most respected sports idols. Never before had any woman whose husband had been attracted to the Princess of Wales openly attacked Diana or publicly accused her of trying to destroy a marriage. Never before had Diana been involved in such a tug-of-love drama over a man.

A smiling, confident Julia would announce later, 'As far as we are concerned, it's over. It's a completely closed shop. That was an episode in our lives and you have to get on with things. Diana's business is her business. What is important is Will and myself. I didn't give him an ultimatum. The decision to end the friendship was Will's alone.'

And Carling insisted that the relationship with Diana had been wholly innocent. 'It was a perfectly harmless friendship with the Princess of Wales. Maybe I was just stupid.'

Forty-eight hours after Julia's declaration that her husband's relationship with the Princess was over, Carling and Diana were seen together at The Harbour Club. And in September 1995, Carling was seen visiting Kensington Palace, apparently to leave two England rugby shirts for William and Harry. The tabloids returned to the offensive, branding Diana 'a home wrecker'.

Throughout the autumn, the battle over Carling continued. Many believed that all three members of the triangle had their own very different reasons for continuing the public fight. Diana, some thought, wanted to demonstrate that she had the power and the sexual attraction to combat any rival, particularly Julia, whom she considered a 'worm'; some believed that Carling thought he and Diana would become an item and that he would walk off into the sunset with a rugby ball under one arm and the Princess of Wales on the other; and others thought Julia Carling was desperate to make the most of a marriage that had gone wrong and was happily making play of the Diana angle for all she was worth.

Ironically, however, there were no winners. Julia

and Will Carling announced after yet another secret rendezvous between Diana and the rugby hero that, with regret, they had 'agreed to spend some time apart'. In reality, their marriage was over. But, just as dramatically and nearly as swiftly, the affair between Carling and Diana came to an abrupt end. Diana, having won the battle, finally realised she was no longer interested in the England rugby hero.

Later, Diana would explain that one of the reasons she cooled towards Carling was that during the height of the public battle, he had showed little enthusiasm for the difficulties associated with their relationship, which she deemed to be a weakness in his character. He had told her that he felt like a cork bobbing about on the ocean rather than taking control of the situation. She didn't like that.

Once again, Diana's love-life was in turmoil, and she had no one to turn to. So she went back to the gym and launched herself into yet more charity work, the therapy in which she always found the security and love she so craved.

# CHAPTER SIX

## 'COMPLEX ... INSECURE ...
## CHILDLIKE ... UNIQUE'

These were the words that Earl Spencer, Diana's brother, used to describe his sister's character during his remarkably powerful speech at her funeral. He was speaking with honesty, frankness and accuracy, for Diana's character and personality encompassed all these traits.

Everyone who spent time with Diana realised only too well that she was a multi-faceted, complex character whom very few people outside her immediate family ever really knew. It seems certain that Prince Charles was never able to fathom what made Diana 'tick' and he would talk to his close colleagues, seeking their advice how best to deal with his wife.

Of course, as most marriage guidance counsellors would recognise, Charles was particularly ill-equipped to deal with someone of Diana's character. Charles had not been brought up by his parents, in any true meaning of the phrase, but by a succession of nannies and governesses, only seeing his parents for an hour or so each morning and each evening. Then he was off to boarding school. And the difficult relationship with his father could not have helped prepare Charles for life with a wife as complex as Diana.

Diana, of course, felt rejection throughout her life. Lord Spencer understood that only too well, for he was only 18 months younger than his sister, and he spoke of the feeling of rejection when their mother quit the family home when Diana was only six years old. Diana referred to that feeling throughout her life whenever she had serious discussions with her friends and she believed that she suffered many crises of confidence as a direct result of it.

Lady Cosima Maria Gabriella Vane-Tempest Stewart was born in the same year as Diana and she became friendly with Diana primarily because they were two of a kind. Her life had been full of many of the experiences Diana had suffered; her parents divorced when she was nine and she suffered the same awful pangs of rejection as Diana. Cosima's marriage also ended in divorce. But when Diana and Cosima met and talked they found in each other a mirror image, almost as though they were sisters. There was an immediate mutual understanding between them, a bond, that lasted until Diana's death.

Cosima recalled, 'When I met Diana, I saw for the first time in someone else's eyes true empathy. The parallel of our experience was exact. It was a Sunday and I was feeling awful for I had just left my two young children at their father's house for the first time. I cried in front of Diana, unable to control myself, and yet in her eyes I realised that she understood what I was going through.

' "Cosi, you'll get used to it," Diana said, speaking quietly.

' "Are you sure?" I replied, and at that moment I believe a bond was formed between us which would never be shaken.'

Later, Diana sent Cosima a present — a candle set in a clay pot. Diana had also attached a note: 'I hope this candle lights some of your darkest moments.'

The beautiful Cosima would say, 'We had both broken away from large, powerful families and we had lost our protection. Both of us were considered "hysterical, unbalanced, paranoid and foolish". Many children from broken homes, as Diana and I were, never get over the sense of rejection; the abandonment sets the tone for the whole of one's emotional life. Our mutual interests included the spiritual and the psychic. Diana did not believe conventionally in God but she and I both sought an explanation for life's endless chaos, pain and drama. The point of seeing psychics is that one has a sense that life is predestined.'

Together, the two mothers would discuss every aspect of their private and emotional lives and the reason for their feelings of insecurity. Together they shared experiences, comforted each other in their dark moments and both knew that the other was always a phonecall away whenever they were needed.

Throughout her life, Diana had great problems in accepting any form of criticism. It wasn't that she believed that she was always right, but criticism embarrassed her, it made her feel inadequate as though she was lacking something. She so hated those feelings that throughout her life her reaction to criticism was to run away, sometimes pretending that there had been no reprimand, that nothing had happened.

It had begun in childhood. When her school work didn't go well Diana would feign illness, thereby earning the compassion of the teachers rather than criticism. And at West Heath, the introvert Diana, lacking confidence and stamina, found difficulty in coping and instead of trying harder, virtually gave up on her education. She failed her first set of 'O'-levels and retook them six months later, failing them all again. Though her father wanted her to persevere, Diana didn't want to know so she went off to a Swiss finishing school instead. Once there, she found difficulty in tackling the French lessons and arrived home six weeks later in tears.

At the age of 17, Diana enrolled as a student teacher at Betty Vacani's dance school, in London, but was criticised for not being good enough. That hurt Diana for she had set her heart on the one career she loved, dancing. Rather than accept the reprimand, however, Diana took off on a skiing holiday and never returned to the dance studios.

All those setbacks had a severe effect on Diana, convincing her that she was a failure in life, and further damaging her fragile self-confidence at a crucial age. One of the main problems was that Diana had no one to encourage her, to push her, to make sure she did work hard at school and face up to the problems and realities of life, for her mother was married and living in London with her second husband.

Diana's failure to accept any type of criticism surfaced time and time again throughout her life. It didn't seem to matter whether people criticised her or simply tried to advise her to do something in a different, more efficient way. To Diana's fragile self-confidence she saw no difference between advice and criticism. That was one of the reasons why so many of Diana's personal staff left her employ. These were not the staff that she inherited when marrying Prince Charles, staff whom she believed were speaking about her behind her back and criticising her. These were staff whom Diana herself hired after interviewing them.

As one put it, 'It was not quite accurate, but word around Kensington Palace was that a member of staff had only to raise an eyebrow suggesting the faintest criticism and he would be out within a week.'

And her attitude to criticism extended to her friends. Throughout her life, Diana became very friendly with any number of people, mainly young women of her own age. With some she formed extremely close trusting relationships, while many others were mere acquaintances. But many of those she favoured fell by the wayside, disowned by Diana because she felt they were criticising her or, indeed, may have criticised her to a third person. Even those whom Diana would phone two or three times a week for months on end would suddenly realise that the Princess of Wales had stopped phoning, that invitations to lunch at the Palace had seemingly come to an abrupt end, with no explanation.

Sarah, Duchess of York, was one of those with whom Diana formed a remarkably close friendship. They were thrown together when Sarah began dating Prince Andrew and, when she also joined the family, Diana and Sarah became even closer. But only from time to time. For months on end they would talk on the phone every day, meet two or three times a week, swap secrets, discuss their marital problems and debate how they planned to escape from the Royal House of Windsor. And yet Sarah herself was to admit that they would frequently fall out, not talk to each other for weeks at a time, and then all would be well again. But with most of her friends, those whom Diana believed had openly criticised her, that was enough for her never to call or write to them again, cutting them dead. It also revealed Diana's stubborn streak.

One of her greatest confidantes, for example, was Rosa Monckton. Diana was not only godmother to one of Rosa's children, but the two went on a private cruise around the Aegean only weeks before Diana died. Rosa Monckton had commented on Diana's lacklustre appearance during an overseas tour with Prince Charles. As a result, Diana cut her dead, and for several months never phoned.

It didn't seem to matter to Diana that such actions resulted in her losing many good friends, many of whom were only trying to be helpful, to show their concern for her, not wanting her to make mistakes that could be picked up by the tabloids and thrown back in her face. Many was the time that the criticism was of the most gentle kind. It didn't matter. To Diana, that was sufficient to banish them from her list of friends.

Her fear and loathing of personal criticism was one of the reasons she adored her compassionate charity work. No one ever criticised her for visiting dying patients, lepers, landmine victims or the small children suffering from cancer and other heart-rending conditions. For all her magnificent charity work, Diana quite rightly won applause and praise from all quarters. And as a result of that praise, she became ever more confident.

It was, of course, this vulnerability which helped Diana to spot the broken-hearted among a group of children or adults, and she would instinctively walk over to them to chat and comfort them. Invariably, her sixth sense was accurate and people who knew the rejected outsider, the one suffering from unhappiness as much as physical pain, would remark on how Diana was able to pinpoint such victims with uncanny accuracy.

Diana even fell out with her own family, including her brother, Charles. When Diana felt that the media attention was becoming overbearing, having reached the point where she would arrive home in tears of anger and frustration at the pack of photographers and tabloid reporters hounding her every move, she decided to move out of London, seeking some peace in her life. She called her brother and asked if she could move back to the ancestral home, Althorp House. The house had automatically passed to Charles following the death of their father. Her brother, however, understandably did not appear to relish the idea of having *paparazzi* camped outside the gates of his home and he told Diana that he did not think her moving to Althorp was a good idea and suggested she find an alternative safe haven. Diana was mortified that her brother, though for the best of motives, had turned down her request in her hour of need, for whatever reason, and their relationship was cooler for some months.

But Diana faced even greater problems when dealing with the Royal Family. She knew they criticised her, sometimes in jest, but she knew in her heart that the Queen and Prince Philip believed that Prince Charles had made a grave mistake in marrying her. They believed Charles had been swept away by the fact that such a beautiful and innocent aristocratic girl wanted to marry him and, mistakenly, that he had believed the words of his great-uncle, Earl Mountbatten, who had advised him to marry a young virgin and educate her to become the next Queen. The trouble was that Diana had proved a handful and he was ill-equipped to cope with a modern young woman who wanted to lead her own life, refusing to accept the strict protocol and tradition laid down by the Windsors.

Diana accepted the Royal Family's teasing of her when she began making speeches in public. She would return home to find Charles and Prince Andrew having a little fun with her delivery, joking about her manner of speaking and trying to mimic her voice. She would blush and poke her tongue out at them but their criticism touched her most vulnerable nerve and she didn't like it.

But when her marriage hit the rocks, when Charles went off with his old mistress, Camilla, when no one in the Royal Family attempted to console her, help to patch up the marriage, or even try to understand what Diana was going through, she felt deserted and disowned. She had produced two heirs for the Windsors; now, it seemed, she was dispensable.

For four years, Diana found solace in the arms of James Hewitt, who massaged her ego, gave her love and affection and restored her confidence. But when Diana tired of Hewitt and once again felt the bitterness of isolation, she felt her old anger returning at the treatment meted out to her by Charles and the Windsors. She aimed her fury not only at Charles and the Royal Family but particularly at Camilla, a woman whom she believed had duped and insulted her, stolen her husband and had treated Diana as a young woman of little or no consequence.

It was in this mood of anger and spite that Diana talked to her friend of many years, the faithful and trustworthy Dr James Colthurst, whom she had known since her teenage years. Their association began in the late 1970s when the pair met during a skiing holiday in the French resort of Tignes. Diana was then a shy 17-year-old while the Eton-educated James was 21 and studying medicine. Indeed, some of Diana's girlfriends at that time believe that James Colthurst, the son of a landed baronet — his father owns Cork's famous Blarney Castle — was, for a while during that early period, in love with Diana, frequently phoning her and visiting her Fulham flat.

And it was James Colthurst to whom Diana first turned when she began suffering the effects of post-natal depression after the birth of Harry in 1984. He would come and visit Diana at Kensington Palace and discuss her problems with her throughout the winter of 1984–85. In those months, Diana came to realise that Colthurst was a man she could trust. Whenever Diana became ill or depressed, or found herself unable to cope, she would call Colthurst who was only too happy to help in any way he could. In 1986, they met formally in public when Colthurst, then a junior doctor at St Thomas's Hospital in London, invited Princess Diana to attend the official presentation of a new scanner for the hospital.

Also at St Thomas's that day was Andrew Morton, a tabloid's royal reporter. He noticed that Diana and James Colthurst seemed to enjoy a strong rapport and, after Diana left the hospital, Morton struck up a conversation with the young doctor. At this time, Morton appeared to feel a closeness to Diana. He would tell other journalists who were detailed to follow Diana's every step that there was a bond between him and the Princess, though they never spoke. He would tell his colleagues that whenever Diana stepped from a royal car or waved at the cameramen, she would always seek out Morton and the two would stare at each other as though secretly communicating.

'See,' Morton would say to whoever was listening, 'Diana's looking at me again ... she's staring straight at me.'

His colleagues, however, doubted that such a bond ever existed, believing that Morton was becoming infatuated with the Princess. Over the next few years, Morton sought out Colthurst and they struck up a friendship, playing squash together and enjoying the occasional meal. Morton slowly gained Dr Colthurst's trust and, through him, Diana would communicate stories she wanted the world to know about. She would also permit Dr Colthurst to inform Morton of any plans she wanted aired publicly.

During 1991, Diana was at a particularly low ebb. Her marriage to Charles had been over, in all but name, for some years and she feared that a legal separation would soon follow. Her four-year affair with James Hewitt was over; her beloved father was not far from death; her mother was living on an island in the north of Scotland and Diana saw a life of unremitting misery stretching into the distance. As she herself put it, 'I felt demons in my head.' She also felt anger in her heart and, in this state of depression and hopelessness, she decided to lash out at those she felt were responsible for her misery.

She talked over the matter with James Colthurst who agreed to become the intermediary between her and Morton. To Colthurst's friends who knew none of this, it now seems extraordinary that a man who had been Diana's friend for so long, who had talked to her about her depression and post-natal problems, should have agreed to such a plan. As an intelligent man and a doctor, who had known her for many years, he would have understood that such subterfuge might not necessarily have been in her best interests.

In the weeks that passed following the revelation that Dr Colthurst was the go-between, no statement was issued or interview given by Dr Colthurst and, as a result, the nation was left to wonder why he had agreed to take part.

What is known, however, is that in 1991 a book deal with the publisher Michael O'Mara was thrashed out. Morton would write down questions and Dr Colthurst would take them to Kensington Palace where Diana would speak into a tape recorder and hand the tape to James Colthurst to pass on to Morton. But she never wanted to meet the royal reporter.

Shortly after the book *Diana, Her True Story* was published in 1992, Diana fell out with Dr Colthurst. Some believe that Diana was outraged, claiming that some of the disclosures she had made on the tape had been blown out of proportion. Diana always claimed that she had *never* attempted suicide but had only thought of taking such a course of action in her darkest moments of despair.

And the story in the book of one of her alleged suicide attempts — throwing herself down the stairs when pregnant with William — filled her with rage and despair that anyone would think for one moment that she would have attempted to kill herself when pregnant.

The publication of that book, and Prince Charles's television interview with Jonathan Dimbleby, confirmed in Diana's mind her desire to give a TV interview as well, putting her side of the story of the royal marriage. She had considered the possibility of assisting with another book but she didn't feel that she could trust anyone sufficiently. She knew such a TV interview would be a gamble but she believed she could carry it off successfully if she knew the possible questions in advance so that her replies could be thought through. Diana also recognised that if she knew, roughly, how she would reply to a question, her TV performance might not look too amateurish.

She kept the *Panorama* interview a secret from everyone, including Prince Charles, her sons, the Royal Family and most of her advisers. She was convinced that if the Royal Family had discovered that she intended to participate in a free-ranging TV interview they would have found a way to stop it. She decided she wanted the interview to go out on *Panorama* because it would give greater prestige and authority to what she had to say.

Diana believed that ever since the marriage had fallen apart in the mid-1980s, Buckingham Palace advisers were keen to keep Diana as low-key as possible. The last thing they wanted was for Diana to upstage Charles, the heir to the throne, and certainly not the Queen. But as the years ticked by, the public and the media became ever more interested in Diana, caring little for the royal duties carried out by Charles or the Queen.

Since the official separation in December 1992, Diana believed that the Royal Family and their advisers had gone out of their way to criticise her and the way she was conducting her private life, forming short-term relationships with married men, conducting relationships in public at a time when William and Harry were becoming more aware of the ways of the world. After the separation, Diana had announced that she was retiring from public life and cancelled her patronage of more than 100 charities. She gave up those charities because she wanted to concentrate on just a few, but she also believed that many of those charities had sought her support simply because she was married to the Prince of Wales. She had also become fed up with what she called 'the boring side of charity work', turning up once a year at an annual meeting, shaking hands with the organisers, giving her name to raise some money and then disappearing for another year.

But, within a few months, Diana realised that staying at home, keeping fit and indulging herself in all types of therapies had become somewhat boring. She realised that she was missing the media attention, the limelight, the crowds, the praise and the warmth and feedback she received during her visits to hospitals, the disadvantaged and the distressed. Her re-emergence into public life, though welcomed by the charities she supported and the hospitals she visited, was certainly not welcomed at Buckingham Palace for, at a stroke, the Royal Family were relegated almost to obscurity in the media as the attention once again focussed almost exclusively on Diana.

And one of the ways Diana returned in style to the front pages of newspapers and magazines was in her capricious choice of clothes. One of the criticisms she believed the Royal Family fully deserved was the way in which they had seemed determined to influence her choice of fashion by the traditions of the family. She resented that interference, though for the first few years of her married life she did toe the line, and accept their advice to a certain degree. Even then, however, she felt that many of the styles she wore did not meet with the approval of the Queen or Princess Anne.

She would recall that at the height of summer with the temperatures in the '80s she was still expected to wear stockings or tights when meeting guests, having drinks at a cocktail party or lunch with the Queen. On one embarrassing occasion, she was even sent from the room where she was chatting to guests before lunch and told to return to her bedroom and put on a pair of tights. When holidaying at Balmoral with the family, Diana would often be politely chastised for wearing casual clothes when it was known that the Queen would be arriving for lunch or tea.

Diana tried to change Prince Charles's attitude to clothes. She tried to persuade him to wear more casual clothing rather than always appearing in suits or, when in Scotland, always wearing a kilt with the correct paraphernalia and never appearing to enjoy

The future Princess.

The young Diana – *(above)* in her earliest years and *(below)* with her brother, the future Earl Spencer.

Prince Charles wins a bride and England wins a Princess in the wedding of the century.

The young couple, early in their marriage, together at
Balmoral, and *(opposite)*, an official photograph taken in
Australia in 1988.

*(Above)* The Princess in Vienna and *(below)* with the new-born Prince Harry.

In France, November 1988.

With Charles in Australia, 1988.

*(Above)* Sporting mums – Diana wins the race at William's sports day in 1989; and *(below)* Wills goes to Wimbledon in 1991.

The Princess always enjoyed sand, sea and sun *(above)* on the Virgin Isles in 1989, and *(below)* on Nevis Island in the Caribbean in 1993.

The smile that captured the heart of nations.

Always the loving mother. With Prince Harry in Majorca, 1988.

Diana at a convention for one of the many charities for which she did so much good work.

Enjoying the music of Luciano Pavarotti at a concert in 1991.

*(Above)* Diana meeting an AIDS patient at Middlesex Hospital. This was a concern that was very close to her heart; and *(below)* another of Diana's frequent hospital visits, this time in Edinburgh.

Visiting the elderly, and receiving flowers on a tour of
Canada in 1991

wearing his clothes, standing as though always on duty, a paragon of protocol. She knew that he was under great pressure to dress correctly at all times and, after a while, she gave up her campaign to change his style.

Diana, too, had felt that pressure. She understood that she was expected to support British fashion houses and with the help of *Vogue* fashion experts she chose many dresses which she liked including designs from Catherine Walker, Bruce Oldfield and Amanda Wakeley. But, as soon as she was free from Charles and the pressure from the Buckingham Palace advisers to conform to the style they thought fitting for a royal Princess, Diana became more daring, dressing exactly as she wanted regardless of protocol.

From that moment, her character shone through in the clothes she selected. She still loved some of the British fashion designers like Catherine Walker and Bruce Oldfield but, freed from the shackles of probity, Diana went wild, flirting with very short skirts, acres of thigh, and rather glitzy German-style designs showing how daring the real Diana could be. She was criticised for wearing ultra-tight black leather trousers, sporting high heels under tight jeans and applying her make up too lavishly. Throughout 1994, it seemed that Diana wanted to show off her legs at every possible opportunity, even, for example while collecting her sons from school. She donned skirts that split to the upper thigh and shocked everyone by arriving at church on Christmas day wearing a split skirt. Some criticised her, bitchily suggesting that her new choice of clothes revealed an immature way of showing any available man that she was on offer. And yet she persisted in wearing her revealing skirts and attracted criticism, and even mockery, from the fashion world. Some had the audacity to describe Diana's fashion taste as that of an 'Essex girl' or TV soap stars. The upper-crust *Tatler* magazine asked, 'Will the real Diana please sit down and dress like a Princess?' Diana took not the slightest notice.

But in her quest to sustain the supermodel image she enjoyed, Diana discovered foreign designers and fell in love with some of them. She chose to wear Chanel, Yves Saint Laurent, Armani and Valentino, but from that time on her favourite would be Gianni Versace. Whenever Versace came to London he and Diana would meet and they would discuss not only his latest creations but also any thoughts that Diana might have for any particular design. Sometimes, when they met Versace would bring along a dress he believed Diana would kill for and, more often than not, she loved his latest design, on occasions buying two of the same creation, but in different colours. They became close friends, which was why Diana was determined to attend his funeral mass in Milan following his murder in July 1997. That day, she wore a classic black Versace shift dress with a single row of pearls.

It was not only in her fashion-conscious styles that Diana wanted to cast aside the taboos the Royal Family had placed on her. Diana was a young woman of the '90s and she showed that in her casual outfits, always going to the gym dressed in tight cycle shorts, sneakers, a sweatshirt and baseball cap. She usually wore the baseball cap as a disguise when driving herself around London because other drivers and pedestrians weren't too sure if the woman driving the car was Princess Diana or not. It didn't matter ...

William and Harry liked their mother in her casual outfits. At home in Kensington Palace, most of the time Diana would wear blue jeans and a shirt, particularly in the winter. She felt, as everyone else did, at ease in jeans. And she would often be dressed that way when other mothers brought their children round to see William and Harry or for tea.

That was Diana being her natural self, the person she liked to be to everyone. But she also believed in her scrapes with palace officialdom that she had to be constantly on guard against her enemies. In her complex personality, Diana believed that 'the enemy' she referred to in her *Panorama* interview — royal courtiers and advisers — had been plotting against her, trying to smear her image with the public and make her appear irrational. She even believed that advisers to Charles and the Queen were conducting a war against her in their efforts to drive her out of the Royal Family.

Diana became certain that senior Buckingham Palace advisers had become so determined to keep her out of the limelight that they were responsible for persuading charity organisations that Diana would not be available to undertake overseas visits though, in private, those same charities had asked Diana if she would be prepared to help them by visiting some of their overseas projects. On every occasion, Diana had said she would be 'very happy' to carry out whatever they wanted, including international trips. When the matter was broached at Buckingham Palace, however, or among senior Foreign Office civil servants, the charities discovered that their ideas did not meet with approval. The Red Cross had wanted Diana to take a high-profile position throughout their year-long 125th anniversary celebrations, participating in a number of Red Cross events around the world in 1995. Within days of the news being published, discreet intervention by Buckingham Palace put an end to the plan. Diana was upset and angry.

Later, Diana would be asked to undertake work as an ambassador on behalf of the British Red Cross. That, too, was diplomatically turned down after the request had been passed to Buckingham Palace. She believed that the powers that be, including the Queen and particularly Prince Philip, were doing their damndest to bury her. So she planned a future for herself. She decided that she would become a roving Royal Ambassador, touring the world, working for any number of organisations including the Red Cross, the Leprosy Society and AIDS charities. So determined did Diana become that she vowed that if the Palace intervened to stop her plans she would move to the United States and carry on her ambassadorial role from there. But first she needed the support of the British public.

The sensational *Panorama* programme was organised in secrecy. The interviews took place in the privacy of Kensington Palace and a breathless world sat in their armchairs on the evening of Monday, 20 November 1995, to await the outcome. The nation was not disappointed. Many viewers were taken aback not only by the content, but also at Diana's performance and the honesty of her replies. Her composure and fluency were remarkable. Polished and articulate, Diana showed no sign of her old self. Gone was the interviewer's flushed and flustered nightmare, with her flat voice, fiddly hands and hesitant sentences. No question took her by surprise and no answers were fluffed.

Her honesty was compelling when she spoke of her eating disorders, of her post-natal depression and the effect it had on her marriage, her adultery with James Hewitt and of her self-mutilation. She said, 'Yes, I did mutilate myself. I didn't like myself, I was ashamed because I couldn't cope with the pressures ... Well, I just hurt my arms and my legs.'

Despite her honesty, which everyone praised, Diana never spoke of any suicide attempts, leaving many to believe that she had, in fact, never attempted to kill herself.

But she did lash out at the monarchy, leaving her most poisoned arrows to attack the Queen, Prince Philip and their advisers.

'I understand that change is frightening for people, especially if there's nothing to go to,' she said. 'It's best to stay where you are. I understand that. But I do think there are a few things that could change, that would alleviate the doubt, and sometimes complicated relationships between monarchy and public.

'I would like a monarchy that has more contact with the people — and I don't mean riding round on bicycles and things like that, but just having a more in-depth understanding. I just say that from what I see and hear and feel on a daily basis in the role I have chosen for myself.'

But Diana's naïveté, her childlike qualities, also came to the fore in that interview when she proclaimed her ambition for the future, wanting to work an an ambassador for Britain, offering her talents to serve victims of society across the world.

'I would like to be queen of people's hearts. Someone's got to go out there and love people and show it ... The perception that has been given of me for the last three years has been very confusing, turbulent and, in some areas, I'm sure, many, many people doubt me. I want to reassure all those people who have loved me throughout the last 15 years that I'd never let them down. That is a priority to me. The man on the street matters more than anything else to me.'

Diana read the following day's newspapers with more interest than for many a year. Most newspapers applauded her 'gut-wrenching honesty' and some felt that the nation had been 'eavesdropping on a confessional, gate-crashing on the burial of a marriage'. Others, more ominously, highlighted Diana's determination 'not to go quietly'. The bouquets and the plaudits flooded into Kensington Palace, the telephone calls never stopped, congratulating her on a 'brave, fearless and wonderful performance'. A Gallup poll taken the following day showed Diana to have risen sharply in the public esteem, with more than 46 per cent thinking more of Diana after the interview than they had done before and 74 per cent believing that she had been right to give the interview. Only 20 per cent thought she should have stayed silent.

Within weeks, however, Diana, too, felt she should not have participated in the programme. She believed she had revealed too much of herself, been too open, made too many confessions and been too scathing in her attacks on Charles and the Royal Family. She wondered whether the interview could even have been counter-productive, making Cabinet Ministers, for example, who had been among her supporters, believe that a Princess who was prepared to appear on an hour-long television programme, confessing all and attacking everyone, was the right person to support in her bid to fly around the world as the queen of people's hearts, upstaging not only the Royal Family but also senior government ministers.

In his tribute, Earl Spencer also touched on Diana's special gift of which the nation knew little, or nothing — her sense of fun.

'To sanctify your memory,' he said, 'would be to miss out on the very core of your being, your wonderfully mischievous sense of humour with a laugh that bent you double. Your joy for life transmitted wherever you took your smile and the sparkle in those unforgettable eyes ... your boundless energy which you could barely contain.'

And that was so true.

It was also what Diana tried throughout her life to give to William and Harry. She wanted to pass on to her sons her sense of humour, her laughter and her zest for life. She loved to hear them laughing, running around the place, having fun. She loved to listen to the sound of their young voices, filled with laughter, enjoying themselves.

One of the reasons Diana became so miserable was because she felt the Windsors had no natural, boundless energy, no sense of fun and very little laughter in their lives. She would complain of never seeing any member of the Royal Family doubled up with laughter, really enjoying a joke, behaving naturally. When Diana would occasionally hardly be able to contain herself for laughing, the only remark she would hear from one of the family was usually 'very amusing', delivered with barely a smile. She was determined that William and Harry would not grow up like that and she hoped that the Spencer genes were that much stronger than the Windsors so that her sons would learn to enjoy their lives rather than spend their adult years checking to see whether they were carrying out their duty, behaving correctly, observing protocol and following tradition.

It is perhaps ironic that Diana, who never grew to like Tiggy Legge-Bourke, the young woman brought in as a friend and nanny to William and Harry, did however share with her a sense of fun, a *joie de vivre*. Six months after the separation, Tiggy, then 30, was officially hired as an assistant to Charles's Private Secretary, Commander Richard Aylard but, in reality, she was Charles's 'girl Friday', whose job it was to take care of William and Harry when they were staying at Highgrove or Balmoral with their father.

Tiggy — whose real name is Alexandra — had a similar background to Diana. She was born and brought up in the country, followed by boarding school and finishing school in Switzerland, the same one that Diana had attended a few years before. Tiggy was popular at school, outgoing, sporty but not an academic heavyweight, attaining only four 'O'-levels. From the boys' point of view, Tiggy was a great asset to the family, and she became rather like an elder sister to William and Harry, riding out with the boys, playing football, swimming, stalking and, if necessary, shooting rabbits!

William, and particularly Harry, became very fond of Tiggy in a remarkably short space of time and, understandably, Diana felt that she had a rival. It was obvious that the boys had fun with Tiggy. Diana would occasionally see newspaper pictures of

William and Harry fooling around with her and obviously enjoying the relationship. The sensible Tiggy, however, would make sure that she did not tread on Diana's toes.

As William and Harry grew up, however, it was thought that there was no need for Tiggy to remain employed by Prince Charles. Fortunately, she did stay on. There are those close to Charles who believe that Tiggy will now assume a very important role in their lives, a woman only a few years younger than Diana, perhaps a surrogate mother, someone whom the young Princes had grown to know and to like in the last five years; someone with a sense of mischief, recklessness and fun about her, just like their beloved mother.

And Earl Spencer, of course, was also correct in his remarkable tribute to Diana when he described his sister as a 'unique' person. Some people believe that if Diana had not existed, it would have been necessary to invent her, so perfect a creature was she. The newspapers and magazines invented a new Diana each and every month and every individual in Britain saw her as they wanted to see her — fashion icon, dancer, blushing bride, mother, saint, flirt or feminist.

The more one examines Diana's life, the more one discovers, that, in turn, Diana was naïve and outrageous, manipulative and innocent, calculating and frivolous, even womanly wise and wanton. It didn't seem important to Diana to know who she was; she careered through life as if on a roller-coaster, finding and dropping friends like confetti, only remaining true to her sons and those she met through her charity work.

Camilla Parker Bowles used to joke about the

problem of being compared to a goddess, but Diana's death at such a young age has created an immortal image of a goddess, for her memory will live on for generations to come. And Diana will be remembered not for her complex, insecure, childlike character, but for her sense of fun and mischief, as well as for her love and compassion for others.

# CHAPTER SEVEN

## THE THREE IN THE MARRIAGE

The words Diana used to describe her marriage during her famous *Panorama* interview will never be forgotten: 'Well, there were three of us in this marriage, so it was a bit crowded.'

She was, of course, referring to Prince Charles, Camilla Parker Bowles and herself, the eternal triangle which Diana blamed for the collapse of her marriage and the associated problems — her eating disorders, her post-natal depression and her feeling of isolation. But it hadn't always been like that.

In fact, at the beginning of her relationship with Charles, when she was a young, immature girl of 19, Diana was keen to meet Camilla, the woman Charles had spoken to her about. She was his 'dear friend' who had supported him during his darkest hours following the death of his great-uncle Earl 'Dickie' Mountbatten. Charles had told Diana something, but not all, about his relationship with Camilla.

Diana knew that they had met years before when she was still a young girl. She knew that some eighteen months after Charles had joined the Royal Navy in 1971, Camilla had married her old flame, a dashing Cavalry officer, Captain Andrew Parker Bowles, a man ten years her senior. They had had two children and Charles had happily volunteered to be the godfather of their eldest child, Tom.

Charles had also talked to Diana of the remarkably close relationship he had enjoyed as a teenager with Earl Mountbatten, his friend, adviser, great-uncle, surrogate father and the man Charles most admired and trusted to give him support and sound advice. Indeed, Charles spoke of Camilla in the same vein, explaining that she was a great woman, a good mother, a first-class cook and a great hostess, who rode to hounds regularly and was well known around Gloucestershire where she lived and hunted.

On one occasion, Diana was heard to say, 'In Charles's eyes, Camilla is Superwoman.'

In most respects, Charles did hold Camilla in high esteem, comparing her even to his mother whom he has always respected, primarily for her dedication to the monarchy and the enthusiasm she still puts into her never-ending job. High praise indeed. But Charles never told Diana of the adulterous affair he had had with Camilla from autumn 1979 until the spring of 1980.

Charles told Diana, 'I will for ever be in Camilla's debt because she saved my sanity.' He was referring to the extraordinarily traumatic effect that Mountbatten's assassination had had on him. Charles was so outraged that the IRA had murdered his great-uncle that he even fantasised about raising an army to take to Ireland to slaughter every IRA man he could find to assuage his anger. He could not turn to his father, Prince Philip, because he knew he would simply be rebuffed as had happened from time to time throughout his developing years. Charles believed he could not turn to his mother, either, for she had far too many other matters to contend with. So he turned to the only person in whom he had complete faith — Camilla.

Charles talked for days and nights with Camilla, pouring out his heart, wondering if life was worth continuing when such awful, dreadful things occurred for little or no reason. So necessary was Camilla's presence at this time that arrangements were made for her husband to fly out to Rhodesia to accompany Lord Soames who was overseeing the forthcoming changeover. Major Parker Bowles would be his ADC and military adviser throughout the six-month transitional period.

Over the following six months, Charles and Camilla became involved in the most passionate sexual relationship. Charles needed Camilla, and her love, to overcome his sense of outrage and guilt that his great-uncle had died for no other reason than being a distant member of the Royal Family. In fact, at the moment of his murder, Mountbatten was enjoying a quiet, peaceful fishing holiday in the Republic of Ireland with his beloved family when the IRA decided to plant a bomb in his fishing smack. Mountbatten had never served in Ireland, never commanded troops or a Royal Naval vessel in Northern Ireland, but the IRA simply wanted the kudos of showing the world that they could murder a member of the Royal House of Windsor whenever they wished.

Diana wanted to meet Camilla and, for his part, Charles wanted to ask Camilla her opinion of Diana and whether she believed Diana to be the young woman he should marry and ask to be his future Queen. Charles and Diana were visiting Highgrove, surveying the restoration work being carried out there one weekend in the summer of 1980, when Charles suggested they go and visit Camilla. That day, Camilla seemed as though she was Charles's elder sister, asking him questions, chatting to Diana and asking her views on several matters as though interviewing her. Diana understood that, for she appreciated the closeness of their relationship.

Understandably, Diana wanted to know more about Camilla, about her family and her background. She could tell by the way Charles spoke of his great friend that she had been quite an influence on him, but she had no idea at that time how close the two of them had been.

Camilla Shand was not from an aristocratic family like the Spencers but they were considered what people politely described as 'gentry'. Her mother, the Honourable Rosalind Shand, was the daughter of the fourth Lord Ashcombe, whose father Thomas Cubitt founded the highly successful Cubitt construction company. Her father, Bruce Shand, became a partner in a Mayfair wine merchants and held the rank of Major in the Second World War with the 12th Royal Lancers. He was a former Master of Fox Hounds and had held the position of Vice-Lord Lieutenant of East Sussex.

By one of the most extraordinary coincidences of history, Camilla was the great-granddaughter of Alice Keppel, who for many years during the latter part of the 19th century had been the mistress of Edward VII, Prince Charles's great-great-grandfather. Although

Alice Keppel was Edward's secret lover, by the time of his death in 1910, the affair had become so publicly acknowledged and accepted that the King's wife, Alexandra, sent for Alice Keppel to join her at Edward's bedside as he lay dying.

The Shands lived in a small Tudor country house in Plumpton, Sussex, and Camilla's childhood was full of fun, love and security, so unlike Diana's. Camilla was a natural tomboy, climbing trees, roller-skating, swimming in the local river and getting into mischief. She also learned to ride at a young age, a sport which she has loved all her life. At the age of ten, 'Milla' (as she was called at school) moved to the family's London home so that she could attend the fashionable Queen's Gate School for girls in South Kensington. She left school at 17 and, like Diana, went off to finishing schools in Switzerland and Paris.

Unlike Diana, however, Camilla would never be described as lovely, beautiful or stunning, but she exuded an earthiness and a confidence which attracted handsome young men. She was also renowned for having stubby, bitten fingernails which looked as though they needed a good scrub and her hair was usually described as 'unkempt'. Her bedroom was always a mess, clothes flung everywhere, and, unlike Diana, she was not renowned for dressing smartly. But the young men who knew her then thought Camilla had raw sex appeal.

At the age of 20, Camilla fell madly in love with Andrew Parker Bowles, who was then seen as one of the most eligible bachelors in London, aged 30, a Cavalry officer with the Blues and Royals and he had a fearsome reputation for dating and bedding young debutantes. Their affair was somewhat stormy because Camilla, who spent much of her life at Andrew's Notting Hill flat, discovered that Andrew continued to date and romance other young woman, much to Camilla's chagrin.

Three years later, during the summer of 1970 and while still dating the handsome Andrew, Camilla met Prince Charles and the two of them found an instant rapport. They enjoyed the same sense of humour and Charles loved her openness and candid approach to life. They both loved horses and enjoyed hunting. Charles, who had just completed three years at Cambridge, gaining a 2.2 BA degree, was a rather shy, nervous young man of 21 while Camilla was by then a mature young woman. They went out to dinner together, they rode to hounds and Charles took her to Broadlands to meet Uncle Dickie, Earl Mountbatten. But within six months of meeting Camilla, the woman who would eventually become his soul-mate, Charles went off to RAF Cranwell to learn to fly. Six months later, he enrolled at the Royal Naval College, Dartmouth, and days before his 23rd birthday, in November 1971, he joined his first ship *HMS Norfolk*.

For Charles it had been a wonderful platonic relationship with strong sexual undertones, but they would not become lovers for a further eight years. Within six months of Charles going to sea, Camilla had become engaged to Andrew and, in July 1973, they were married at the Guards Chapel in London. In December 1974, Camilla gave birth to their first child, Tom, and Charles readily agreed to become the boy's godfather. Charles never forgot Tom's birthday, sending him a present every year. Four years later, Camilla gave birth to a baby girl, Laura.

In August 1979, however, the killing of Earl

Mountbatten shattered Charles's young life. Camilla wanted to know the details and, one evening, Charles told her exactly what had occurred.

That August day, Dickie Mountbatten, then a sprightly 79, took the helm of the family's small, 30-foot boat, *Shadow V*. On board were his daughter Patricia and her film producer husband John (Lord and Lady Brabourne) and their twin 14-year-old sons, Nicholas and Timothy, as well as John's mother, the Dowager, Lady Brabourne. A young local Irish lad, Paul Maxwell, went along to help. As the fishing smack cleared the harbour of Mullaghmore and slowed to approach the first lobster pots, an IRA bomb exploded beneath Mountbatten's feet. The boat disintegrated, killing Mountbatten, Nicholas and Paul Maxwell outright; Lady Brabourne, 82, was fatally injured. The only survivors were John and Patricia Brabourne, who suffered fractured legs, and Timothy who was also severely injured.

Prince Charles was in Iceland at the time, enjoying a quiet fishing holiday with his friends Lord and Lady Tryon. Numb with shock and grief, he went for a solitary walk. Dale Tryon found him sitting by the side of a fjörd, sobbing uncontrollably. He had never felt such a loss.

After Mountbatten's funeral, when Charles delivered a moving and remarkable tribute to his beloved Uncle Dickie, he felt dispirited, desolate and alone. There was only one person he felt he could turn to, only one person whom he believed would understand and give him the comfort and emotional security he craved, his old flame, his close friend, Camilla. Over the following six months, Charles took control of his life again and decided on his future. But during that time he also became involved with Camilla, enjoying an all-consuming, passionate love affair which he would never forget.

But Diana would not know until some years after her marriage to Charles that during the time Charles and Camilla spent together, Charles had implored Camilla to divorce her husband and marry him. He didn't care what the Queen or her advisers would say; he knew that he wanted to marry her, and only her, for she was the one person who could make him happy as well as understand his complex character in the context of what had happened in his life. The level-headed Camilla, however, never entertained the idea for one moment.

She pointed out to Charles in no uncertain terms that the drama over the abdication of King Edward VIII in 1937 had been over the same issue, his determination to marry a divorced woman come what may, even it that meant surrendering the crown of England. And Camilla stressed that the furore over the abdication had come within a whisker of destroying the House of Windsor. Camilla knew that was the only way she could make Charles understand the gravity of the situation he was proposing. She also knew that Charles's sense of duty to his mother and the House of Windsor would not permit him to take such a risk. After much argument and debate, tears and turmoil, Charles reluctantly agreed. He had to put all that behind him and go in search of a bride.

Within weeks he had met Diana.

Whenever Diana confessed to the fact that she was no saint, that she had made mistakes in the marriage as well as Charles, that some of the blame for the breakdown was hers, Diana was, in fact, referring to those early years with Charles when she had not fully appreciated the life he led and that he had to lead as Prince of Wales. She had only seen the picture painted of Charles in the tabloid press of his action-man image; playing polo, skiing, parachuting, sailing, swimming, hunting, flying aircraft and helicopters, and on his holidays shooting, stalking and fishing at Balmoral. It came as quite a shock to her that Charles had to run the Duchy of Cornwall, spend time as Patron of the Prince's Trust and carry out royal duties, meeting Ambassadors and dignitaries, attending official lunches and dinners, opening factories, office blocks, schools and hospitals, as well as dictating letters by the dozen to people who constantly wrote to him on a myriad of subjects.

It was during those years of marriage that Diana, through frustration and loneliness, had given Charles a hard time. She never stopped demanding his presence at the Palace or begging him to stay with her rather than attend to his royal duties. She would beseech him to take care of her personally, rather than leave her to the advisers, footmen, ladies-in-waiting, maids and servants whose duty it was to care for her every need. And the more Charles left her to go about his duties, the more angry and frustrated Diana became and the more she took it out on the only person she could — her husband.

Diana's frustration with Charles reached a crescendo after William was born and again after Harry's birth. She liked to have Charles spend time with her and their children, even when they were babies. She loved having Charles around to chat to her while she fed the boys or played with them. She hated the thought that every morning Charles would suddenly have a queue of people waiting to discuss the day's events with him, make decisions, sort out programmes, make appointments, when all Diana wanted was for Charles to spend time with her and the babies. Those were the occasions when Diana would be heard screaming at Edward Adeane, Charles's Principal Private Secretary, a quiet, intellectual courtier who had never been shouted at in his entire life. Later, Oliver Everett, one of Charles's great polo friends, a young man who gave up a promising career at the Foreign Office to return to royal service, tried to help and advise Diana to settle into life as a member of the Royal Family. For two years Everett and Diana got on famously, but she believed he was spending too much time with Charles. She demanded that Everett go and, reluctantly, Charles had to ask one of his best frineds to leave.

Having been responsible for the dismissal of many good and loyal members of staff, Diana did manage to form friendships with a select few. One of these was Alan Fisher, one of her butlers. At first, Diana welcomed Fisher as a breath of fresh air. They would chat together, fool around together and Fisher would tell Diana the latest jokes as well as the gossip among the servants. But he went too far, swearing in front of her and telling her to stop being 'foolish' or 'ridiculous'. In the end, of course, he received his marching orders, but only after Diana and Fisher had indulged in some face-to-face screaming matches.

Diana realised that she was 'driving Charles to distraction' — to use his phrase — but she could not help herself. She had no idea that life in the Palace was going to be so restrictive. What she rebelled against was the fact that she was never permitted to go out on her own, not even in a car, without at least one bodyguard walking with her or driving with her and never, but never, leaving her alone!

She had hoped that the arrival of William and then Harry would solve many of her problems. Now she had her own family, two wonderful little boys to care for, drool over, kiss and cuddle, feed and bath. But after the arrival of Harry she became ill, suffering from quite severe post-natal depression and she felt awful. She spoke to her mother and to her sisters, she called in her great friend, Dr James Colthurst, and she sought advice from other specialists. She talked to Charles about her moods and her lethargy but he never understood. He would advise her to hand the babies over to the nurses and nannies and go to bed and rest. But that solved nothing.

Diana's mood swings became worse and she became almost desperate. One minute she would feel reckless and hot-headed, irresponsible and audacious, as though standing on the edge of a volcano; the next she would be plunged into despair and melancholy, not knowing where to turn or whom to turn to. Charles was totally out of his depth. He called in doctors and specialists and, with their medication and assistance, Diana slowly began to recover.

But the root cause of the depression, her life in the Palace and the unhappiness she felt in her marriage, did not go away and, as a result, her depression manifested itself with Diana blaming herself for what had gone wrong. As a result, she stopped eating and her irregular eating habits became more serious. Finally, she was diagnosed as suffering from *anorexia nervosa*.

In desperation, Charles turned to Camilla for advice. He knew little or nothing of such illnesses, of post-natal depression or eating disorders. He hoped Camilla would be able to advise him, tell him what to do and help save his relationship from disaster. But Camilla barely knew Diana and thought it better if she did not become directly involved. During the next few months, in the summer of 1985, Charles returned to Camilla again and again, talking to her, picking her brains, trying to fathom out how he could break the deadlock and cure Diana.

The more time he spent with the sensible, down-to-earth Camilla, the more Charles began to realise how pleasant it was to chat quietly over a cup of tea or a meal, walk in the country with the dogs enjoying the peace and freedom of life away from London, Kensington Palace and his demanding young wife. And the more time he spent with Camilla, the more Charles realised that, after all, there was nothing more he wanted in life than to spend the rest of his days with the woman he had fallen for during those traumatic months following the murder of his great-uncle. He realised what a grave mistake he had made in believing that he could find true happiness with another woman, even someone as lovely and dynamic as Diana. During the autumn of 1985, Camilla and Charles became lovers again.

It was the following year that Diana learned the truth. For some months, she had had her suspicions as Charles spent increasing amounts of time at Highgrove. Instinctively, Diana knew that Charles was seeing Camilla once again and when Charles finally admitted that he was seeing her, the truth of his former relationship with her came out. For the first time, Diana knew the facts about Charles's longstanding relationship with Camilla, and she was devastated. Her eating disorders returned with a vengeance and Diana became ill with *bulimia*. She would binge uncontrollably, and then have to run to the bathroom to be violently sick.

She would sit in bed alone at night realising that all was lost. Now she had even lost her husband to another woman. She believed she was useless and hopeless at everything. There was nothing, save producing her wonderful young sons, that she had done with her life and now she could not even keep her own husband happy at home. At that time, Diana felt she had driven Charles away because of her outrageous behaviour. She began to feel that she might indeed be mentally unstable, that she might eventually be put into a home for the mentally ill. Some of the time she blamed herself for the breakdown of the marriage; at other times Charles, but increasingly she began to lay the blame at the door of Camilla.

In fact, by removing the blame from herself Diana unwittingly helped in her own recovery. Now there was someone else to blame for what had happened and she began to feel more confident. Instead of feeling dreadfully morbid and dejected, Diana became angry; angry both with Charles and, more particularly, with Camilla. The anger gave Diana strength and with that strength came confidence.

And, like a breath of fresh air, Sarah Ferguson came into her life with her bubbly nature, high spirits and devil-may-care attitude to life. Sarah found a glum, down-in-the-mouth Diana whose marriage was going through hard times and whose husband had run off with his former mistress. Sarah's attitude was to take hold of Diana and shake her, to tell her to get out and start enjoying life and she would help her. The tonic worked. Diana began to meet different young people, go to parties, chat with dashing young men, even attend public concerts and films with them. But these brief encounters would soon end as Diana tired of them. But she persisted and, within months, she had met the charming James Hewitt. Within a matter of months, Diana was enjoying her now well-documented affair with the young Cavalry officer.

Officially, of course, both Charles and Diana had to pretend to the world that all was still well with the marriage. In their capacity as the Prince and Princess of Wales, they had to attend royal functions together, entertain foreign dignitaries, Prime Ministers and Presidents and carry on in public as though all was well between them. But Diana hated the idea that she should feign happiness, that they were a happily married couple when, in reality, she had come to loathe her life and resent her husband. And she wondered who they were fooling. The Press had heard the rumours of discontent, and knew that life inside Kensington Palace was far from harmonious, and they noted that Charles was spending more and more time at Highgrove while Diana was living alone in Kensington Palace. What the Press did not know at this time was that Charles was having an affair with Camilla, and that Diana was having an affair with an unknown Cavalry officer.

In public, however, Diana found it increasingly difficult to look charming, happy and high-spirited when undergoing official royal duties. She still dressed beautifully, she still attracted the photographers and the headlines, but the newspapers and the public sensed that something was wrong. Whenever Diana and Charles travelled abroad, Diana took the opportunity to look bored and unhappy, hoping that the cameras would catch her black moods and downcast expression, so that the British public would know what a miserable life she was leading. In private, Charles would chastise her for such appalling behaviour, particularly as they were the guests of another nation, representing Britain and the Royal House of Windsor. But each and every time Charles reproached Diana for her behaviour, Diana would tell Charles that he was to blame, that it was all his fault, because he had run off with his old flame.

Their foreign tours became the focus of attention to such a degree that Charles and the Queen, backed by senior courtiers, knew that the marriage could not last without bringing increasing disrespect to the Royal Family. They knew that Diana was the most popular Royal, and that the rumblings in the Press would soon explode into full-scale disclosures of Diana's misery and that Charles and the Royal Family would take the flak. In talks within the Royal Family, Prince Charles made it abundantly clear that there was no future in the marriage. It was over. He wanted nothing more to do with Diana and she wanted to see as little as possible of Charles. Before any books appeared detailing the troubles in the marriage or revealing Diana's anger, frustration and illnesses, a decision was taken that a legal separation would have to be organised in a bid to limit the eventual damage.

Charles had found his love and his future in Camilla. For Diana, however, the future seemed bleak. And she did not know whether she would have the strength and determination to continue her life alone.

# CHAPTER EIGHT

# MINES KILL CHILDREN, DON'T THEY?

The campaign to rid the world of anti-personnel landmines had become Diana's great crusade from the autumn of 1996 until her death. Indeed, the cause had become so crucial to Diana that she was prepared to go anywhere, see anybody, and use her influence in any way necessary to force a worldwide ban.

Diana believed that the anti-personnel mine was nothing less than an evil attack on the innocent of the developing world. What appalled her was that nothing had been done to stop their production, or their use, although politicians and generals were fully aware that 26,000 people, many of them children, were being killed and maimed each year by such mines.

Diana's interest began during 1995, which marked the 125th anniversary of the British Red Cross. It had been intended that she would take a high-profile role in events being staged throughout the year to celebrate the anniversary but, as she had only recently decided to withdraw from the limelight and the patronage of more than 100 charities, the idea had been frowned upon by advisers at Buckingham Palace.

Mike Whitlam, Director-General of the British Red Cross, had been involved in discussing with Diana what part she would play in the celebrations and one of the matters discussed was the thorny issue of landmines.

'That seemed to strike a chord in her,' Mike Whitlam commented, 'but because of the situation, it was decided that she would play no major part in our celebrations. She did, however, ask to be kept informed if there were any developments on the issue of landmines.

'We sent her videos, photographs and reading material. Some of the videos were horrifying, showing footage of children and adults who had lost an arm, a leg, a foot or half a face in anti-personnel landmine accidents. The photographs also pulled no punches. The videos also showed the excellent work being carried out by Red Cross volunteers, doctors and specialists who were carrying out wonderful work helping amputees.'

Towards the end of 1996, the film producer Lord Richard Attenborough approached the British Red Cross, asking if they would be interested in highlighting the film première of his film *In Love and War*. Understandably, the Red Cross was interested, seeing this as a great opportunity to promote their campaign to ban landmines. Mike Whitlam believed that Diana would be interested in being the première's star guest, providing the high profile needed to push the campaign. As a result, Lord

Attenborough wrote to Princess Diana asking if she would attend the premiére. She jumped at the opportunity.

Diana told Mike Whitlam that she would do anything the Red Cross wanted if it might bring about a ban on the production and use of landmines. What she hadn't told him was that her sons William and Harry had seen some of the photographs of maimed children, showing appalling injuries and loss of limbs, and had discussed the issue with her in some detail.

Later, Diana would reveal that at one point, Harry had asked her, 'Mines kill children, don't they, Mummy?'

The concern of her sons was another reason why Diana was determined to do all in her power, to help in any way she could, to rid the world of landmines. Once again, she studied the papers and the details of the many types of anti-personnel mines until she had attained a good working knowledge of the subject and the problems involved in tracing, finding and destroying them after they had been laid. She knew that the primary problem was that, in developing countries, no maps had been kept by armies laying the mines so that no one knew exactly where they had been buried. She understood that it was because of the random laying of mines that so many people were killed and maimed each year.

Following the film premiére, Diana told Mike Whitlam that if an opportunity arose to highlight the gruesome effect of landmines, she would be ready to travel anywhere in the world, if he thought it might help the cause. It was then that she volunteered to travel to Angola in the early part of 1997 so that she could meet some of the victims of landmine incidents.

But Diana had some demands of her own. 'She told me that she wanted her visit to Angola to be a working tour,' Mike Whitlam explained. 'She wanted no high profile, no meetings with government ministers and she didn't want to pack any posh dresses for meetings or official dinners. She told me that she wanted to travel light, taking only jeans and a few shirts.'

As ever, the world's Press followed and pictures of innocent, seriously injured children all but killed in landmine accidents made front-page news in the papers and heart-rending footage on television screens around the world. Those pictures of Diana, Princess of Wales, comforting child victims, propelled the landmine issue to the centre of political agendas in the western world.

In Angola, Diana saw for herself the extent to which minefields hindered aid and development and caused such tragedy for thousands of refugees seeking to return to their homeland. She met in both Angola, and later in Bosnia, those who had been mutilated by anti-personnel mines and realised the urgent need to restore through orthopaedic work their ability to live more or less normal lives.

Demands for a worldwide ban on the manufacture and use of anti-personnel landmines had been gathering pace for two years or more but the pictures of Diana holding young victims catapulted the issue into the living rooms of ordinary people. For the first time, the silent majority took note and the demands for action gathered pace, forcing governments to address the issue and take positive action. Suddenly, banning landmines was an issue at the forefront of people's minds and the voters were not prepared to take 'no' for an answer.

The Canadian Government had taken a lead in pushing for a landmine ban. For years, the Canadians had been persuading governments around the world to address the issue. The Nordic countries responded positively, as well as those developing nations whose people were suffering appalling injuries and loss of life due to the mines exploding daily in the country and desert regions where recent wars had been fought. But in the developed world, particularly among NATO countries, Russia and the former Soviet bloc, as well as China, the arms lobby and the military were fighting a rearguard action. They wanted their armies to have the use of mines whenever necessary. The Generals argued that if mines were laid correctly, with every mine laid diligently recorded on a map, there was no danger to civilians because all could be simply removed when necessary.

All that was true. But the Red Cross, and other more concerned governments, were worried that mines were laid by armies in developing countries with no recourse to detailed, accurate records. It was the manufacture and sale of mines to irresponsible governments and warring factions that caused the problems and the thousands of injuries and deaths each year. The Red Cross argued that laying anti-personnel mines had become an ethical issue which the world's major governments had to face.

By 1996, many western governments accepted that the laying of landmines had become a moral issue but many, including the all-powerful United States and Russia, were not prepared to stop the production and sale of anti-personnel mines, as well as their use, unless there was an agreed worldwide ban.

The International Red Cross had been reporting the increase in deaths and injuries caused by landmines since the 1970s. Other non-government agencies had also noticed the increase. Since 1979, the International Red Cross has manufactured 100,000 prostheses for 80,000 amputees in 22 countries. Much of its work had been in Cambodia, Afghanistan and Angola. Since the end of the Angolan civil war, when landmines were laid randomly, the IRC had fitted 1,550 new amputees with prostheses. It had given Afghanistan 600 wheelchairs and 6,000 pairs of crutches — that covered only a tiny proportion of the victims who needed help.

The IRC insisted that nearly all these horrific injuries were occurring in countries with very low incomes, so that the maimed could never receive help for their conditions without outside assistance. The vast majority of maimed people in developing countries were therefore left to a life of abject poverty and wretchedness, unable to work or care for themselves.

Across the developing world, voluntary organisations have been at work for years. The Red Cross, the Cambodia Trust, Motivation, Power, The Halo Trust and The Mines Advisory Group have been clearing mines and caring for the maimed and wounded in a number of countries, including Afghanistan, Angola, Bosnia, Cambodia, Chechnya, Laos, Mozambique, Sri Lanka and the Sudan.

They needed someone to highlight the appalling effects of laying landmines, someone who could combine a high profile with compassion, bringing the attention of the world to the problem. No politician or organisation had the image or the mass appeal necessary to grab the attention of the international media.

Diana's visit to Angola, when she was pictured taking part in the destruction of a landmine, began the campaign, but later, when the TV cameras showed Diana cuddling and chatting to young victims, those pictures touched a raw nerve in viewers across the world. People began to take notice, voters began to question their politicians, and those in power, particularly in the western world, realised that something had to be done to placate the growing awareness and anger at the effect those mines were having on the innocent children living in far-off countries. It was also true that many of those mines had been manufactured by western arms firms and exported by western governments to the developing world.

There was no need for Diana to say a word when she visited Angola early in 1997, except to call for a worldwide ban. She preferred the horrific pictures to tell the story. Those photographs also showed the need to stop the laying of landmines which were causing so much pain and so many deaths to so many innocent people each year.

But despite the Angolan visit, some nations, including the United States, Russia, China, India and Pakistan, were still holding out against the Canadian Government's efforts to persuade all nations of the world to sign a draft treaty outlawing the use of anti-personnel mines. But the tide had turned against those reluctant nations. Across the world, a total of 1,000 non-government agencies in 60 countries had joined the campaign to outlaw these evil, indiscriminate weapons.

In August 1997, Diana agreed to visit Bosnia where increasing numbers of people, including children, had been the victims of landmines laid during the horrific ethnic wars of the 1990s. Diana had cut short her romantic holiday with Dodi Fayed to fly to Bosnia with the Red Cross in an effort to keep the landmine campaign to the forefront of people's minds. Once again, the photographs and the TV footage revealed the full horror of the effect random laying of mines can have on a community. She also heard some horrific stories related through interpreters.

Diana shared a birthday cake with a little boy named Hamic who lived outside Tuzla, one of the centres most affected by the war. Hamic had lost both his feet when he stepped on a landmine. He had no idea who Diana was, a young woman dressed in blue jeans and a white shirt, who sat with him, held his hand and cuddled him like his mother did. But he was fascinated by the television cameras, the photographers and their equipment as they huddled around him taking pictures.

She spoke to many victims, both young and old. Many of the tales they told were grisly, as they related in detail what had happened and where the explosion had occurred — none of them were in mine-designated areas, showing the total disregard of those involved in the fighting.

All the interviews were unhurried. After her first one, Diana told the representatives organising the visit that she would not hurry any of the interviews because she felt that letting the victims tell their stories in their own words might help towards their recovery from the traumas they all must have felt.

Usually, such meetings are strictly timed with little deviation permitted. Diana said it didn't matter how long her conversations lasted; no one was to hurry the victim or suggest that the party move on, for whatever reason. For most of the time, Diana hardly said a word. This time she was simply listening, for they all seemed to want to talk about their injuries and what had happened when the mines exploded. A translator sat next to her explaining everything. It was on this trip that Diana showed the patience many people had suggested she lacked. In some areas of her life, Diana would have agreed with them, but not when it came to hearing the experiences of the unfortunate victims, who needed a willing listener to give them the time to tell their stories.

One of the most moving accounts was from a young Muslim widow whose husband received fatal injuries while out fishing one day. The widow and her late husband's mother sat either side of Diana, talking about the 29-year-old man who had been killed. His two young children sat at their feet and asked three times when their father was coming home. The young widow told Diana, 'He was a good man and we had such happy times together. He was a good father, too.'

As the women wiped away their tears, Diana instinctively knew what to do. She reached out and held their hands, clutching them for some time until the women had regained their composure. Some of the journalists present turned away, too, emotionally overcome by the pain of the two women.

Remarkably, there was laughter, too. Two young lads, both aged 12, had each lost a leg in landmine explosions, one when he was walking through the woods near his home, the other as he was carrying bricks to help rebuild the family home. The two lads had never met before but now, both suffering from the same disability, they had become instant friends. They both recounted their stories to Diana but, somehow, unbelievably with laughter. And they told her that a loss of a leg was not to going to stop them enjoying life. One day, they both had ambitions to play football!

Whenever Diana was talking to children, whether ill or injured, in hospitals or homeless, she would feel a thrill if they managed to smile and to laugh, overcoming their wretchedness while talking to her. She knew that many of them had little to laugh about but she believed that laughter helped them enormously in overcoming their feelings of dejection. Laughter to Diana was of prime importance, because it broke down all other barriers and helped the children to hope again, and begin to believe that the future might not be so bleak.

Two weeks after Diana's death, representatives from 100 nations met in the Norwegian capital, Oslo, to sign a treaty banning the future use of landmines. The final document would be signed in the Canadian capital, Ottawa, whose government put such effort into organising the worldwide treaty.

Diana recognised, however, that she was merely a figurehead in the campaign, reserving her praise for the charity workers who spend their lives tending the maimed and the injured and those brave men and women who spend their lives finding, unearthing and destroying the mines in lonely, isolated places around the world.

A mine action team comprises a leader, a mine awareness officer, one survey officer, eight deminers/surveyors, one medical assistant and a driver. A sum of £60,000 is needed to fund one team for six months. Some of the money that has been contributed to Diana's Memorial Fund will go towards supporting those teams that have the unenviable, death-defying task of clearing the mines, and some money will provide crutches and prostheses for the amputees.

In October, the campaign to ban landmines received the final accolade when it was awarded the Nobel Peace Prize. The Norwegian Nobel committee said the £600,000 award would go in equal parts to the International Campaign to Ban Landmines and to Jody Williams, the campaign co-ordinator. They had, the committee said, started 'a process which, in the space of a few years, changed a ban on anti-personnel mines from a vision to a feasible reality'.

Princess Diana would have thoroughly approved, not because she had been involved in the campaign, but because ordinary people and non-government agencies had forced politicians around the world to accept the need for the ban. There was only one point at issue and Diana helped to highlight it — more than any other military weapon, the landmine kills or mutilates at random long after hostilities have ended.

# Chapter Nine

# Diana and Dodi

It was during night-time walks along the deserted beach at St Tropez in the summer of 1997 that Diana became involved with Dodi Fayed, the 42-year-old playboy, erstwhile film producer and eldest son of Mohamed Al Fayed, the billionaire owner of Harrods, the Knightsbridge store.

On numerous occasions, Mohamed Al Fayed had offered his villa in the South of France, the Castel Sainte Térèse, to Diana for her to use as her own, a place secluded from *paparazzi* and patrolled by bodyguards where she could stay as long as she wanted in peace with William and Harry. At first, the invitations came through Raine, Earl Spencer's second wife, who is a director of Harrods International. Until the summer of 1997, Diana had always declined.

But her beach holiday with William and Harry the previous year had been an unmitigated disaster, due primarily to the attentions of freelance photographers who not only discovered the exact location of their holiday villa but would spend the days and nights camped nearby, their intrusive lenses forever trained on the terrace leading from the villa to the swimming pool. Indeed, during that holiday the boys stayed out of sight in the villa for most of the time, because they did not want to provide the photographers with the pictures they so desperately wanted. In the end, Diana cut short the stay and the three returned to London, mightily fed up that their family holiday in the sun had been ruined by the rude attentions of the prying photographers who, seemingly, did not care a damn that they were ruining the family's summer break.

The memory of that disastrous holiday was one of the reasons why Diana accepted Mohamed Al Fayed's invitation to use his St Tropez villa and with it the staff, which included bodyguards, quite capable of keeping away any unwanted intruders, including photographers. Diana had met Dodi Fayed from time to time but they had never been more than mere acquaintances. Their first brief encounter was in 1986 when Dodi's polo team met the Prince of Wales's team in the final of the Harrods Cup at Windsor Great Park. It was Diana who presented the winner's trophy that day.

Mohamed Al Fayed suggested that his eldest son, Dodi, could use the villa's fisherman's cottage on the beach, 200 yards from the main villa where Diana, William and Harry stayed. It was suggested that Dodi could provide some adult company for Diana in the evenings, as well as ensure that no photographers would be permitted to get close enough to take any pictures. She readily agreed.

Quiet, polite and unobtrusive, Dodi was every inch the perfect gentleman throughout that holiday, dancing attendance on Diana when requested and playing rough-and-tumble games with the boys in the swimming pool during the day. Occasionally, Diana would invite Dodi to take lunch with them on the terrace or inside the villa when the sun was too hot. On a few occasions, he dined with them at night, but for most of the time he would remain discreetly at a distance, only speaking when asked questions directly. The last thing he wanted to be was the overbearing, uninvited guest.

Diana and the boys also had the use of the Fayed's magnificent yacht, *Jonikal*, and the boys thoroughly enjoyed running all over it, inspecting the cabins and the crew area as well as taking it in turns to sit at the wheel. The boys were allowed to roam the yacht at will, so unlike the times when they were aboard the Royal Yacht, when they had to obey strict rules. They swam from it, borrowed the *Jonikal* tender and dived and jumped into the sea, enjoying the beautiful clear, deep waters of the Mediterranean, a world away from the more polluted beaches. And they had the time of their lives.

It was while they were enjoying themselves on the yacht that the *paparazzi* were able to capture Diana and the boys, the only time they were pestered by the photographers during the entire trip.

Sometimes, in the late evening, when William and Harry had gone to bed exhausted, Diana and Dodi would sit together, sip wine and chat. And Dodi, in his inimitable way, would make Diana laugh. It was Dodi's ability to make Diana laugh that first attracted her to the man she had only seen as quiet and polite and somewhat lacking in character. But she had misread the man and the more time they spent together on that holiday, the more Diana relaxed and the more she realised that she was becoming attracted to him. And she loved Dodi's quiet, mid-Atlantic accent, telling friends later that she found his voice not only beautiful, but sexy. All this she would tell those few intimate friends on her return to London.

And there was more. Once or twice towards the end of the holiday, Dodi and Diana took late night walks along the beach, wearing no shoes, but walking in and out of the warm sea as it lapped gently along the beach.

'That was the best holiday I have ever had in my entire life,' was Diana's verdict on her return to London in July.

At first, her remark was taken to mean that she had enjoyed her time with the boys, the time she always called 'special' because she loved being with them watching them grow up, having fun, laughing with them, chatting to them about everything and encouraging them to be themselves. This time there had also been no interference, no photographers at the villa and a wonderful sense of freedom.

Three weeks later, to everyone's surprise, Diana and Dodi flew out from Stansted Airport together on a Harrods Gulfstream jet for a cruise around Corsica and Sardinia aboard the *Jonikal*. They spent six days together getting to know each other. They visited Monte Carlo for an evening, undetected by the Press and spent some time on the island of Corsica, dining secretly at a number of exclusive resorts. Their days were spent visiting quiet coves and swimming in private, away from the lenses of the *paparazzi* who spent the time chasing their quarry, mostly without success.

Only once were the couple compromised and that was when the Italian photographer Maro Brenna snapped them, producing the famous photograph which will forever be called 'The Kiss'. The photograph was grainy and out of focus, but other pictures taken the same day showed that Diana and Dodi were enjoying their time together, relaxing on board the yacht.

Diana had only been back in London for a few days when she took off once more for another Mediterranean cruise, this time with her old friend Rosa Monckton, the President of Tiffany & Co and wife of Dominic Lawson, the editor of the *Sunday Telegraph*. Diana and Rosa Monckton had been close friends for years. Diana was also godmother to the second of Rosa Monckton's two daughters, Domenica, aged five. Diana and Rosa flew out to Greece on board the Harrods Gulfstream jet, which had been put at their disposal by Mohamed Al Fayed.

Many royal-watchers believed that Rosa Monckton had hurriedly organised the cruise so that she could 'knock some sense' into her good friend Diana, as there were many so-called cool heads in London who rather frowned on what they saw as Diana's budding relationship with Dodi. Nothing could have been further from the truth, for this private cruise, away from it all, had been planned months before. Some were concerned about the implications of Mohamed Al Fayed's alleged involvement in payments to disgraced former Conservative MPs he had named, which had caused some eyebrows to be raised around Westminster and Whitehall in 1996. It appeared, however, that Diana couldn't have cared less about those political repercussions; she was spending time with Dodi and, the more she saw of him, the more involved she became.

The question many were asking was 'Will it last?'and no one could answer that question. All the British newspapers, and some magazines, understandably delved into Dodi's past, trying to figure out the origin of his attraction for Diana, Princess of Wales, as well as trying to decide whether he was a suitable companion. Dodi told Diana that she could trust him because his given name, Emad, translated from the Arabic means 'someone you can depend on'.

Though it appeared that Diana was enjoying the most wonderful summer, she was not altogether sure that Dodi would be the man for her. In some ways, she was uncomfortable with him. She resented the fact that Dodi appeared to believe that he could 'buy' her love, lavishing many presents on her, both large and small, but nearly always expensive. Nor did she like the fact that Dodi kept telling her how generous he was being to her, repeatedly talking of the presents he had bought her and asking her what else she wanted him to give her. Diana would tell Dodi that she wanted nothing material from him.

And Diana would tell one or two friends that because Dodi was so generous she felt obliged, in return, to buy presents for him, to show her appreciation and to prove her love for him by constantly giving material things rather than enjoying time together and the simple pleasures of life — enjoying each other's company, being together because they wanted to be together. She would complain that Dodi had problems understanding that mentality but she supposed that it was simply a cultural difference. As a child, Diana had not been spoilt with toys or presents, except at Christmas or on her birthday. It was all so foreign to her. And she, too, had carried on that same tradition with William and Harry, not wishing to spoil them. But she did give Dodi a present which, to her, showed that she was falling in love with him — a pair of gold cufflinks that had belonged to her father. Those who knew Diana realised that she would not have given him such a treasured gift if she had not become romantically involved.

When Diana was searching for some little presents to take back home to the boys after her wonderful cruise alone with Dodi, he had volunteered to buy them whatever presents they wanted, but Diana refused to let him, saying that she didn't want him to start spoiling the boys, that as their mother, she felt it important to retain some control.

The £130,000 ring from Repossi's 'Tell Me Yes' range was the last present Dodi bought for Diana before the fateful night, but no one knows whether she was ready to receive such a ring or would have worn it. Indeed, no one knows whether the question of marriage had ever been suggested or discussed, only that Diana considered her relationship with Dodi to be 'marvellous'.

And there was one other matter worrying Diana. During their first romantic trysts, Dodi had made Diana laugh and that had been one of his most endearing attractions. But Diana had already begun to feel that the jokes that Dodi cracked to make her laugh were ones that he had used before with other women and, the more time she spent with him, the less fun their relationship became. To Diana, that was not a good sign for she knew that without laughter and mischief, enjoyment and impulsive gestures, she would soon tire of the man. She felt that her married life had been boring, exacerbated by the strict traditions of the family she had married into. She knew that she could not survive another such long-term relationship, and she didn't want to inflict that sort of life on William and Harry either.

Dodi Fayed's mother was Samira Khashoggi, sister of the billionaire international arms dealer Adnan Khashoggi, but when Dodi was only two years old, Mohamed Al Fayed and Samira separated and later divorced. It was Adnan Khashoggi who helped his brother-in-law Mohamed to start up in business, putting him in charge of his furniture importing concern in Riyadh, Saudi Arabia, when that nation was enjoying an extraordinary boom due to the billions of dollars pouring into the country from oil exports.

Left in the custody of his father, Dodi was to lead a somewhat nomadic life, attending boarding schools in Switzerland and spending his school holidays in France, Egypt or Britain, either with his mother or his father. His summer vacation was sometimes spent on yachts or in holiday villas along the Mediterranean coast. His education was supervised by another uncle, Salah Fayed.

At the tender age of 15, while still at school at Switzerland's famous Le Rosay, Dodi would invite his close schoolfriends for weekends in London where he had been bought his own Mayfair flat. He had also been provided with his own Rolls-Royce and his own chauffeur and bodyguard. Dodi and his friends would fly to London, spend a couple of nights in Mayfair enjoying the freedom of London's nightlife, before returning to school before lights out on Sunday evenings.

In the early 1970s, Dodi attended parties thrown by American youngsters studying at the American School in St John's Wood, London, and even then, while still a teenager, he would spend his time making himself as attractive as possible to the American teenage girls who gathered every Friday and Saturday night at the Aristocrats, a pub in George Street, off

Baker Street in London. Dodi would appear there regularly, always ensuring that his ultra-cool Trans-Am Mustang was parked directly in front of the pub and in full view of the girls.

It was during 1972 that Robert Eringer, a writer who now lives in the United States, first met Dodi. 'He must have been just 17 and had only recently passed his driving test. He was quiet and reserved but he loved to be noticed. If I remember correctly, he wasn't very bright at his school studies but he knew how to attract the American girls. Some of them came from Merrymount, the all-girl American School in south London, and these girls would come to the pub most Friday and Saturday nights. It was the 'in' meeting place at that time for all young Americans living and studying in London.

'And he was popular with the girls. We thought his popularity stemmed from the fact that he always had plenty of money, even then. Most of the time we hardly had the money to buy a pint of beer, but Dodi, on the other hand, would buy round after round of drinks for the girls. Understandably, we were jealous, especially as he would always drive away at closing time with the most beautiful young woman in the pub that night, while we would trudge to the Tube. We nicknamed him 'Dodo' because we thought he wasn't very bright, but that was probably unfair.'

From hanging out at the Aristocrats, Dodi moved on to the London club scene, spending two or three nights a week at London nightclubs. At that time, he had also earned a reputation as someone who consistently attracted the most beautiful young girls and who openly flashed around lots of money. In the late 1970s, he would tip the doorman and the barman £20 each — a considerable tip for a teenager in those days — and the manager would always make sure that 'Mr Dodi', as they called him, had one of the best tables in the place, usually close to the dance floor where he could eye the girls. As a result, of course, Dodi was very popular and would usually leave the clubs with a beautiful girl on his arm. What was noted, however, was that he hardly ever arrived at any of these clubs with a girl, preferring to meet and 'pick up' girls. It seemed to his few male friends that Dodi was not particularly interested in having a steady girlfriend but preferred instead to date different ones all the time, as though trying to impress as many people as possible with his attractiveness to women.

He would also take friends, including girlfriends, to his other homes in Gstaad, Sardinia and the South of France for holidays. It was a typical, rich-kid lifestyle.

On leaving school, however, his father decided that Dodi should have a more disciplined life and, as a result, he attended Sandhurst, the school for potential army officers near Aldershot, where his father hoped he would be transformed into an archetypal English gentleman, well-mannered, courteous and a credit to his family. He left there in 1974 to be commissioned into the United Arab Emirates Air Force as a Lieutenant but Dodi, instead of going to live in Arabia, was given the job as a military adviser at the UAE's London embassy. But that career would not last for long. He wanted something more glamorous, more rewarding. As a young, good-looking man Dodi's first love, however, remained the pursuit of beautiful women and he decided that moving to Hollywood, the mecca of beautiful, if somewhat plastic, young women would be his realisation of heaven on earth.

With the active support of his beloved father, who had always shown an interest in the film industry, which Dodi apparently shared, he decided to forge a career as a film producer. At the age of 23, he set up his own film production company, Allied Stars.

Dodi's principal claim to fame was finding backers, including his father, to invest in a film he truly believed would be a winner, *Chariots of Fire*. Dodi's faith in the film, in which he contributed a remarkable 25 per cent towards the cost of production, was rewarded and that film became his passport to the inner sanctums of Hollywood. Later, he invested in the pop music film *Breaking Glass* (1980), *The World According to Garp* (1982), the children's film *Hook* and *The Scarlet Letter*, as well as a couple of other lesser-known films.

He would never become, however, a hands-on film producer but would remain discreetly in the background giving his support to those artists and film-makers in whom he had faith. Far more to Dodi's taste was living the Hollywood life of a film producer, the provider of the means to make films, the man whom the stars and the starlets loved to spend time with, enjoying the producer's lifestyle, entertaining, dining and clubbing together. Dodi would also gain recognition from the Hollywood *cognoscenti* for the parties he threw, for he had a knack of being able to invite along the rich, the famous and the Hollywood moguls as well as the stars and starlets who would give the parties glamour.

During his years in California and New York, where he later kept an apartment, Dodi dated some of the most beautiful women in the world of films and showbusiness, including the actresses Brooke Shields, Daryl Hannah, Britt Ekland, Patsy Kensit, Joanne Whalley and Prince Andrew's former girlfriend, Koo Stark. He also dated supermodel Marie Helvin, the singer Lynsey de Paul and Frank

Sinatra's daughter, Tina. And one of the young women he showed great interest in was the beautiful Princess Stephanie of Monaco.

His only foray into marriage, however, occurred in 1986 when he married the American model Suzanne Gregard. The marriage, however, only lasted eight months. It is believed that Suzanne's divorce settlement was a most handsome £1,000,000. Since those days, Suzanne has never mentioned a word about their relationship but she had talked magnanimously about him. Some friends believe that Dodi's brief marriage occurred as a direct result of his mother's early death. She died of a heart-attack while undergoing a minor operation. His mother had always been his closest confidante, one of the most stable relationships of his life, and Dodi did marry shortly after his mother's death.

One woman who knew Dodi throughout his adult life was Barbara Broccoli, daughter of film producer Albert 'Cubby' Broccoli, the James Bond film-maker. They met when Dodi was only 16 and still at school.

'He was like a brother to me,' Barbara would say. 'I was only 11 when we first met and even then Dodi was keen on films. He used to visit my father's film sets and it was probably from those small beginnings that he began his love affair with the big screen. Through the years, we became close friends and would speak on the telephone a couple of times a week.'

Barbara Broccoli recalled Dodi's marriage break-up. 'Dodi was romantic ... he led from the heart ... even when his marriage failed after only eight months, he was philosophical about it, never negative.'

Barbara would also discuss with Dodi what she believed was his need to settle down, get married and have a family. Dodi would tell her, 'My life is already blessed with so many children — my little sisters and brothers and others.'

When news of Dodi's affair with Diana hit the headlines, their relationship suffered a little with the news of an American model, Kelly Fisher, 31, claiming that Dodi had jilted her for the Princess.

Kelly Fisher immediately filed a lawsuit through the Santa Monica Superior Court claiming unspecified damages from Dodi Fayed for breach of contract, fraud and damages for a dishonoured cheque.

Her lawyer, Gloria Allred, one of America's most powerful women's rights lawyers, commented, 'We would like Princess Diana, who has suffered greatly in the past, to know of Miss Fisher's experiences with Mr Fayed so that she can make an informed decision regarding her future and that of her children.

'We understand that Mr Fayed's holiday with the Princess took place while Mr Fayed was still in an intimate relationship with Miss Fisher. To compound matters, my client learnt about Mr Fayed's betrayal, not from Mr Fayed, but instead from the "kiss photo" that was published and circulated around the world to Miss Fisher's utter dismay, shock and shame. She was especially devastated because, just a few weeks earlier, she was on Mr Fayed's yacht in St Tropez.'

In her statement, a weeping Miss Fisher said that she and Dodi Fayed met in Paris in 1996 and travelled the world together, staying in London, Paris, California and New York. He agreed to pay her £320,000 in 'pre-marital support' and promised to marry her in 1997 and buy her a house at Malibu Beach, California. At a press conference called by her lawyer, Kelly Fisher showed reporters a huge sapphire diamond engagement ring she claimed had been bought for her by Dodi Fayed.

In her lawsuit, Miss Fisher claimed that Dodi Fayed had agreed to pay her £320,000 in return for her cutting back on her modelling engagements. But, she claimed, all she received from Dodi was a cheque for £130,000 which bounced. She claimed he then wired her £38,000 with a promise to pay the rest later, but never did.

Miss Fisher claimed that after the 'kiss photo' was published, she had tried to talk to Dodi but had been told 'never to contact him again'.

The media investigation of Dodi's affairs threw up serious questions over a string of allegedly unpaid bills and taxes in the United States. Enquiries revealed unpaid bills and a number of lawsuits filed against him. At the time of his death, most of the negative information was derived from sources at the United States Internal Revenue Service and the California Department of Revenue. Both government and state agencies had Dodi under active investigation in the months before his death.

The Collections Branch of the US Internal Revenue Service named Emad ( Dodi's correct birth name) Fayed, case number 95701342 in the Los Angeles District of California, owing a federal tax lien of US$93,059 (approx £55,000) from 28 April 1995. The Los Angeles County Recorder of Deeds also had a Californian state tax lien — case number 941102395 — against Emad Fayed for US$25,714 (approx £16,000) dated 8 June 1994.

Despite concern for Diana because of the reports of Dodi's alleged misconduct, many of those who had known him were positively gushing in their praise of the new man in Diana's life. At the time of his death, Dodi appeared to have everything he could ever have wanted, including a castle in Scotland, homes in

Switzerland, New York, Los Angeles, Dubai and Italy. He also appeared to have unlimited use of the Fayed family's £15 million yacht, *Jonikal*, a Sikorski helicopter and a Gulfstream executive jet — everything a rich playboy could want in what appeared to be his never-ending pursuit of some of the world's most sought-after women.

Except for his involvement with Kelly Fisher, it appears that all Dodi's girlfriends considered him to be a gentle, quiet and generous man. Barbara Broccoli considered Dodi to be 'the sweetest, kindest, gentlest man who took infinite care about his friendships'. He must have been somewhat remarkable because he appears to have had the incomparable gift of remaining on good terms with the great majority of his former girlfriends and lovers.

And Dodi had passionate affairs with motor cars, too. At the age of 18, he was given a British Ferrari concession in Surrey called a Modena, after the town in Tuscany where Ferraris have been made for two generations. He also owned and drove a 180mph Ferrari shortly after he was old enough to hold a British driving licence. A few years later he was believed to own £1 million worth of classic cars, including at least one Rolls-Royce and an Aston-Martin. During his last couple of years in London, he preferred to drive a Range Rover; in Paris, a Mercedes. In California, however, he struck quite a pose in Beverley Hills by roaring around in a £65,000 US army jeep that had been used in the Gulf War against Saddam Hussein.

Did Dodi love fast cars because he liked driving at speed? Ever since the tragic crash, people who knew the man have debated this important issue and most of the evidence seems to indicate that he not only loved fast cars but also enjoyed driving fast. Barbara

Broccoli, his long-time friend, insisted after his death that Dodi was 'terrified of speed', 'obsessive about safety', 'hated fast cars' and was 'paranoid about drinking and safety'.

Details emerged of Dodi's involvement 15 years ago in a frightening high-speed car chase through Manhattan after a party at the home of his uncle, Adnan Khashoggi. Dodi is said to have ordered his driver to 'outrun the chasing photographers'. While Dodi sat in the front ordering the driver to 'lose them, lose them', the actress Koo Stark and Jack Martin, a close friend, feared for their lives in the back. At one point, they were flung to the floor as the car careered through the city at speeds of up to 95 miles per hour.

Jack Martin recalled, 'It was a long time ago but I remember that drive really well. We had been at a party and had dropped off Claudia Cohen and Christopher Reeve when Dodi saw a car full of *paparazzi*. They gave chase. We reached great speeds down Madison Avenue and there was the repeated call to "lose them". I won't deny that trip was scary.'

Indeed, employees of the Surrey concessionaires recall that Dodi Fayed took part in classic Ferrari races on British race tracks, wearing fire-proof overalls like all the other drivers. Other employees recalled Dodi enjoying the speed of driving the beautiful road Ferraris at speed, too. Indeed, Dodi enjoyed being a dare-devil, always attracted to the more dangerous sports and always involving speed and action.

One of Dodi's great loves was skiing. He had learned to ski 'like a demon' when at school in Switzerland and he always adored the hair-raising sport. One of the reasons he took up polo was because of the challenge and danger of the sport. Dodi also enjoyed speedboat racing, particularly the danger of 'rough seas'. He never suffered any serious injuries in his many and varied sporting activities except for the odd fall at polo, but he did once fall out of a helicopter in Sardinia breaking a hip and several ribs.

In the world of Hollywood films and showbusiness Dodi became a casual cocaine user. During the parties frequented by the stars, film makers and the hangers-on, snorting cocaine was as common as having a drink. Indeed, for many who had decided that alcohol was not good for their health or their looks, cocaine would become their preferred drug when in company. This was Dodi's set; these were Dodi's friends and he joined them in their use of the banned drug which, in the Hollywood of the late 1980s and 1990s, was widely accepted as the norm in showbusiness circles.

Whenever Dodi visited London, he would always spend a few nights a week at Browns nightclub in Great Queen Street near the Aldwych, a venue where, most nights of the week, a number of rock stars and their partners would gather to chat and while away the hours. Browns was Dodi's favourite, his most preferred club in London and he became a very popular member — the staff loved him. When he arrived at the club he would tip the doorman £100 each time he visited, and the barman would also receive a £100 tip. Understandably, Dodi was respected by the management, too. Most evenings, however, he would relax in a private room upstairs above the dance floor where he would entertain his guests, which usually included the most beautiful young women, sitting in sofas around a coffee table chatting and drinking. Sometimes he would dine there and stay until 3.00-4.00am, spending between £500 and £1,000, buying rounds of drinks for his friends. Dodi visited the club, where he felt very much at home, and stayed for several hours only a week before the tragic crash.

Throughout the 1990s, the drug scene spread to the great majority of clubs in and around London. At some, taking drugs was the norm; at others, any sign of drug-taking would result in being asked to leave. But at the great majority of clubs, smoking marijuana and taking Ecstasy or speed was taken for granted. At the more exclusive, members-only clubs like Browns, though, drugs were never permitted, although it was accepted that some guests had been known to use cocaine. Dodi was one of those users.

But the Hollywood playboy was well known for having an unusual drinking habit which meant that the barmen earned their substantial tip during the evening's shift. Dodi would order a bottle of vodka and have it delivered to his table. He would pour himself a measure and drink it, sometimes sipping the vodka, at other times following the Russian habit, emptying the glass in one gulp. But Dodi would then push away the glass and ask for a fresh one. During a few hours' drinking, he would probably use 20 or 30 glasses. Those who noted this peculiarity believed it showed considerable paranoia, in this case an abnormal tendency to suspect and mistrust others as though fearing someone might 'spike' one of his drinks.

And for years before Dodi met Diana, he had a fear of photographers. Because photographers were not permitted in Browns, for example, *paparazzi* would often wait outside at night hoping for a picture of a well-known artist or star arriving or leaving. If Dodi saw photographers standing outside, he would order his chauffeur to drive on, though the photographers would not have recognised Dodi or, until recently, wanted to take his picture. In London's nightclub circles, a picture of Dodi on his own would not have earned the photographers a penny if they submitted his picture to any newspaper or magazine, for no editors would have had the slightest interest in printing a photograph of Dodi Fayed. But they would have used his picture if he had been accompanying one of his many Hollywood film stars. Once again, his actions suggested paranoia.

Those who knew Dodi well believe he had a soul-searching relationship with his father, who loved him deeply. Dodi had grown up adoring his mother, whom he regarded as his closest confidante, and he had also been influenced by his uncle Adnan Khashoggi. Some of those friends believe that, in his formative years, Dodi felt as close to his illustrious uncle as to his father, who was busy building his fortune in Saudi Arabia, as Adnan Khashoggi's protégé.

In fact, Dodi would tell his friends that he felt he didn't know his father as well as he might. They would talk on the telephone every week or so, but Dodi always felt that he had let his father down. He believed his father wanted him to follow in his footsteps and make a success of his life, and earn a fortune, rather than waste time enjoying a luxurious lifestyle with Hollywood stars.

His father encouraged Dodi to become involved in Harrods, inviting him to try his hand at anything he might like to do. Mohamed Al Fayed would have loved his son to follow in his footsteps, to run the Knightsbridge store with as much care and attention as he lavished on his pride and joy. Dodi did occasionally work at the store but he was never happy doing so. Unlike his father, Dodi much preferred his life back in Hollywood where he felt more at home in the relaxed atmosphere of California rather than what he perceived to be the stuffy regimen of London.

After Sandhurst and a spell at the UAE embassy in London, Dodi still had no wish to live near his father but preferred to seek his fortune in Hollywood. But when Mohamed Al Fayed became successful financially and bought Harrods, he was then in a position to exert more influence over his spendthrift playboy son who, despite the odd success, was never wealthy in his own right.

Dodi had homes he could use all over the world, a range of cars, money to spend on any number of beautiful women, the capacity to dine in the most expensive restaurants, to play polo, to ski and to drive speedboats, and to indulge in snorting coke. But the reason he had a string of debts in America, mainly for unpaid rent on homes he leased here and there, was that he appeared to have no ready cash sufficient to pay for his extravagant lifestyle.

Dodi Fayed was not rich and good looking, but he was courteous and generous to a fault, particularly with women, showering them with gifts and tokens of his affection. And he dressed impeccably, though his style became more Versace than Saville Row.

In Diana, Dodi realised that she could provide him with the status that he had always craved, a status which no longer required the help or assistance of his father. Of course, that is not to suggest that Dodi was not hugely attracted to one of the world's most adored and desirable women, but there were other benefits to a love affair with Diana, Princess of Wales. There were even more benefits if the couple became engaged. Marriage would have provided Dodi with the cachet he had always strived for and had never been granted — the key to unlock Hollywood's high-flyers, as well as a social position all America would envy.

Engaged to Diana, dating her, or having her live with him in California for several months a year, Dodi would be the toast of Hollywood, welcomed at every party, invited to bring his beloved Diana to every dinner table, ball and social event and, more importantly, Dodi would have been offered a seat whenever big money films were being considered. Hollywood film-makers would have asked Dodi to co-produce their films and Dodi's bank balance would have rocketed. In one leap, Dodi would have proved to himself and, just as significantly, to his father, that he was worth his salt and was capable of making a success of his life.

Dodi didn't even consider the cachet such a marriage would have brought him in England for, unlike Mohamed Al Fayed, he didn't mind whether he was considered a member of English society, an American or from any other nation. He simply wanted to prove himself, earn enough money to provide himself with all the accoutrements of luxury and never have to rely on his father financially again.

To Diana, the very fact that Dodi's parents had separated when he was so young, as her parents had, meant that there was an automatic bond between them for they had both grown up feeling a loss, a void in their lives which could never be filled by anyone else.

What surprised and confused many people, including those who knew Diana well, were the reasons why she seemed to have fallen in love so suddenly and so dramatically with an Egyptian playboy/film producer, a man with a string of past lovers to his name, the son of the billionaire owner of Harrods.

The question on many people's lips in the summer of 1997 was why the beautiful, angelic Diana could not find a decent Englishman to fall in love with. Many drew a comparison with the love affair and marriage of Jackie Onassis, the widow of US President John Kennedy, who angered, shocked and dismayed public opinion across America when she married the Greek billionaire shipping magnate, Aristotle Onassis. Hate-mail piled up at her Manhattan apartment; television commentators criticised her for greed and vulgarity and, to some, Jackie became a traitor to her country.

Even though five years had elapsed since the assassination of her husband, America felt hurt and angry that the former President's wife had found it necessary to turn to an ugly, overweight, ageing Greek shipping tycoon to find love. Many asked whether it was, in fact, love or, as they suspected, that Jackie had found a means of escape as well as financial independence. Jackie adored luxury, needed security and wanted to evade what she described as America's 'oppressive obsession' with her and her children. But the marriage, for all Ari's claims of 'pure happiness', was to end in recrimination and rancour and Jackie was not even bothered when her husband renewed his affair with the opera star Maria Callas. When Onassis died, Jackie, at 48, became one of the world's wealthiest women.

Diana, Princess of Wales, had always tried to keep her romantic liaisons secret, away from the Press and the all-important *paparazzi* so that she could conduct her love-life in private away from the glare of the limelight. Diana had always been a shy, reserved person and never one to wear her heart on her sleeve. But, suddenly, here was a new Diana, happily revealing to the world her love for a divorced man whom she had only really known for a couple of weeks. It seemed extraordinary.

It was Diana herself who took the trouble to take a motor-boat from the Al Fayed's St Tropez eight-acre complex where she was holidaying with her sons and, dressed only in a leopard-skin swimsuit, to tell the Fleet Street tabloid reporters, 'You will have a big surprise coming soon from the next thing I do.'

At the time, nobody had the slightest idea what Diana was referring to but most believed it concerned her charity work. It did not. She was referring to Dodi.

Many wondered whether Diana cared that the world was given an opportunity to witness her new found love in 'the kiss' photographs — and the other pictures of them lounging on board *Jonikal* together in swimsuits — which were taken during Diana and Dodi's Mediterranean cruise a couple of weeks later. Some thought she was happy that those photographs found their way into the world's newspapers.

On their return to London, Diana was again photographed, this time visiting Dodi's Mayfair apartment in Park Lane for dinner, dressed in a low-cut navy-blue dress. She appeared happy that night to see the photographers waiting to take her picture.

Forty-eight hours after returning from Bosnia where she spent three days visiting and talking to children and adults maimed by landmines, Diana was photographed with Dodi one more, after the couple had flown in a Harrods helicopter 160 miles for a private session with psychic Rita Rogers, a key adviser to both Diana and the Duchess of York. On that occasion, Diana and Dodi posed for the photograph which was taken by a schoolgirl.

And again, Diana was happy for the Press to know that, on 21 August, the couple were flying from Stansted Airport to Italy where the Al Fayed's 200ft yacht, moored at Portofino on the Italian Riviera, was waiting to take them on yet another Mediterranean cruise. Indeed, the Press were informed of all the details concerning the dates and times of both their departure from England and arrival in Italy by Dodi's personal aides. Now, the relationship had progressed to a quite different level, for Diana obviously wanted everyone to know that they were an item, a couple in love who wanted to spend as much time together as possible, in private.

Since the collapse of her marriage to Charles, and the four-year relationship with James Hewitt, Diana had been unable to find true love anywhere, just a succession of people she felt attracted to, loved for a while and then either discarded, or from whom she would split in acrimony and tears. Those who cared for Diana, her few true friends, desperately wanted Diana to strike up a strong relationship with an Englishman, preferably, a man of unimpeachable, even exquisite, reputation and standing in the world who was respected by all; a man of taste with discretion, the quiet confidence of success, solid British values and the wit and wisdom to be a good stepfather to the young Princes.

Some maintain that Diana could not find such an Englishman because the man would never want to live in the glare of the public limelight, photographed at every turn, his entire former life scrutinised, his every friend, both male and female, questioned and quizzed about his former life and loves. His reputation and credentials would be examined under the microscope in case, just in case, he had been guilty at some time of some tiny indiscretion or misdemeanour. And what Englishman worth his salt would want his photograph taken every time he poked his head out of a door or left home to travel to work?

And there was another point.

The sort of aristocratic Englishman who could have provided Diana with the financial wherewithal, the privacy and the luxury she obviously required, more than likely lived the languid life of the landed gentry, buried away in the country with muddy spaniels, erratic central heating, solid food and hearty outdoor pursuits; everything, in fact, that Diana abhorred. It was difficult imagining Diana loading a gun for her new man on a cold November morning in driving rain, or making the tea for the village cricket team every Saturday in summer when she could have been lying in the sun, aboard a yacht in the Mediterranean or, during winter, enjoying a 'nouvelle cuisine' lunch in an intimate London brasserie.

Those who criticised her new relationship, whether through snobbishness, racism or real concern over Dodi's suitability, failed to understand why, in the end, only a non-Englishman would do. Though Diana was born to landed privilege, a member of the aristocracy, in later years she recast herself as a citizen of the new classless society. It was, though, an illusion. It is true that Diana preferred modernity, meritocracy and status conferred by achievement and excellence rather than breeding. To have married a British aristocrat would have put her back where she started, while an ordinary, middle-class executive was always out of the question.

She needed a man outside the social hierarchy, but who understood it; someone scornful of starchy formality, but who could handle a polo pony; someone exuding the relaxed hospitality which she loved, but who would not eventually complain that, in reality, he preferred his port and gun-dog to this fame nonsense. In fact, the man needed to be an outsider like her, but with the wealth to provide her with the luxuries she enjoyed, the security she craved, the jets, helicopters and cars she fancied. He could provide the privacy she required and would never challenge her image as the world's most adored person.

She could imagine becoming Lady Diana Fayed of St Tropez, Los Angeles, London, Gstaad and other centres of such style with yachts and jet skis, Hollywood glitter and charity causes, underwritten by an indulgent billionaire father-in-law.

And so Diana found love with an Egyptian playboy, so well versed in the art of attracting beautiful women that she quickly found herself enjoying his every attention to such an extent that she wanted the world to share their love.

But no one would know whether Diana was enjoying a wonderful, crazy summer of madness or seriously thinking that her sons would approve of her marrying Dodi Fayed, for without their approval it is most unlikely that Diana would have agreed to go through with such a marriage.

# CHAPTER TEN

# THE PRINCESS AND THE PAPARAZZI

Nothing could have prepared the young Diana for the extraordinary attention photographers, reporters and television cameramen would give the innocent kindergarten assistant in the weeks and months when she was enjoying the earliest tender moments with Prince Charles during the summer and autumn of 1980.

I knew her at that time after we met on the polo ground at Windsor Great Park and later at Cowdray. The first time we met was during half-time at a polo match when we were both treading in, when spectators and players alike are encouraged to walk on to the pitch and tread in the divots thrown up by the galloping horses. As I walked around finding large divots, I noticed this young, fair-haired teenager, dressed in jeans and a white shirt, diligently trying to tread in the divots but wearing thin-soled, light pumps.

'I don't know whether those light shoes are man enough for the job,' I said and the young woman looked up and smiled.

'Am I doing it correctly?' she asked.

'Yes, but make sure you stamp in the ground around the divots, too,' I suggested.

She had another go. 'Is that better?' she asked with a smile.

'Yes,' I replied, 'but I would wear boots next time.'

Later, I asked friends about the identity of the blonde-haired young woman, and was told that she was Prince Charles's latest girlfriend.

Two or three weeks later, I was again treading in and felt a tap on my shoulder. It was Diana.

'Are these any better?' she enquired with a broad smile, and I looked down to see that she was wearing small, ankle-high leather boots.

'Better than last time,' I suggested, 'but I think it would be better if you wore proper polo boots like these.'

'I couldn't wear boots like those,' she said laughing and we walked back to the stands chatting about the ponies, the game and the inclement weather.

It was a joke that she never forgot and would often remind me of the time I had frowned on her footwear. From those beginnings, I would occasionally chat to Diana during polo afternoons, primarily because the more she was seen as Prince Charles's girlfriend, the less people risked talking to her, as though they might annoy the Prince of Wales.

Even then Diana seemed cut off and she didn't like it. She enjoyed being the centre of attention. Whenever I wandered over to chat, she was always happy for the company, ready to talk about anything rather than feel like the proverbial wallflower, left to her own devices, while the polo set chatted and mingled together and got on with the game.

Some years later, I was walking through the Harvey Nichols store in Knightsbridge and, as I turned, I saw this woman whom I recognised standing by the lift.

'Oh, hello,' I said automatically, 'how are you?' before realising it was Diana, Princess of Wales. 'I'm awfully sorry,' I said, 'I thought I knew you. I do apologise.'

I was just about to walk away when she said, 'Excuse me, but I do know you, don't I?'

'Well, we used to meet at polo, if you remember,' I replied.

'Of course I do,' she said laughing, 'you used to check my footwear to see if I was wearing the correct gear.'

'Sort of,' I said, feeling somewhat foolish. 'Anyway, how are you? Enjoying the life?'

She looked me in the eye as though unsure how to answer the question and, in her inimitable way, held the look, as though imparting a confidence. She ignored the question.

'I don't go to polo so often now,' she said smiling, 'not now I have two boys to look after.'

'You should,' I said, 'they would love it ... lots of children do.'

'That's a point,' she said, 'I'll bear it in mind.'

She touched my arm lightly. 'Take care,' she said.

'Take care,' I repeated. And she was gone, the lift doors closing as she stepped inside to be whisked to the higher floors.

Diana's wonderful innocence became apparent the first time she was photographed as the young woman whom the world believed would become the Princess of Wales. And from that moment in 1980, when she was captured on film at the Young England School in Pimlico, south London, Diana has never been able to escape the picture, when she was filmed standing somewhat sheepishly with a child on one hip and holding the hand of another; a beguiling young woman wearing a flimsy cotton skirt.

From that time until the moment of her death, the media never left her alone. Throughout the autumn and winter of 1980–81, Diana tasted the life of a celebrity, hounded by photographers and reporters whenever she appeared in public. They would chase her down the street asking innumerable questions, demanding answers she could not provide and prying into her love-life with Prince Charles. In those first few months, she withstood the media onslaught with remarkable equanimity, always smiling and trying to be friendly at the same time as giving nothing whatsoever away.

As she parked her little Mini she would hope to avoid the waiting cameramen who seemed to be camped outside her block of flats. She would rush into the apartment at Coleherne Court in Earl's Court and slam the door shut, as though reaching a sanctuary which the photographers could not invade.

On her return home, Diana would not appear agitated or annoyed but would apologise to her other flatmates for the nuisance her love affair with Charles was causing them. It was typically Diana, forever thinking of others while ignoring the fact that she was taking the brunt of the intrusion into her private life.

One story, however, infuriated and saddened her, as well as causing a major problem for Buckingham

Palace advisers. The story, which appeared in the *Sunday Mirror*, was gratuitously demeaning, with no basis in truth whatsoever.

The tabloids were always searching for stories on Charles's girlfriends. In September 1980, six months before the official engagement, and well before the Press or the public realised that Diana would be the chosen bride, the paper ran an exclusive front-page story claiming that Diana had been driven to the royal train when it was in a siding overnight in Wiltshire and she had spent the night with Charles. What angered Charles above all else was the sullying of Diana's reputation. In the House of Commons, a motion was tabled by 60 MPs 'deploring the manner in which Lady Diana Spencer is treated by the media'. The Fleet Street editors were called together, along with senior members of the Press Council to discuss the problem of the media intrusion into Diana's private life. It was the first such meeting in the council's 27-year history. It would be the first of many such scandalous, muck-raking stories 'invented' by Fleet Street tabloids to sell their papers, but the 'train story' was a hard lesson for the trusting Diana.

The constant badgering of Diana could not continue and she was forced to quit her job at the kindergarten due to the constant presence of photographers around the school, hindering her work and annoying the parents who did not like having to walk their children through a bunch of Fleet Street and freelance photographers every day. The teachers were loath to let Diana go because she was so popular with the children in her care, but they did not appreciate the constant attention and they reluctantly thought it better if Diana left. Of course, she understood, only too well, but it would be the start of a never-ending phenomenon in her life, changing her plans and her intentions simply because of the unbearable pressures of the world's media.

Even in those early days, she learned to take evasive action whenever possible, dodging around corners and into shops if she saw any photographers heading towards her. Sometimes, however, the constant newspaper pressure got to Diana and, in the autumn of 1980, the 19-year-old Diana cracked and was photographed in tears after being chased along the street by *paparazzi*. Her mother, Frances Shand Kydd, appalled at such behaviour, wrote an irate letter to *The Times*. But it made little difference.

But despite the ever-present attention of photographers, Diana and Charles did manage to continue their relationship, sometimes arranging to meet in the homes of friends. Stephen Barry, Charles's faithful valet for 12 years, and a face unknown to the tabloid photographers and reporters, took a central role in this cat-and-mouse game as Charles was determined to outwit the 'rat pack', the nickname given to those journalists and photographers who earned their living from trailing Diana. By now they had begun to follow Diana's every move.

In his book, *Royal Service*, Barry described how he used to wait at Buckingham Palace for Diana's phonecalls. When he picked up the phone, she would simply say, 'It's Diana,' give the address where she could be found, and he would drive over to collect her. Diana would usually take a taxi from her apartment in Fulham to her mother's, sister's, or a friend's apartment. Once the chasing rat pack were satisfied that she had arrived at her destination, Barry would then arrive to drive her to Buckingham Palace or wherever they were meeting. Later, and very discreetly, he would return her to her flat, stopping immediately outside. Most of the time the ruse worked perfectly, so that the great majority of her meetings with Charles went unrecorded.

On some occasions, Diana would take taxis to a friend's house and, once again, wait until the rat pack disappeared before hailing another taxi to her intended destination and the rendezvous with Prince Charles. Some of the time she enjoyed the game, but as the newspapers became convinced that an announcement of their engagement was imminent, the pressure became acute.

Considering that she was literally under siege, Diana managed to cultivate a remarkable relationship with some individuals from the pack, those men and women who preferred to be called 'members of the royal Press Corps'. She would occasionally talk to them, take them into her confidence and even joke with them. The cynical rat pack not only began to trust the shy young girl, but nearly all of them were won over by her natural charm. In truth, it was remarkable how the young, trusting Diana dealt with the Press at that time. She understood that they were simply doing their job, an attitude that tended to disarm them. But she also confided to her flatmates, 'I am terrified of them. Everywhere I turn, they are there, poking their cameras at me, asking me questions, following me whenever I step outside. I don't know how I am going to cope.' But cope she did.

Indeed, newspapers soon began almost to fawn over her. She was packaged and presented in a way that guaranteed her a place in the hearts of the general public. The magic ingredient which the world wanted to believe and which the media hyped out of all proportion was Diana's 'common touch'. *Common* in this case meaning she had not been brought up as an aristocrat but as a normal, ordinary member of Britain's upper-middle class. She had shopped in the January sales and travelled by bus and Tube. She had queued at the local supermarket, done her own laundry, ironing and cleaning and had even worked as a cleaner and a nanny. The public was led to believe that the Prince's eye could have fallen just as easily on any pretty girl.

Of course, this was nonsense. Diana might have enjoyed an 'ordinary' schooling and down-to-earth lifestyle but, in reality, her pedigree was faultless. She had descended from a long-established aristocratic family and was, in fact, very distantly related to Prince Charles through Henry VII, James I, Charles II and James II. As far as breeding goes, Diana could hardly have been more suitable.

The day of the announcement of Diana's engagement to Prince Charles both released the pressure and, in that moment, confined her to a life behind walls which her temperament and character found entirely alien to the lifestyle she loved. At a stroke, her freedom ended for ever. In retrospect, it is easy to see that Diana was never suited to the strictures imposed on the life and privacy of a Princess and, in truth, she was never able to cope with it.

Almost immediately, Diana moved all her personal belongings from her Coleherne apartment into a small suite of rooms in Clarence House, the

Queen Mother's home opposite St James's Palace and just 200 yards from Buckingham Palace where Charles lived in his suite on the first floor. But that arrangement would not last for long.

This was a time when both Charles and Diana were in love and wanting to spend as much time as possible in each other's company. Charles arranged for another suite of rooms to be opened for Diana next to his in Buckingham Palace and, unknown to the prying eyes of the world, Diana moved all she needed into Buckingham Palace.

It was there that they became lovers and they would spend every night, all night, together in Charles's rooms enjoying a wonderful, magical time together.

Diana was given her own personal police bodyguard who would drive her around London, leaving Buckingham Palace through various exits so that the photographers had no idea where or when they could capture her on film. Within a matter of weeks, they gave up hunting her, only managing to get pictures of her when she accompanied Prince Charles to an event, or attended a royal engagement with him. In the early summer of 1981, Diana also accompanied Charles to several polo matches but each time he played, the swarms of photographers made a nuisance of themselves and, occasionally, upset Diana. Even then they would creep close to her, their long lenses sometimes only a few feet from her face as they clicked away, making it impossible for her to relax and enjoy herself.

In the end, the ordeal became too great and a couple of weeks before the marriage she was pictured leaving the polo ground in tears in her Jaguar car. The following day, the newspapers had a field day, showing the tears and the confusion on Diana's face but apparently unconcerned that they had caused those tears by their intrusion into her private life. At the time, no one in the media complained about the behaviour of the tabloid photographers.

On that occasion, the tabloid Press revealed that Diana was simply suffering from pre-wedding nerves. That was totally untrue and they knew it. Her tears were due entirely to their constant attention, with photographers clicking away only a few feet from her for the previous hour. Apparently, it seemed, Diana was fair game.

Diana, of course, adored the photographs of the wedding and of the pictures taken at Balmoral where she and Charles posed and chatted to reporters shortly after their return from their Mediterranean cruise on the Royal Yacht.

Within three months of returning home, an official announcement from Buckingham Palace revealed that Diana was pregnant. The nation rejoiced and wished her well but reports were leaking from the Palace that all was not well with the royal marriage. As a result, tabloid editors ordered their royal reporters and photographers to 'stake out' the Palace and follow Diana's every move as closely as possible, snapping her whenever she ventured out. In fact, Diana was having problems settling down to the life of a Princess, having to attend royal functions and being left on her own in the huge, cold, uninviting Palace that was now her home. Reports leaked out revealing a lonely, unhappy Diana walking the corridors on her own, her walkman clamped to her ears, listening to pop music.

Fearful for Diana's well-being and that of their unborn child, Charles broached the subject with his mother, asking her to take the Fleet Street editors into her confidence and suggesting that they give Diana some breathing space.

As a result, the Queen's Press Secretary, Michael Shea, an urbane former diplomat, formulated a plan for the Queen which he hoped might work. On a Tuesday, 18 days before Christmas 1981 and four-and-a-half months after the wedding, the editors of national newspapers, television and radio were invited to Buckingham Palace to discuss with Shea how to balance the very real public interest in the Royal Family — and in particular the Princess of Wales — with their need for privacy. It was the first meeting of its kind in 25 years. No demands were made at that meeting and no orders were issued. But after painting a picture of an immature Princess in turmoil, Michael Shea suddenly announced to the gathering, 'Now you are about to meet the most anxious mother-in-law in the land,' and the media executives were ushered into the presence of the Queen.

This was indeed a precedent which quite surprised and flattered the editors. She chatted informally to them. The Princess, she said, felt totally beleaguered. There was concern, too, about the effects the relentless hounding might have on the young mother-to-be, who had not been subjected to continuous public exposure and scrutiny since early childhood, unlike other members of the Royal Family. The Queen explained that Diana was finding it difficult to cope and the people who loved and cared for her had become anxious.

The Queen also told them how she feared the

long-term effects of such unprecedented and zealous Press harassment, and she was worried that if the Press didn't calm down, Diana's anxieties about the media might continue in the future, when she would be playing a more important role in the life of the country.

The subject of photographers pursuing Diana in the village high street in Tetbury, near Highgrove, was raised. The Queen pointed out that the off-duty Princess could not even step outside her car to buy a packet of wine gums without coming face to face with a lens or two.

Until Diana arrived on the royal scene, the Press used to observe a voluntary code of conduct that left the Royal Family in peace while they were on holiday. But all that had been abandoned in the scramble to get exclusive pictures of the young Princess. Michael Shea said that it was hoped that this tradition might be resumed immediately and that the editors might consider the private life of the Princess *private*, and not use material from freelance or foreign photographers that invaded her privacy. In essence, the Queen was appealing to them to control the rat pack.

For a while after this meeting, Fleet Street did leave Diana alone, but she had become such a hot property that it wasn't long before they once again had their prying, intrusive lenses trained on her as soon as she set foot outside her new home in Kensington Palace. The reason was simple; magazine editors reported at this time that a cover of Diana in colour boosted their circulation by a remarkable 10 per cent.

Throughout her two pregnancies and in the

early months of motherhood, Diana withdrew inside the protective walls of Kensington Palace and pictures of her were few and far between. But, whenever possible, the Press continued to intrude on Diana's private life. In February 1982, a private holiday in the Bahamas was ruined by photographs taken with a long-focus lens showing the pregnant Princess wearing a bikini. Though the photographs were taken without her knowledge or her consent, two Fleet Street tabloids printed the sensational pictures. The team of photographers who now spent their waking hours following every step Diana took, made note of the fact that large sums of money changed hands for those pictures which were syndicated around the world. This was the moment when the royal *paparazzi* took off in earnest. They were to affect her life severely and dog her every move for the rest of her days.

Some months after the birth of Prince Harry in September 1984, however, rumours of strife within the royal marriage began circulating. It was noted that Diana was looking thin, painfully thin, and people wondered if she was suffering from *anorexia nervosa*. The media noted that she was looking increasingly unhappy; gone was the fun-loving girl of the earlier years and in her place was a morose Diana with no sparkle. Throughout the late 1980s, newspaper reports revealed alleged details of troubles between Charles and Princess Diana.

At first, these reports were dismissed as fictitious, dreamed up by a tabloid press determined to dramatise the slightest problems in the marriage. But then Diana herself began to show by her actions that all was not as it should be between her and Prince Charles.

Many of those photographers who have followed Diana over the past ten years of her life, since her marriage problems became apparent, refuse to accept that they have always been at fault when dealing with the world's most photographed woman. They maintain that on many occasions Diana wanted her photograph taken, indeed, needed the *paparazzi* to show the world the problems of her life, how she felt, illustrating the restrictions that made her life almost unbearable.

Diana was on first-name terms with many of the 'Press Corps', particularly when having drinks with them at the official media cocktail party at the start of an overseas official visit. She would joke with them and tease them, she would learn some of the 'in-jokes' which the photographers shared amongst themselves and she would call some of them by their nicknames, which made them all laugh. Generally speaking, those that she came to know well did not cause Diana too many problems; she accepted that some of them were simply doing their job and she respected that. But there would always be eager new recruits to the ranks of the *paparazzi* who were determined to make a name for themselves, and make their fortune, and it would be these freelance photographers who caused Diana the greatest torment.

On many informal occasions, the photographers would wait for Diana to go to her health club or snap her out shopping. She understood that they would take a few shots and then they would disperse, leaving her to go her own way without any further intrusion. That she didn't mind; that she accepted. What annoyed and frustrated her, sometimes to the point of tears, was when one or two photographers continued snapping away, their lenses inches from her face, when there was no need to be so aggressive. Some photographers learned the rules of the game they played with Diana, but others refused to accept that there were ever any rules; that she was there for them to snatch pictures and, if possible, make their fortunes. Those photographers didn't care about Diana's feelings or her privacy — these were the troublemakers.

As Diana became more independent of Buckingham Palace and her advisers, she began to become even more friendly with certain selected members of the Press and even some *paparazzi*. Diana retained a remarkably close relationship with Richard Kay, the *Daily Mail* reporter she phoned the night before she died. She would sometimes telephone them, and inform them of her plans well in advance, so that they would be in position to photograph her. She would also talk to a few journalists, telling them of her problems with the Royal Family or putting her side of the story if rumours of an affair hit the headlines. For the most part, this relationship worked well until, occasionally, the photographers would pop up unexpectedly when Diana had not informed them of her plans. That upset and annoyed her.

After her separation from Prince Charles in 1992, Diana began inviting editors and senior executives of all newspapers to lunch at Kensington Palace. She would insist that all comments made during the lunch were off the record and, to their credit, the editors agreed. They also realised that if they had revealed details of such lunches they would never be invited back. And Diana would woo those men, flatter them, make them feel there was a special relationship, a one-to-one contract. She would look them straight in the eye, flirt ever so slightly and make a fuss of them. She made them feel important, massaged their egos and won them over like puppies having their tummies tickled.

Clive James, the journalist, TV reporter, wit and raconteur, revealed some time after Diana's death that 'to know the Princess of Wales — her goodness, her foibles, her mischief, her strength — was to love her', and that was on the strength of a few lunches with her! Undeniably, it seemed that Diana was capable of wrapping these privileged editors and journalists around her little finger. James maintained in an article for *New Yorker* magazine, 'The tacit bargain was: You tell me what you can't tell anyone else and I'll tell you what I can't tell anyone else, and then neither of us can tell anyone else what we said.'

He continued explaining her technique: 'I suppose it was a mind game. There must have been dozens of other people that she played it with, but she infallibly picked those who would never break her deal. She would make each of her platonic cavaliers believe, or at any rate want to believe, that he was the only one.'

During some of her lunch parties, Diana would usually hand out some riveting titbits of gossip or information knowing that the editors could not repeat the story for then they would have broken her confidence. And that was Diana's technique — she brought the editors into her confidence. In some respects, Diana copied the infamous political 'lobby system' where information is given to political journalists and commentators on the strict understanding that the person giving the information

— whether the Prime Minister or some lower rank — will only quote the news as coming from 'a government source'. Everyone, of course, knows what goes on, but no one breaks the unwritten agreement.

If an editor or journalist was part of Diana's 'lobby', they fully realised that to break that would meant they would never again be invited to lunch or phoned at their office to be briefed, by her in person, about a particular subject. And, undeniably, the editors were flattered. They were privileged, handed information by Diana personally, the world's most glamorous Princess.

This lobby system continued until her death. As one anonymous editor put it, 'The *quid pro quo* with Diana was that, in return for access to her private office, you would be broadly sympathetic to her charity work, and by and large we were.'

Diana needed the tabloids as well as the broadsheets to support her charity work because she had formulated a plan for her future, one which necessitated their support, the people's support, and later, she hoped, the support of ministers and members of parliament. Ever since her separation from Prince Charles, Diana wanted to become someone in her own right, someone the people respected, not because she was or had been the Princess of Wales, but someone whom everyone would respect for the work she carried out.

Diana was aware that her charity work received acclaim not only among the general public but also among many of the 'movers and shakers', including a broad range of politicians who believed she was an influence for good. Somewhat naïvely, Diana had hoped after her separation that she would be permitted, maybe even encouraged, to take on more worldwide charity work and that was one of the reasons why she dropped more than 100 of her patronages so that she could concentrate on issues that took her to other lands and thereby broadened her popularity.

In the end, she wanted to become a world figure, taking her charity work across the five continents and thereby achieving her ambition to become someone who had won respect and acclaim for the work *she* carried out alone, with none of the credit belonging in any way to the House of Windsor. That was one of the principal reasons she took up the issue of landmines, for that charity work took her to the very edge of serious political activity, for which she hoped she would eventually be taken seriously, and perhaps move further away from the image of the glamorous Princess with the pretty face. One of the calamities of her untimely death was that Diana was robbed of that success at the moment it seemed her ambition would be fulfilled.

Many will suggest that Diana was driven to take the tabloids into her confidence because she had become so distraught at being married to the Prince of Wales and that she did indeed feel like a prisoner trapped within Kensington Palace. It would appear that in all her subsequent dealings with the tabloids, the aim was to put herself in a favourable light, and if that meant painting others in a less favourable light, then so be it.

And there were odd occasions when Diana was very happy that the ever-present photographers were at hand. The moments when Diana could show the world her true feelings towards her husband as the marriage fell apart were few and far between. But occasions did arise and the photographers obliged, making front-page pictures for the tabloids and even some broadsheet quality papers, who had to acknowledge that the royal marriage was in serious difficulties.

In January 1988, Charles and Diana toured Australia and photographs taken during that overseas trip showed a most unhappy, if not downright miserable, Diana. She certainly made sure as she posed for photographers that no one back home could be left in any doubt that she was not a happily married woman. The following year, Charles and Diana toured the Middle East and, once again, photographs of them together, such as the one taken at an afternoon's camel racing in the United Arab Emirates, showed a sullen, unhappy Princess of Wales.

And her poses would become even more exaggerated, making it clear to everyone who saw the pictures in publications around the world that Diana was no longer in love with her Prince. The fairytale story was shattered and Diana wanted the world to realise it. During a royal tour of Canada in the autumn of 1991, Diana was seen looking bored, barely managing to raise a smile for the photographers. Back home, the tabloids had a field day, speculating on what they saw as the writing on the wall for 'Charles and Di'.

And in 1992, during a royal tour of India, two occasions arose which left no doubt that the royal marriage was on the rocks. Firstly, after playing in a polo match in Jaipur, Charles went to kiss Diana, as usual, in full view of the photographers, the dignitaries and the thousands who had turned out to watch. Just as his lips were about to kiss her cheek, Diana turned away and Charles was left kissing thin air. It was no accident.

Days earlier, Diana had posed for the royal photographers, those accompanying the royal couple on their official tour, sitting quite alone in front of the famous Taj Mahal, the monument to love built on the banks of the sacred river in Agra. Earlier, Diana had toured the monument whilst Charles was hundreds of miles away attending the rather less romantic Forum of Indo–British Industrialists.

There were also many, many occasions when Diana had wished there had been no *paparazzi* present to catch her unguarded moments, during which she would become tearful or frustrated with their constant hounding. In April 1991, Diana broke down in tears in Newcastle while visiting residents in a programme for housing the homeless and, on other occasions, Diana would become distressed for no apparent reason. Usually, however, the tears would flow only when she was being pestered by photographers who would not leave her alone. Indeed, some *paparazzi* deliberately went out of their way to hound Diana in a determined effort to make her break down in tears, thus ensuring that their pictures would be sold around the world. The fact that Diana was suffering at those times meant nothing to the small, greedy bunch of photographers who only wanted to get rich quick.

The night of Wednesday, 29 June 1994, was a date that Diana never forgot because she knew that her former husband, Prince Charles, was to be interviewed on national television in the fullest and frankest two-hour interview he had ever given. Diana had no idea what he was going to say but she had no doubt that the front pages of all papers the following day would be filled with Charles's words, his views and his statements.

She had accepted an invitation that evening to a gala banquet at the Serpentine Gallery in Kensington Gardens only a few hundred yards from her apartment in Kensington Palace. Dressed in a breathtaking off-the-shoulder, above-the-knee, black chiffon Valentino dress, she dazzled the 250 guests, who had paid £150 a head towards the £1.5 million gallery renovation. Diana's photograph showing her smiling, relaxed and confident appeared in every newspaper the following morning, competing with Charles's television appearance for space.

Diana had not been aware that evening that during the interview, Charles would confess to adultery. Charles bared his soul that night in the most revealing documentary ever made about a member of the Royal Family, confirming that he had been unfaithful to the Princess of Wales but only after the marriage had 'irretrievably' broken down. But her magnificent entrance at the gallery that evening, looking so confident, was a personal triumph, a triumph that she was happy the photographers caught so brilliantly on film.

Though the *paparazzi* may have been intrusive and upsetting throughout her marriage, many considered their behaviour towards Diana in the last few years of her life to have descended into cruelty. They pursued her relentlessly, determined to capture pictures when she was in the company of any man, married or unmarried, with whom there was a vague possibility that she might be having an affair.

In her famous BBC *Panorama* interview, Diana had confessed to adultery with Captain James Hewitt. Every subsequent man seen in Diana's presence was also, therefore, believed to have been having an affair with her. It was unjust, unfair and, most of the time, untrue. But that didn't seem to matter. Any photograph of Diana with a man sold well overseas, even if the same photograph barely received any newspaper space in Britain. Some Italian and French newspapers and magazines wanted to believe that Diana was a very sexually active young woman and they needed the pictures to prove their argument. The *paparazzi* were only too happy to oblige. The fact was that, much of the time, the photographers knew her relationships to be perfectly  innocent, but they still photographed them together and sold the pictures as though revealing a new lover in Diana's life. It was cheap, despicable and scandalous. But the photographers didn't care at all.

Behind-the-scenes political pressure had begun to be applied to newspaper proprietors and their editors. Every time Diana broke down in distress, and the pictures were carried in one or more of the tabloids, public anger surfaced and editors began to have second thoughts about keeping their own staff photographers trailing the unfortunate Diana from dawn until midnight. So, as a magnanimous gesture, they decided they would no longer hound the Princess of Wales and announced their intentions to their readers, hoping to gain credit and praise for such a bold, selfless decision.

In reality, it was all a sham.

Fleet Street's tabloid picture editors were ordered

to make sure that their paper never missed a good picture of Diana. They were ordered instead to do deals with *paparazzi*, promising them hefty payments for good pictures of Diana. The photographers who followed Diana also knew that if they secured a sensational picture — for example, kissing a lover in a compromising situation — then there was no limit to the payment. No contracts were drawn up, no deals were signed, but the unwritten agreements were crystal clear: the newspapers would still get their pictures and the *paparazzi* would get their money.

As a result, a coterie of seven or eight photographers across the world began to organise and circulate information on the playgrounds of the rich and famous worldwide. They also agreed to control and sell the circulation of each other's material. They were organised, shrewd, multilingual and sometimes smartly dressed, and possessed the social graces to ease their way to the world's exclusives. This tight group — almost a *mafiosa* — have the regular haunts of the rich and famous sewn up.

One such is Jason Fraser, 30, a well-known and determined *paparazzo*, who built up a reputation and a fortune not just as a photographer but also as an agent, brokering snaps from foreign photographers dependent on him for getting the best price in the lucrative British tabloid market. The 'Kiss' pictures of Diana and Dodi — taken by the Italian photographer Mario Brenna — earned nearly £5 million worldwide, but it was Jason Fraser who negotiated the sales in Britain.

Days before Diana's death, Jason Fraser justified his pursuit of the Princess saying, 'I think she, like everyone else, is entitled to a certain degree of privacy but she abdicated a certain amount of that when she started briefing journalists. Understandably, she wants to put her views across but, if you are going to forge those close relationships with journalists, you have to understand that other journalists will want to correct the imbalance.'

He went on, 'Given the fact that this latest holiday with Dodi must have been her tenth this year, what are we to do? Are we just to photograph her on the few days she is in Britain? Are we to ignore a story which, as well as being highly entertaining for the majority of readers, actually has a constitutional impact as well? We are looking at the development of a relationship between Diana, Princess of Wales and Dodi Fayed. If she married him, he would become stepfather to the future king.'

And Fraser maintained that he was not in the *paparazzi* business solely for money. 'I really do it because I find it thoroughly enjoyable. It allows me to live very much on the edge and to do things that other people only dream about. It's that adrenalin rush. I take a certain amount of risks but I do get a buzz out of hanging out of helicopters.'

But the death of Diana on the morning of Sunday, 31 August 1997, apparently having been chased along the streets of Paris by a gang of *paparazzi*, meant that whatever an inquest's verdict on the causes of her death, whether the driver was drunk or suffering from the combined effects of drugs and drink, the tabloid press would have to take its share of the blame. And yet, within hours of her death, some tabloids forgot that their papers had ever carried *paparazzi* pictures. Sir David English, Chairman of Associated Newspapers and editor-in-chief of the

*Daily Mail* was one temporarily affected by this amnesia, inexplicably forgetting that only three weeks earlier, the *Daily Mail* had used 18 pictures of Diana and Dodi taken by the Italian Mario Brenna. Others, like Stuart Higgins, the editor of the *Sun*, which had over the years sometimes given the Princess a rough ride, wrote a piece suggesting that he had been her most dependable friend and ally.

The *Daily Telegraph* wrote in a leading article days after her death that some tabloids treated Diana 'with bestial cruelty'. It went on, 'The fact that they also published many articles of slavish adoration of the Princess makes their cruelty only more refined, more cynical. It is almost past belief that organs which harried her and defiled her now claim to be the guardians of her flame.'

Indeed, so angry and upset was Diana's brother, Earl Spencer, that he withdrew the editors' invitations to her funeral, believing that his sister would not have wanted them there. 'My two sisters, my mother and I felt very strongly that Diana would not have wanted any of the national tabloid Press to be present at the funeral. I therefore contacted the office of each editor and asked them to observe the family's wishes on Diana's behalf. I am very grateful that they have all agreed that it would be inappropriate for them to be there.'

The death of Diana, however, once again threw up the great controversy which had raged through Britain ever since Diana entered the public arena of British life 17 years ago — privacy and the Press. Her death created unprecedented pressure for a new law to protect privacy. The anguish at the manner of her death turned to anger at those who tortured her during her life — the photographers who followed and bullied her incessantly, and the journalists who sneered at her and tried to put her down.

As Diana herself put it in an interview with the French newspaper *Le Monde* only months before her death, 'The Press in Britain has always misrepresented me in my attempts to help people. I can think of any number of occasions when I have been attacked by the Press because I dared to help other people. They attacked me for hugging AIDS victims, for my visits to Imran Khan's cancer hospital in Lahore, Pakistan, and for wearing make-up during a visit to a hospital operating room during a heart transplant operation.

'The Press is ferocious. It forgives nothing, it only hunts for mistakes. Every good intention is twisted, every gesture criticised. I believe that abroad it is different. I'm welcomed with kindness when I'm overseas. I'm taken for what I am, without prior judgements, without looking for blunders. In Britain it's the opposite. And I believe that in my position, anyone sane would have left a long time ago.

'Over the years, I've had to learn to rise above criticism. But the irony is that it's been useful to me in giving me a strength which I did not think I had. That's not to say that the criticism hasn't hurt me. It has. But it has given me the strength to continue along the path I've chosen.'

But it was intrusion into her private life that angered Diana even more and she, more than anyone, suffered from constant harassment by photographers and reporters. No one doubted, and Diana bore witness to the fact, that intrusion into privacy can, and does, cause serious harm. The loss of privacy can cause more damage to its victims than theft of property. Yet it is a harm for which there is no legal remedy in English law. The hypocrisy of many of the defences of the current régime of self-regulation in the Press — the right to know, the right to publish the private matters of people in the public eye — seems to be obvious to everyone except the journalists who put those defences forward. Editors who criticise the failings of self-regulation to ensure high standards of behaviour in other areas — the Stock Exchange, the police, the medical profession — seem unable to appreciate just how hollow their protestations that journalists can be trusted to look after themselves sound to the public.

But a privacy law is extremely difficult to formulate. In some European countries privacy laws even forbid the publication of information which voters should know about the politicians who are seeking their votes. But Diana's principal complaint was not the invasion of her privacy but the harassment and bullying techniques of certain photographers, most of them freelance. The new law on harassment, which has just come into force, makes such behaviour a criminal offence. That is a start.

Three weeks after her death, a tough privacy code was unveiled. Lord Wakeham, Chairman of the Press Complaints Commission, announced a series of the most radical changes to Press regulation since the commission's inception. It included proposed rules covering a person's private life, the treatment of children and harassment. The package was agreed by Fleet Street editors following Diana's death.

One of the main aims of the proposals was to drive the *paparazzi* out of business. Lord Wakeham claimed that if all the proposals were adopted, Britain would have the toughest code in Europe. Lord Wakeham said that the industry should prohibit the publication of pictures obtained through 'persistent pursuit' or unlawful behaviour, which would cover both staff and freelance photographers. 'I am thinking of pictures obtained by freelancers who break the traffic laws, commit trespass or stalk their prey,' he said. The Commission hopes that this would end the market for pictures taken by the sort of photographers who persistently pursued Diana.

But the key concept of the new code should be privacy. It is expected that the re-drawn definition of a person's private life will encompass their home life, relationships, medical records and personal correspondence. Children should now receive greater protection, including, particularly, Prince William and Prince Harry. They will not be the subject of stories or photographs while in full-time education, even if their parents are famous, unless there is an overriding public interest.

In the aftermath of the tragic death of Diana, the Press knew that they had to act to allay the public's real concern over many of their intrusive activities. Many people worried that the first proposals carried no sanctions whatsoever against transgressors, though there were calls for those contravening the rules to be forced to pay substantial amounts of money to charity. Despite the new moves, sceptics wondered how long the tabloids would, in fact, respect the new code. We shall see.

# CHAPTER ELEVEN

# THE FINAL DAY

Diana began what would be her last day ever in Sardinia. Dodi and Diana had woken early and decided to go for one last swim before heading back to London. They took the *Jonikal* tender, a small motor-boat, and sped around to a cove nearby before slipping into the warm waters of the Mediterranean for an early morning bathe.

But while they were splashing about and enjoying themselves in blissful privacy, a small boat, packed with *paparazzi*, approached and their secret swim was discovered. Bodyguards in another boat confronted the photographers and asked them to go away and respect the Princess's privacy, but they refused, telling the security guards that they had every right to sail into the cove. They also told the guards that they would not go away because they were engaged in making their living and should be allowed to do so unhindered.

As Les Wingfield, one of Dodi Fayed's most trusted bodyguards, explained, 'We tried to appeal to their better nature but they didn't want to listen. They were determined to stick around and take pictures of Diana and Mr Dodi together. There was nothing we could do.'

Annoyed and fed up that the photographers had stolen their privacy once more and refused to leave them alone, Diana and Dodi decided to end their swim and speed back to the privacy of the *Jonikal*, moored at the jetty of the exclusive Sardinian resort of Cala di Volpe, on the Costa Smeralda, for a shower before breakfast.

Diana and Dodi remained on board in the seclusion of their yacht, relaxing in the sun and having a light lunch out of sight of the troublesome *paparazzi*. Diana had intended to remain in Sardinia with Dodi until Sunday before flying back to see her sons who were flying down from Balmoral to spend 48 hours with their mother at Kensington Palace before returning to their boarding schools. But the chasing pack of photographers made them change their plans. Indeed, if it had not been for the *paparazzi* Diana and Dodi would never have visited Paris that day.

Instead, they travelled by road to Sardinia's Olbia Airport, managing to avoid the photographers who believed them still to be aboard the *Jonikal*. They had decided to fly to Paris — one reason being that Diana wanted to buy some presents for William and Harry to give them at Kensington Palace on Sunday afternoon. Diana always took home presents for the boys when she had been travelling overseas and would try to find items which they really wanted, sometimes spending hours choosing the gifts. As the photographers had made their stay in Sardinia all but impossible, they decided to have their last romantic night together, dining out in Paris and staying the night in the privacy of Dodi's apartment.

But the Italian *paparazzi* discovered that the Harrods jet had left Sardinia and telephoned their photographic agencies in Paris. A number of quick calls to the control towers of airports around Paris quickly confirmed that a Harrods Gulfstream jet was indeed due to land at Le Bourget at 3.20pm. The agency chiefs were fairly certain that it was Diana and Dodi's plane.

Gamma, one of the biggest French photo agencies, sent photographers, including one of their most respected cameramen, Romauld Rat, a large, softly-spoken man with the reputation of being a top class *paparazzo*. He said later, 'This was not a very important assignment because of the number of photographs that had been taken of the couple in the South of France and Italy. It would have been just another picture of them arriving at an airport and leaving in a car.'

Dressed in a light, beige trouser suit with a black cotton T-shirt beneath, Diana stepped from the aircraft wearing her Versace sunglasses and accompanied by Trevor Rees-Jones, one of a number of security guards who had been employed by Mohamed Al Fayed to protect Diana and Dodi. Rees-Jones was the man who joined them for their fateful drive later that night. Les Wingfield had also accompanied Diana and Dodi on the flight from Sardinia. Also waiting on the tarmac was Rat and five other photographers, and they snapped away at the group as they disembarked from the plane.

Waiting on the tarmac next to the aircraft was a chauffeur and a black Mercedes 600SEL owned by the Ritz. There was also Henri Paul, the deputy chief of security at the Ritz, a man well known and trusted by Dodi Fayed. He drove the back-up car that afternoon as the two vehicles made their way to the hotel in the Place Vendome. They were escorted by French police for a few miles and then they continued on their own.

The *paparazzi* gave chase on motorbikes and in cars. Les Wingfield would say later what happened on that journey.

'A black Peugeot came from behind, overtook our vehicle and then slammed his brakes on, forcing us to slow right down. The guys on the motorbikes then came up on either side of the Mercedes and began snapping away at the Princess.' Rat, however, would later deny that this had occurred.

Les Wingfield, an Englishman, sat beside Henri Paul in the back-up car. Although Wingfield had worked for Mohamed Al Fayed for five years he had never met Paul. He commented later, 'Henri Paul drove well on that journey into Paris. He seemed a nice guy.'

On the way to the Ritz, the convoy of two cars stopped briefly at the Villa Windsor, the house where the Duke and Duchess of Windsor had lived for many years before their deaths. Mohamed Al Fayed bought the lease on the substantial, detached French mansion in the Bois de Bologne for £4 million and had spent a further £25 million modernising, refurbishing and redecorating the beautiful house. It had private apartments on the top floor for the use of his family and friends. The two cars then headed for the centre of Paris and the Ritz hotel which Mr Al Fayed had bought and restored to its former glory at a cost of more than £100 million.

This time, Diana and Dodi managed to evade the pack of photographers in pursuit by driving to the service entrance at the rear of the hotel, in the Rue Cambon, arriving at around 4.30pm. The couple spent the next two hours relaxing in the luxury of the Imperial Suite, the Ritz's largest and most impressive set of rooms. Diana ordered tea and had her hair done and they chatted about their future plans.

Royal Holidays. *(Above)* In Lech, one of the Princess' favourite skiing resorts, with William and Harry; and *(below)* in Majorca the previous year with King Juan Carlos and Queen Sophie of Spain.

*(Above)* A family together – sports day at Ludgrove School in 1995; and *(below)* Diana carries the ashes of her father, Earl Spencer. She is accompanied by her siblings Jane, Sarah and Charles.

*(Above)* Diana pictured alone at the pyramids; and *(below)* despite her fame, Diana was always a caring and fun mother.

At a mosque in Cairo, Egypt.

Dressed to perfection, a mum to be proud of.

*(Above)* With her mother, Frances Shand-Kidd; and *(below)* white-water rafting with William and Harry in Colorado.

The Queen of Hearts in Hungary *(above)*, and in Derbyshire *(below)*. Diana's kindness reached every corner of the world.

In Zimbabwe with the Red Cross, 1993.

The Princess on the beach.

*(Above)* Winner of the 1995 Humanitarian of the Year
award; and *(opposite)* on the same trip, visiting the Pio
Manzu International Research Centre in Italy.

*(Above and opposite)* In Angola with the Red Cross.

Diana tells the world's press of the purpose of her
visit to Angola.

The event that shocked the world. Charles, Harry and William examine the flowers laid at Balmoral in memory of Diana.

A nation grieves. The funeral of Diana, Princess of Wales,
6th September, 1997.

At 6.30pm, Dodi, accompanied by two security guards, crossed the Place Vendome to an exclusive jewellers, Repossi. One of the reasons the couple had come to Paris that day was to look at two rings, which Dodi had seen in the store's Monte Carlo branch. He wanted to present one to Diana. Later that day, a diamond ring was delivered to Dodi at the Ritz.

At 7.00pm, Diana and Dodi left the Ritz, once again using the service entrance in the Rue Cambon, but this time the photographers were ready. The moment was captured on film. Diana, her hair looking smart after a week of swimming and sunbathing, was still dressed in her beige trouser suit, and the couple were once again guarded by Trevor Rees-Jones and Les Wingfield. Also seeing them off that evening was Henri Paul but he was now off duty and, after Diana and Dodi had left, he drove away from the Ritz in his black Mini.

What Henri Paul, the 41-year-old Ritz security officer who had worked for the Al Fayeds for six years, did during the following five hours, is not known. Paul, a former pilot in the French Air Force who spent most evenings after work drinking and socialising in the gay clubs of Paris, was known to be a heavy drinker, though the autopsy on his body showed that his liver was in good condition for a man of his age, with no sign that he was suffering from the effects of an excess of alcohol and nothing to suggest that he was, in fact, an alcoholic. Some employees at the Ritz talked of Henri Paul as a man who was a steady and heavy drinker who would occasionally collapse from over-indulgence. What is certain, though, is that his employers never had cause to discipline him for excessive drinking or even drinking while on duty. He had proved himself to be a reliable security officer, diligent and hard working.

And yet, according to the autopsy, Paul had

consumed at least ten glasses of wine during the evening — nearly two bottles — without having had anything to eat. The examination showed that there was no food whatsoever in his stomach. Blood tests carried out on his body revealed that Paul was more than three times over the French legal drink-drive limit, the analysis showing 1.8 grams of alcohol per litre of blood, more than twice the British limit, indicating that he had drunk more than a litre of wine.

That was not all. Ten days after the crash, the French Prosecutor's office issued an official statement that a search for toxic chemicals in Henri Paul's blood had revealed 'therapeutic levels of a medication whose active ingredient is fluoxetine, and sub-therapeutic levels of a second drug whose active ingredient is tiapride'. Fluoxetine is the active ingredient in Prozac, the commonly-used anti-depressant. Official guides to medicine say that the drug can have a number of side-effects including drowsiness, nervousness, anxiety, confusion, dizziness, thoughts of suicide, movement disorders and violent behaviour.

The second substance, tiapride, is commonly prescribed to treat behavioural disorders and involuntary twitching, and aids the management of acute alcohol withdrawal symptoms. The pharmaceutical journals state that the drug can alleviate distress, improve abstinence and drinking behaviour and facilitate re-integration within society following a detoxification period. Moreover, all drivers under the influence of one or both of these drugs are advised to treat them with caution.

Diana and Dodi's destination that evening was Dodi's private apartment just off the Champs Elysée, a 15-minute drive from the Ritz. No one appeared to notice the Princess and her friend Dodi as they drove slowly along the Champs Elysée in the thick of the nose-to-tail Saturday evening traffic. But, once again, photographers were staking out the apartment waiting for their quarry to arrive. The bodyguards stopped some photographers taking pictures and a dispute flared up.

Les Wingfield would say later, 'We asked the photographers to back off a little, to stop crowding the Princess and to give the couple some space, pointing out that in that way they would get better pictures of the couple. Some of the photographers accepted that but others wouldn't, obviously keen to provoke a reaction from us. Those photographers physically assaulted us, poked and hit us with cameras. It was obvious they were annoyed because we had stopped them taking pictures when the couple arrived.'

Later that evening, Diana herself discussed the behaviour of the *paparazzi* with her bodyguards. Les Wingfield recalled, 'She was upset a couple of times because of the way the Press were acting, and the way they were driving. She was concerned that one of the *paparazzi* would fall off a bike in front of one of our cars. They were only riding small motorbikes, easily manoeuvrable so they could zoom in and out of the traffic.'

Meanwhile, Henri Paul who had a small apartment in the Rue des Petits Champs, not far from the Ritz, was relaxing off duty. He was well known in the bars and restaurants of the area and most barmen considered him a social drinker. No one thought of him as an alcoholic.

That night, Dodi planned to take Diana to one of his favourite Parisian restaurants, Le Benoit, but they decided against the venue because the restaurant had a large glass window looking directly on to the street.

With the *paparazzi* in hot pursuit, they thought that was taking too great a risk so they decided to eat back at the Ritz.

Dodi had left the ring at his apartment knowing that they planned to stay the night there. As they left the apartment shortly after 9.30pm, the couple were once again photographed by about a dozen *paparazzi*. Dodi was wearing blue jeans, a casual, light tan suede jacket over a shirt, but with no tie; Diana was dressed smartly in a long black jacket with a black silk top and white trousers. A dozen photographers in cars and on motorbikes followed them back to the Ritz.

Pierre Suu, from the Sipa Photo Agency, was one of those photographers following the small convoy. He recalled, 'I remember one of the bodyguards opening the back door of the Range Rover that was following the Princess's Mercedes and gesticulating to us to stay behind their car and not to act aggressively. We kept our distance and there was no trouble. He gave us the 'thumbs-up' sign, indicating that we were co-operating and that there was no problem. We were not harassing them, although there were 15 motorbikes following the car. This was regular procedure in Paris. There were 15 photographers following simply because it was Diana. Major celebrities visit Paris all the time and similar procedures follow ... it happens all the time. But none of them was as big a celebrity as Princess Diana.'

Les Wingfield, who escorted the couple back to the Ritz, recalled what happened when they returned to the hotel. 'We unlocked the car doors and got the couple out. We were immediately surrounded by about a dozen photographers who jostled us, coming within a couple of feet of the couple, shooting away with their cameras. Some were aggressive, others were OK.'

The hotel's security cameras, both outside the main

entrance to the hotel and inside the lobby, captured what happened. *Paparazzi* can be seen surrounding Diana and Dodi as their bodyguards guided them through the dozen or more photographers who seem determined to get yet one more shot of the couple.

Pierre Suu maintained that when they went inside, Diana did not appear to be upset by the photographers' attentions but Dodi tried to shield his face from the cameramen. Neither spoke during the short ten-second walk from the car to the hotel entrance. Once inside, an angry Dodi, now fed up with the constant attentions of the photographers, asked Les Wingfield to go outside and try to persuade the photographers to go away. Dodi knew that the footpath immediately in front of the Ritz is the private property of the Ritz and he was entitled to demand that the photographers leave.

Diana and Dodi made their way to the hotel's Espadon Restaurant where Diana ordered her last meal, roast turbot garnished with dried seaweed and seasonal crispy vegetables. From the neighbouring dimly-lit Ritz bar, she would have been able to hear the pianist playing such romantic melodies as 'You Must Remember This'. But the couple felt uneasy sitting at their corner table while other guests looked on, unable to keep their eyes off the Princess. The waiter who served them noticed that Diana appeared ill at ease. After finishing their main course, they left and went upstairs to the Imperial Suite. It was 10.15pm.

At about the same time, Henri Paul arrived back at the hotel, parking his car near the front entrance. A phonecall had alerted him to return to take care of Diana and Dodi, whom he hadn't expected to see back at the hotel that night. Pictures taken by the hotel's security cameras showed Henri Paul walking through the swing doors and then walking away from the camera while buttoning up his double-breasted suit jacket. Later, Ritz executives would claim that the pictures proved that Henri Paul was sober, chatting easily and in control of his actions.

Les Wingfield, who remained on duty all that night, said later, 'There was nothing about his demeanour which would have suggested to me that he was drunk. He was the same as he had been that afternoon ... sober.'

However, Henri Paul had been known to drink in the hotel, according to one member of staff who preferred to remain anonymous. 'We had seen Henri Paul well under the influence at parties, not perhaps completely drunk but well away. He was also not a professional driver. This year, around 1 May, there was a drinks reception and it was the same thing. He arrived in the lobby, drunk, still upright but laughing and talking nonsense. Then he went into his office, fell over and cut his nose.'

By 10.30pm, about 15 photographers were standing outside the hotel in the Place Vendome and a crowd, varying between 150 and 300 people, gathered when they heard that Diana, Princess of Wales was expected out at any moment. A photographer from the Sipa Photo Agency, Nicolas Arsov, was there. He recalled, 'There were many people standing around waiting to get a glimpse of the Princess.'

During the next half-hour, Henri Paul walked out of the front hotel and talked to photographers, telling them what was happening. He seemed in an expansive mood.

Pierre Suu would comment later, 'He did not appear drunk or anything. But it was weird that he should keep coming out and giving us information about the couple's movements. He had never done that sort of thing before. He was looking happy, excited, saying things like, "She is coming out in ten minutes." As a result, we did not wholly believe him and some photographers decided to watch the back of the hotel in case they slipped out of the service entrance.'

A few minutes after midnight, Dodi and Diana left their hotel suite and made their way downstairs. Dodi was informed that 12 photographers were waiting at the front of the hotel and he came up with a plan. The two regular cars would stay at the front and so would their drivers. A black Mercedes, not an armoured one, was summoned from the hotel garage and ordered to take up a position at the rear of the hotel. Dodi arranged that Henri Paul would drive the Mercedes carrying him and the Princess, and Les Wingfield was told to make a show at the front of the hotel, flashing the five minute signal, making it seem that the couple would soon be leaving.

The security cameras show Dodi and Diana waiting at the back door of the hotel with Henri Paul. Dodi is leaning against a wall with his arm around Diana's waist as they waited for the Mercedes to arrive.

According to the Ritz employee who was prepared to speak anonymously, no one at the Ritz ever said 'no' to the Fayeds. 'If Henri Paul had been told to drive Dodi then he would have done so with no questions asked. He would never have said "no" and he would certainly have never said "no, I can't, I've been drinking." '

At 12.20am on Sunday, 31 August, Dodi's plan swung into operation and Diana and Dodi left the privacy of the Ritz and made their way to the Mercedes waiting outside. They got into the back of the car while Henri Paul took the wheel and Trevor Rees-Jones, their only bodyguard that night, sat in the front passenger seat. As they walked forward, their attention was drawn to three men standing some way off, the three photographers who had stationed themselves watching the hotel's rear entrance. Dodi's plan had failed.

There has been speculation that Henri Paul goaded the photographers, telling them that they would never catch him. There is also speculation that Dodi Fayed told his trusted security officer Henri Paul to 'lose' the photographers and yet more which suggests that it was Henri Paul's decision alone to try and outpace the chasing *paparazzi*.

Outside the entrance to the Ritz, the photographers' mobile phones rang, alerting them that the couple had left the Ritz; the two decoy cars moved slowly out of the Place Vendome, while other *paparazzi* leapt on to their motorbikes and scooters and tried to pick up the trail.

Romauld Rat of Gamma said later, 'Some of the photographers were working in teams and we knew that the photographers who were working behind the hotel had disappeared and I realised that the couple must have left by the back entrance. I got on to my motorbike and set off to find them.'

As Henri Paul turned out of the Rue Cambon, only one photographer was giving chase and he was on a scooter. But coming towards the Mercedes was the photographer Romauld Rat, riding pillion, with his camera at the ready. He turned round and caught up with their car as it stopped at lights.

He recalled, 'At the intersection of the Place de la Concorde and the Champs Elysée I saw the Mercedes with the Princess and Dodi Al Fayed inside. Just as I arrived behind the Mercedes, it set off very quickly and several other photographers had caught up with us. I was first away at the lights, with *paparazzi* in a Fiat behind and two other photographers on motorbikes following. As the Mercedes gathered pace along the road beside the River Seine, we all dropped back, unable to keep up with it.

'It was a well-known route for chauffeurs trying to out-run the Press. I believe the Mercedes must have reached speeds around 80mph. I never saw the car again, it was too far ahead.'

The Mercedes had driven fast around the Place de la Concorde, one of the busiest roundabouts in Europe, and swooped down the Cours la Reine at the south-west corner of the Place. The road dips towards the route which runs along the Seine and leads to the underpass next to the Pont de l'Alma. Henri Paul saw his chance and put his foot flat to the boards of the Mercedes. The car, capable of speeds up to 135mph, responded instantly and within a few hundred yards the Mercedes was believed to be speeding in excess of 120mph. On that stretch of the narrow, winding road leading beneath the Pont de l'Alma, there was a speed limit of 37 mph!

Drivers entering the tunnel first veer slightly towards the right and then the road dips down to the left before straightening out. The road has a slight camber and there are no crash barriers on either side, just concrete posts on the driver's left side and a wall on the right.

Exactly what happened is not known and may never be. But, for some reason, Henri Paul lost control of the vehicle at high speed, crashed into the third concrete column, bounced off and then smashed almost head-on into the thirteenth column, spinning the car 180 degrees until it came to rest against the wall on the right side of the tunnel. The vehicle was a tangled mass of metal, the roof caved in almost to the level of the bonnet. The front was badly mangled though the back was relatively intact.

Dodi Fayed and Henri Paul, who were both on the left side of the vehicle, died instantly. Diana, severely injured, had been thrown around the interior but appeared, at first sight, to be not too badly injured. Their bodyguard, Trevor Rees-Jones, despite being the only person in the car to be strapped in, was seriously injured, the lower part of his face badly damaged. He was also suffering from internal injuries.

What caused Henri Paul's loss of control remains unclear but it was not directly caused by the photographers on their motorbikes and scooters because they were some 200 metres behind.

Romauld Rat arrived about 40 seconds after the crash and three other photographers arrived some seconds later. Rat, a qualified first-aider, recalled, 'We drove past the car and parked the motorbike. I jumped off the bike and ran towards the car. At that moment, I thought they must all be dead. I was shocked. After a few seconds, I got a grip of myself and went towards the car. I opened one of the car doors, the only one I could open, the rear right-hand side one, to see what I could do to help them.

'When I opened the car door, I could see that the chauffeur and Mr Al Fayed were clearly dead and that there was nothing I could do for them. I leaned over the Princess to see if she was alive. I reached over and tried to take her pulse and when I touched her, the Princess moved ... she was breathing.

'I spoke to her in English, saying "I'm here ... be cool ... the doctor will arrive." '

One of the most serious allegations made against the photographers at the scene that night was that not one of them ever phoned the emergency services for help.

Romauld Rat commented, 'I did not call the emergency services myself, simply because after I looked into the car I heard someone say that they had called the emergency services. That's why I didn't call them; one call was enough.

'Later, when a doctor arrived who was passing the scene of the crash, I stepped back and allowed him to get on with his work. It was only then that I fell back into my role as a journalist and began taking pictures.'

A couple of minutes later, a car approached on the other side of the tunnel carrying Dr Frederic Mailliez, a French emergency doctor who had just finished work, and his American friend, Mark Butt.

Butt recalled, 'It was a beautiful night and we had just passed the Eiffel Tower. We were travelling down into the tunnel below the Pont de l'Alma when we saw smoke ahead. We could see that there had been a crash but that there were no emergency services there, so we immediately stopped the car and jumped out to assess what was going on.'

Dr Mailliez took up the story. 'I could see immediately that there were two people dead and two civilian people injured. I ran back to my car, phoned the fire brigade and the ambulance services and told them to send two ambulances. I took my emergency equipment from the boot of my car and ran back to the scene.

'There was a volunteer fireman treating the passenger in the front seat of the car so I treated the young lady who was in the back of the car. At first I had no idea that she was the Princess of Wales.'

Butt said that when he first arrived on the scene there were only two or three photographers, but within a couple of minutes there were between 12 and 15 of them. He judged that they were all professional cameramen because of the equipment they were using and the way they were operating.

Dr Mailliez said that he remembered the photographers working very close to him as he examined Diana, but he was not distracted from what he was doing. 'They didn't bother me, they didn't hamper me,' he said.

The first two police officers on the scene made a confidential report later stating that some of the photographers at the scene were 'aggressive and obstructive'.

Butt remembered one photographer, a tall man, who approached the Mercedes and 'virtually stuck his camera in the car' as he took photographs of the Princess of Wales.

At 12.32am — eight minutes after the crash — the fire brigade arrived. Three minutes later, their trauma unit arrived at the scene.

Laurent Sola from the LS Presse Photo Agency said later that two of his photographers arrived at about the same time, took some photographs inside the Mercedes and left immediately. He said later, 'Two of our photographers took 30 to 40 pictures. A police officer told them, "OK, you've done your job, now go away." And they left immediately.'

Fifteen minutes after the crash and when all the emergency services had arrived, Les Wingfield and the decoy vehicles, followed by other photographers, came across the scene as they passed over the Pont de l'Alma. He said, 'I immediately used my mobile to check whether Diana and Mr Fayed had arrived at the apartment. They told me they had not arrived, nor had they heard from them. I expected that they were late arriving because of the accident. I thought that they had probably taken a detour.'

That night, six photographers and one driver were arrested by the French police at the scene of the accident. They were all placed in a police van and taken to the nearest police station. Later, they would be charged with manslaughter and for failing to help the victims of an accident, an offence in France.

The two photographers from LS Presse returned immediately to their agency, knowing that the pictures of the injured Diana, and her dead lover Dodi Fayed, could be priceless. They were keen to get them on to the computer as quickly as possible so they could be offered around the world.

Sola said later, 'For two hours we discussed whether we should distribute these pictures around the world or not. When we saw the pictures, showing that she did not appear to be badly injured, we decided to distribute five of them. We did not distribute any pictures of Dodi or anyone else in the car. When I started to market those pictures it was impossible to imagine that Princess Diana would die. In these pictures, you can see Diana's face behind the front seat. And her face is intact.'

One hour after the accident, the ambulance carrying Diana moved slowly away from the scene. It had taken doctors that long to stabilise the Princess and then take her to the waiting ambulance. Fearing that Diana might suffer a heart-attack, the ambulance drove slowly to the nearby Pitie Salpetrière Hospital, one of Paris's leading accident and emergency hospitals.

When examined in theatre by a team of doctors and surgeons, the severity of Diana's injuries rapidly became apparent. She was suffering heavy blood loss, broken ribs and multiple lacerations. Recovery from her main injury, a torn pulmonary vein, which carries freshly oxygenated blood from the lungs to the heart, is rare and is possible only through immediate hospital treatment. Even if her life had been saved, heart surgeons believe it is likely that she would have suffered permanent brain damage as a result of the loss of blood circulation.

First attempts to revive her by external heart massage took place at the scene of the accident and it is believed that she suffered her first heart-attack while still in the car. She was still unconscious when she arrived at the hospital. Once inside the theatre, she suffered another heart-attack and an urgent thorocotomy (surgical opening of the chest) revealed a major laceration to the left pulmonary vein. Damage to such a major blood vessel will usually cause a patient to bleed to death very quickly.

After establishing that Diana was suffering from heavy internal bleeding, a team of 12 doctors carried out the thorocotomy to the left side of her chest, giving access to the heart and lungs. The doctors entered through the breastbone. The surgeons quickly found the leakage which they succeeded in repairing. Throughout the operation Diana was given 20 pints of blood and other fluids, pumped into her so that they would enter her bloodstream as fast as possible. While surgeons worked on repairing the laceration, others took it in turns to pump her heart manually, grabbing and squeezing it to keep the blood pumping around her body.

Despite these heroic attempts to save her life, including both internal and external massaging of her heart for two hours, no circulation was restored and the death of Diana, Princess of Wales, was declared at 4.00am Paris time on Sunday, 31 August.

# Chapter Twelve

## Aftermath

The first devastating news that Diana, Princess of Wales, had been involved in an accident was telephoned by the duty officer of the French Interior Ministry to his counterpart at the British Embassy in Paris. Immediately, the duty officer informed the British Ambassador, Sir Michael Jay, and then flashed the news through to the Foreign Office in London. Those first reports stated that the Princess had been injured, though not seriously, and that her friend, Dodi Al Fayed, had died along with the driver.

After Diana had reached the hospital, and the extent of her injuries became known, further phonecalls were made to London and the decision was taken to inform the duty officer at Buckingham Palace that Downing Street believed Diana's injuries now appeared to be life-threatening and, as a result, the time had come to inform the Queen, Prince Charles and the rest of the family. They were enjoying their long summer break at Balmoral Castle in Scotland and William and Harry had joined their father there two weeks before.

Buckingham Palace telephoned the duty police officer at Balmoral, the man in charge of security during the night who also acted as duty telephonist. He immediately called the duty valet who went along to Prince Charles's rooms. Shortly after 2.00am, Charles was woken by a knock at his door and told the grim news. He immediately phoned Buckingham Palace and asked to be kept informed of any developments. He phoned Sir Robert Fellowes, the Queen's Principal Private Secretary, her closest adviser, who was also staying at Balmoral. Together, they decided to wake the Queen if Diana's condition deteriorated further. Charles had been informed in that first phonecall that Dodi Al Fayed had died in the crash along with the driver.

An hour later, the news came through that Diana had died. Charles was informed that she had sustained serious internal injuries in the crash and had never regained consciousness. He was also told that the security officer, Trevor Rees-Jones, was the only survivor and that doctors at the hospital considered his injuries to be non-life threatening.

Prince Charles immediately called his mother on the castle's internal phone system and she asked him to see her immediately. Charles dressed hurriedly. A few minutes later, Prince Philip, asleep in his own bedroom, was informed and he joined them in the Queen's suite of rooms. Charles told them everything he knew. Nothing is known of that conversation.

What concerned all three of them was how and when the news should be broken to William and Harry. There was grave concern how Harry, only 12, would take the news and so it was decided that the boys, who slept in adjoining bedrooms, should not be given the devastating news of their mother's death until they had woken as usual at around 7.30am.

After the Princes had been awake for about ten minutes, Charles, now shaved, showered and fully dressed, went to see them to break the news. It is not known what went on during those ten minutes or so when Charles spent time alone with the boys. He then took them to see the Queen and Prince Philip, who by then had dressed for the day. Nothing is known of that initial family meeting.

In the early hours of the morning, before the boys had been informed, Charles spoke to Earl Spencer at his home in South Africa, as well as Diana's sister, Lady Jane Fellowes, who is married to Sir Robert, and Lady Sarah McCorquodale. Prince Charles told them that he intended to fly to Paris to recover the body that day. Both sisters asked that they, too, should be allowed to accompany him so that they could bring back Diana's body together. Charles agreed.

Sarah McCorquodale took the responsibility of phoning their mother, Frances Shand Kydd, at her isolated home, a whitewashed bungalow on the island of Seil, 15 miles south of Oban in the West Highlands of Scotland where she has lived for the past eight years.

A Roman Catholic convert, Mrs Shand Kydd, who had left her three young daughters and baby son in 1967, spoke to her parish priest after hearing the news of Diana's death.

The priest, Father Sean MacAulay, of St Columba's Cathedral in Oban, said, 'She was in a terrible state, but she is a very, very strong woman, a brave woman. I can never find the words to describe the strength that woman has. The death of a child knows no words we can say that will ever comfort a parent.'

Islanders visited Mrs Shand Kydd throughout the day, delivering flowers and messages of condolence while Diana's mother spent most of the time watching television, absorbing all the evidence and the words of sadness which filled the screens and the airwaves throughout the day.

The British people, however, were unaware in their misery that Diana's death had caused the most remarkable row ever heard in royal circles. At Balmoral, a meeting took place shortly after breakfast, attended by the Queen, Prince Charles, Prince Philip, Sir Robert Fellowes, three other senior advisers and two senior Palace Press spokesmen.

It was during this first meeting that arguments broke out between members of the Royal family. Newspaper reports talked of clashes between the Queen and Prince Charles over the funeral arrangements. Allegedly, the Queen argued that Diana's body should be taken to a private mortuary rather than remain in a royal chapel. According to some newspapers, the Queen also argued that Diana should be given a private family funeral as she was no longer a member of the Royal Family. Later, these allegations would be denied in the strongest possible terms. The Buckingham Palace Press spokesman, speaking with the authority of the Queen, angrily denied the allegations which were described as 'simply untrue' and 'pure mischief-making'. Indeed, a Palace official specifically rejected any suggestion that the Queen opposed arrangements as to where the Princess's body should lie, and added that the funeral plans were agreed 'with the close and willing co-operation of the Spencer family.'

All that is true. The Queen was never involved in any controversy over Diana's funeral arrangements.

However, there *was* the most almighty row at that first family meeting. A furious disagreement grew between Prince Charles and his father Prince Philip and, throughout, the Queen sat silent listening to the violent quarrel between her husband and her eldest son.

Prince Philip, who believed that Diana had become a liability to the Royal Family, first objected that an aircraft of the Royal Squadron should be sent to Paris to bring back Diana's body. He argued that as Diana had left the Royal Family she was now no longer entitled to the use of an aircraft of the Royal Squadron.

The relationship between Prince Charles and his father has always been strained. It was one of the reasons why Earl Mountbatten acted as Charles's surrogate father because of the lack of close affection Prince Philip had shown his eldest son, the heir to the throne.

On this occasion, however, Charles saw red and became angry with his father, annoyed that he should be so stuffy about the memory of Princess Diana. Charles gave Prince Philip no respite stating that, if necessary, he would personally pay for the cost of the aircraft but he was determined that it would be from the Royal Squadron and that, in death, he would make sure that she received every respect that would have been shown to a member of the Royal Family. Prince Philip was taken aback by the force of his son's argument and the manner of his attack.

Then, when a discussion took place over where Diana's body should rest before the funeral, Prince

Philip suggested that her body should not lie in a royal chapel but in a private mortuary or one designated by the Spencer family. Once more, Charles turned on his father, telling him that such a suggestion was 'unacceptable'. Charles told him that he had decided that Diana's body should rest in the chapel at his London home, St James's Palace, 200 yards from Buckingham Palace. Charles knew that his father had to agree to that.

It was during this argument, when Sir Robert Fellowes took the side of Prince Philip, that one of Charles's senior advisers turned to Sir Robert with his famous remark: 'You can go and impale yourself on your own flagstaff.' That single remark, made in front of the Queen, reveals the depth of anger prevailing during that stormy meeting.

It was at that point that the Queen intervened and agreed that Prince Charles should make the arrangements for the return of Diana's body to Britain, the suitable resting place and, with the Lord Chamberlain and the Spencer family, should be responsible for the funeral arrangements. It was decided that no further decisions could be taken until Earl Spencer had returned from his home in South Africa. He was expected to arrive in London early on the Monday morning.

Two hours after the stormy exchange, the Queen, with Charles, William, Harry and Prince Philip all drove to Crathie Church for the Sunday morning service they always attend when staying at Balmoral. The Queen Mother, 97, also went with them. She has always had a warm, gentle relationship with both William and Harry who love and admire her.

The boys, dressed in grey suits and black ties, sat

either side of their father for the drive to and from the church. Their faces were expressionless; there were no tears. Their tears had been dried earlier but there would be more that day. Time and again that Sunday, and over subsequent days, the boys suddenly burst into tears, shocked and overcome by the weight of their grief.

To those few sombre parishioners waiting outside the church, it seemed extraordinary that the young Princes had somehow, in those few hours, adopted the tradition that monarchy must do its duty, no matter how unexpected or shocking the circumstances. William and Harry showed extraordinary courage. They stepped out of the car into the greyness of the overcast morning, their faces pale, their eyes expressionless. They stood for a moment in silence as other members of the family emerged from the group of black vehicles and then walked into the tiny church for the hour-long service.

Prince Charles's staff had contacted Jane Fellowes and Sarah McCorquodale who flew to Aberdeen. After rows of seats had been removed from the red and white BAe 146 aircraft to make space for the coffin, the three of them, escorted by bodyguards and three advisers, flew directly to Paris.

Britain awoke that morning — Sunday, 31 August — stunned by the unimaginable news of Diana's death. Most people learned of the news from the radio because nearly every radio station had dropped their schedules to concentrate solely on the events in Paris.

Others, living near churches, awoke to hear the bells tolling slowly, the sound of one muted bell every minute, a centuries-old custom announcing a tragedy.

On hearing the news, many families gathered

around their television screens, desperate for news and the pictures that told of the horrific events of the night. Photographs of the twisted Mercedes were flashed on the screen every few minutes, driving home the point that the Princess had indeed died in the accident.

In their shock and disbelief that morning many people mumbled the same words wherever and whenever they met, 'I don't believe it ... I can't believe it.'

No one wanted to believe that Diana, Princess of Wales, the person many people held most dear outside their immediate family, had been killed in such an extraordinary, senseless road accident. It did not matter that very few of those people grieving that day had ever met the Princess or spoken to her. She had managed to overcome that hurdle. The general public had taken the young woman to their hearts; they had rejoiced and wept tears of joy at her wedding in 1981; they had watched her grow thin as she suffered from her eating disorders; and their hearts had gone out to her when her marriage to Charles irretrievably broke down.

But it had been during the last five years of her life — since the official announcement of her separation in December 1992 — that the great mass of the British people had been won over by Diana. Her magnificent work for charity, her dedication to the disadvantaged and homeless, to lepers and orphans, to cancer patients, AIDS victims and those maimed by landmines had touched a chord in the nation and their respect and admiration went out to her in a way that the British people had never managed for any other members of the Royal Family.

The first flowers were laid outside Buckingham Palace in the early hours of that Sunday morning by night workers going home to sleep. These few were followed in the next few hours by a steady stream of people, a stream that became a river and then a flood as a huge number of British and foreign mourners arrived to pay their respects in a remarkable, overwhelming display of love and grief for the Princess. They went to Kensington Palace, Diana's home since her marriage in 1981, and to St James's Palace, Charles's official London residence, and they came with flowers, a never-ending river of people queuing in stunned silence to lay their wreaths and to say their 'farewells' to the young woman they had come to love.

By lunchtime on Sunday, the Princess's home at Kensington Palace in West London became an unofficial shrine, a place to which people flocked in their thousands to lay flowers, cards, messages and even some personal tokens, such as toys or items of clothing.

Tens of thousands came to London that day, numbed by the news, reacting in the only way they could, bringing mementoes to the Princess who had been taken away from them in an underpass in the centre of Paris while being chased by a dozen or more *paparazzi* who hounded her every step.

And it wasn't only the British people who came to pay their last respects to the people's Princess, but also Americans, French, Germans, Italians, Spanish and Japanese. Anyone and everyone who was visiting London that weekend wanted to share their sorrows.

The silence in London was eerie. The only sounds were of children's voices and the gentle sobs of people mourning. Never before had such a scene been witnessed in London. The stiff upper lip which is supposed to be a natural part of the British character had gone, to be replaced by an open display of grief. People held handkerchiefs and tissues to wipe away their tears, overcome with compassion and regret. Most talked in hushed whispers as though they were in church, while others cried, unable to believe that Diana was dead. Some knelt in front of Buckingham Palace, rosaries in their hands, praying for Diana's soul and asking God for forgiveness for the way she had been treated in her lifetime.

And the people who made their way to the royal Palaces that day, by road, rail, bus and Underground, were overcome by the sheer numbers of fellow mourners who had also decided to visit the capital to pay their respects. One woman spoke for many when she said, 'Diana knew she was loved, but even she could never have imagined scenes like this. Finally, we've shown her how much we loved her, but too late. She's been taken from us, taken from us by those bastard photographers.'

Most of the tributes were small bunches of lilies, carnations, sunflowers or roses, some with magazine photographs of the Princess attached to them, most with cards bearing simple tributes:

'I was so sorry to hear the news. Lots of love.'

'In memory of a beautiful person, Queen of Hearts.'

'You were a real Princess. I will miss you so much.'

'Born a lady. Became a princess. Died a legend. God bless you.'

'To our Queen of Hearts, an English rose.'

'To Diana, the brightest spark who gave us love. Rest in peace.'

'Our candle in the wind. Eternal love.'

'We loved you. Now we will miss you.'

One card read simply, 'No, no, no.'

Buckingham Palace set up a page on its Internet site for people to send condolences. The black-bordered page, featuring a picture of the Princess, concluded, 'Thank you for your kind message of condolence for the sad loss of Diana, Princess of Wales.' Messages flooded in from around the world.

At Tetbury in Gloucestershire, close to Prince Charles's home at Highgrove, worshippers wore black ties while the Cross of St George flew at half mast on the Church of St Mary the Virgin.

'Everyone is just numb,' said the local priest, the Reverend John Hawthorne. 'Diana was often seen around the town, in the street and in the shops, and the people here will feel they have lost someone from the town.'

Meanwhile, people laid flowers at Diana's family home, Althorp in Northamptonshire. At a church service in the nearby village of Great Brington, Betty Andrews, 76, housekeeper and cook at Althorp when Diana was growing up, said, 'She was just an ordinary, shy little girl. She would come in from boarding school, plonk her bag on the kitchen table and raid the larder. She and her brother Charles would clean me out — Yorkshire pudding, cold potatoes, the lot.

'The thing I remember most was her ordinariness. She wanted to help me cook and often she ate with the staff rather than at the family table. Even after I retired, she kept in touch, and would always pop in to see me during school holidays. She was a wonderful, warm person.'

And she recalled other memories. 'I remember Diana as a teenager, such a lovely, bubbly girl, always full of fun. I feel that I've lost a daughter.'

In the warm, sultry, afternoon sun, groups of people sat in Green Park, St James's Park and Kensington Gardens, families and friends, all talking about Diana and the wonderful person she was. They looked downcast, miserable, their faces drawn, their eyes reddened with tears, their voices breaking with emotion when they spoke of her. It seemed that they didn't want to leave or return home, as though leaving would betray her memory, and many hung around for hours watching others mourning and weeping in turn.

A man walked past pushing a bicycle and he shouted at the top of his voice, startling many around him, 'Ban all landmines ... we love you, Diana,' and along the rows of people sitting in the park there was spontaneous clapping and cheering; and the clapping was caught up by others, by hundreds of others, as the man walked across the park shouting his demand.

And the grieving did not only occur in public but also in the privacy of churches and chapels, synagogues and mosques. People knelt and prayed and sobbed quietly to themselves and then got to their feet and, before leaving, lit a candle of remembrance for the Princess.

But in London, in particular, there was anger, too. Those photographers and TV cameramen working around the royal Palaces that day were sometimes the object of abuse and insults as the public vented their fury on the Press in particular, and the media in general. They knew in their hearts of the distress which photographers had caused Diana in her lifetime. They had seen photographs of her breaking down in public, crying with frustration as yet another cameraman poked his long lens in her face and snapped away when all she wanted was to be left alone, in peace.

During that first day of anguish and mourning, reports were coming out of Paris of the part the *paparazzi* had played during Diana's last day. The news bulletins on radio and television reported the disgraceful antics of the photographers, allegedly hindering police and the emergency services, climbing on the car's bonnet and wrenching open the door of the car so that the photographers could get better close-up pictures of Diana, sprawled unconscious on the back seat. The idea that photographers could act in such an inhumane manner caused revulsion and anger.

And Les Wingfield, the security officer who had spent the past week with Diana and Dodi trying to protect them from the *paparazzi*, was in no doubt that the people responsible for the deaths of Diana, Dodi and Henri Paul were those photographers who chased them from the Ritz that night.

He would say later, 'If anyone is to be blamed for their deaths, it is the people who were hounding them. There had been an escalation for the whole period we had been away. And it came to a head that day after we landed at Le Bourget, all the way to the Ritz.'

In Paris, however, a trend has developed among the *paparazzi*, who now believe that celebrities, including politicians, who venture out on to the street or drive through the city are fair game. They play a sort of hide-and-seek within which, the photographers claim, the local celebrities understand the rules.

Because the French privacy laws are the toughest in Europe, French photographers believe that when celebrities venture out into public places, it is open season. Hounding celebrities from motorbikes and scooters is a sort of Gallic Russian roulette, where the most enormous risks are taken to capture someone on film, dodging in and out of the speeding traffic and riding at excessive speed through the heart of the city, totally ignoring legal limits.

The photographers sometimes hire the most daredevil motorcyclists to carry them, while they ride pillion, camera in hand, ready to snap whoever might be their intended victim that day. Such reckless riding was developed as a result of the photographers and TV cameramen who ride pillion to cover the famed Tour de France cycle race, during which the motorcyclists weave skilfully in and out of the hundreds of competitors and spectators.

The French *paparazzi* believe that they have a God-given right to harass, chase and hound any celebrity whenever and wherever they like, as long as they are not intruding on that person's privacy. And it is unusual for the photographers to come to blows with security men, though arguments often develop when they are chasing a celebrity. Usually, after the photographers have taken a few snaps, they will happily return to their agencies to develop and then sell their latest photographs.

But Princess Diana was different. The *paparazzi* knew that a good picture of Diana and Dodi kissing, cuddling or being affectionate in the back of a car was a photograph they could sell around the world for hundreds of thousands of pounds. It was not often that the Princess of Wales visited Paris as a private individual and the photographers were determined to get as close as possible to their quarry, whatever the risks or the consequences. As with every politician or celebrity, including Diana, the photographers were totally unconcerned about the feelings of the person they were hounding. In their view, that was the price the victim had to pay for being a celebrity, a film star or even a Princess.

But on the day of Diana's death, her brother, Earl Spencer, laid much of the blame fairly and squarely on the shoulders of the *paparazzi*, the photographers and the tabloid Press whom Diana quite openly 'hated and feared'.

Within hours of the news, Earl Spencer issued a bitter, ferocious attack on the Press, an attack which had the backing of the British people.

He said, 'All those who have come into contact with Diana, particularly over the last 17 years, will share my family's grief. She was unique. She understood the most precious needs of human beings, particularly those who suffered. Her vibrancy, combined with a very real sense of duty, has now gone for ever.

'It is heartbreaking to lose such a human being, especially as she was only 36. This is not a time for recriminations, but for sadness. However, I would say that I always believed the Press would kill her in the end. But not even I could imagine that they would take such a direct hand in her death as seems to be the case.

'It would appear that every proprietor and editor

of every publication that has paid for intrusive, exploitative photographs of her, encouraging greedy and ruthless individuals to risk everything in pursuit of Diana's image, has blood on their hands today.

'My heart goes out to the families of the others killed in this accident. Above all, my thoughts are with William and Harry and with my mother and two sisters, who are showing tremendous bravery in the face of this tragedy.

'I would ask you please at this time to respect the fact that Diana was part of a family. And among the general mourning of her death, realise that we, too, need space to pay our final respects to our own flesh and blood. For that we will need privacy.

'Finally, the one consolation is that Diana is now in a place where no human being can ever touch her again. I pray that she rests in peace.'

Meanwhile, in Paris, Prince Charles, Sarah and Jane were met at the Villacoublay military airfield by President Chirac, whose presence signified the national sense of shock that so profound a tragedy should have occurred in the French capital. The royal party was escorted by *gendarmes* to the Pitie Salpetrière Hospital where doctors had fought in vain to save the Princess. The Prince thanked doctors, surgeons and staff for their efforts. French pallbearers, led by a Catholic priest, carried the body to a hearse outside the hospital. And President Chirac offered the nation's condolences to Charles and Diana's sisters before they left the hospital on their journey home.

Nineteen hours after the car accident that claimed her life, the Princess's body arrived back in Britain at RAF Northolt in west London, the coffin draped in a Royal Standard. A ten-man bearer party from the Queen's Colour Squadron of the RAF Regiment escorted her body from the aircraft to a waiting hearse. From there, it was taken to a private mortuary in London to be dressed and placed in a lead-lined coffin, before being taken to the Royal Chapel at St James's Palace where it remained until her funeral six days later.

Prime Minister Tony Blair and Defence Secretary George Robertson were present at Northolt when Prince Charles stepped from the aircraft. Also watching the arrival were Lord Airlie, the Lord Chamberlain; Lord Bramall, Lord Lieutenant of London; Group-Captain Peter Hoskins, the station commander; Air Marshal David Hurrell, Air Officer Commanding 38 Group; and the station chaplain. After the hearse had been driven away, Prince Charles once more climbed aboard the BAe 146 for the return flight to Balmoral so that he could be with William and Harry.

Earlier, Tony Blair, at his constituency in Sedgefield in the north-east of England, said, 'I feel like everyone else in this country today. I am utterly devastated. Our thoughts and prayers are with Princess Diana's family, particularly her two sons. Our heart goes out to them. How many times do you remember her and in how many different ways with the sick, the dying, the children and the needy? When, with just a look or a gesture that said so much — more than words — of her compassion and her humanity?

'We are today a nation in a state of shock, in mourning, in grief that is so deeply painful for us. She was a wonderful and warm human being, although her own life was often sadly touched by tragedy. She touched the lives of so many others in Britain and throughout the world with joy and with comfort. We know how difficult things were for her from time to time. I am sure we can only guess that.

'But people everywhere, not just here in Britain, kept faith with Princess Diana. They liked her, they loved her, they regarded her as one of the people. She was the People's Princess and that is how she will stay, how she will remain in our hearts and in our memories for ever.'

From all corners of the world, the great and the good, and thousands touched by Diana's charity work, spoke of their 'shock' and 'devastation' at her death.

President Bill Clinton said, 'Hillary and I knew Princess Diana and we were very fond of her. We are profoundly saddened by this tragic event ... I will always be glad I knew the Princess. I admired her work for children, AIDS victims and for getting rid of the scourge of landmines.'

Chief Emeka Anyaoku, the Commonwealth Secretary-General, said, 'She was loved and admired across all the nations of the Commonwealth and was emerging as a potent symbol of our common humanity in her evident commitment to others less fortunate than herself.'

Russia's President Yeltsin said, 'Diana was loved by the people of Russia. Many exceptional projects that touched the lives of ordinary people have been put in practice in Russia with her direct participation.'

President Mandela of South Africa said in a message to the Queen that the Princess 'would be sadly missed as a warm, compassionate and caring person'.

And Mother Teresa, who was herself to die only a week later, said, 'She was extremely sympathetic to poor people ... and very lively and homely.'

Pakistan's former cricket captain, Imran Khan, recalled Diana's work to raise funds for his Shaukat Memorial Hospital for Cancer. 'She achieved unprecedented heights in the service of mankind. May God give us strength to carry on serving humanity as a tribute to her memory.'

And there were countless other tributes from world leaders, church leaders and from her many friends whose lives she had touched, all referring to Diana's wonderful charity work, her warmth and her compassion.

But perhaps some of the most poignant tributes came from those countries like Afghanistan, Cambodia, Angola and Bosnia, where landmine victims are still being maimed and killed every hour of every day.

Jasminko Bjelic, 23, from Tuzla in Bosnia, who lost his left foot when he accidentally trod on an anti-personnel mine, said, 'She was our friend. When she came to Tuzla three weeks ago we asked her to tell the world about the horror of landmines and she said she would do everything to get a worldwide ban.'

Diana visited Bosnia in August 1997 as part of her personal campaign in support of an international ban on landmines. The visit had been organised by the Washington-based Landmine Survivors Network. Many of the victims she met during her visit to outlying villages had no idea who she was.

One woman, Andjelija Kresic, told Diana how her husband had lost both his feet to a landmine in 1992. She would say later, 'Diana immediately stood up, held my hands and looked me in the eye. She understood immediately how I felt. When a neighbour asked what this woman, whose identity she did not know, had brought me, I told her she had brought warm words, the most important thing anyone can bring.'

Another villager, Plamenko Priganica, 37, a man who lost his leg to a landmine, when told of Diana's death, said, 'My whole family is crying. She came here to help us, to help all mine victims. She did not deserve to die.'

It was on that same day that Dodi Fayed, the man who seemed to have won Diana's heart in just a few weeks, was buried in accordance with Muslim custom. His body was flown to London, his coffin draped in a black cloth with gold lettering, and he was taken to Regent's Park Mosque in London where hundreds attended a 25-minute service. Family mourners, led by his father Mohamed Al Fayed, then escorted his body to Brookwood Cemetery, near Woking, in Surrey, for a private family burial.

Later in the week, a spokesman for his father said that the owner of Harrods had personally passed on Diana's 'final words and requests to the appropriate person at a private meeting'. The day before Diana's funeral, Mr Al Fayed had met Diana's sister, Lady Sarah McCorquodale, and passed on Diana's final words. The Spencer family were astounded at the message, describing the alleged request as 'preposterous'. The family decided not to tell the public what those words were. Weeks later, however, Thierry Meresse, the Communications Director of Pitie Salpetrière hospital, where doctors tried in vain to save Diana, said, 'The Princess was unconscious on arrival and then she had a heart-attack. She was not capable of speech in her last hours. It is utterly untrue to suggest that she was.'

Meresse insisted also that Michelle Bollet, the nurse allegedly named by the Fayed camp as the employee who carried the Princess's dying words, did not exist. 'It is an invention by the entourage,' he added.

In fact, the final words Diana was alleged to have uttered were, 'If I die, I want to be buried next to Dodi.'

But the Spencer family are convinced that Diana made no last request and uttered no such words.

Within hours of her death, Paris became a city of rumours. Within days, a blizzard of information was pouring into French newspaper offices and TV stations, and finding its way on to the Internet. At one time or another, the French journalists revealed to readers and viewers that the speedometer of the Mercedes was stuck at 123mph; traces of cocaine had been found in the car; and that a £130,000 ring had disappeared. But the most persistent rumour that was still being recycled in French magazines six weeks after her death was that Diana was pregnant. One French magazine, *Voici*, 'revealed' to its readers that a tell-tale hormone had been present in Diana's blood showing that she was pregnant. Even the prestigious *Paris Match* reported that a coded message from the French authorities to Whitehall gave 'highly sensitive' blood test findings, suggesting that Diana was indeed pregnant.

Weeks later, after police investigators had stated categorically that there was no other car involved in the fatal crash, it was revealed that they were searching for a Fiat Uno after fragments of plastic from a Uno tail-light had been found at the scene. There was also the discovery of a scratch on the door of the Mercedes which, apparently, had been made by another car.

But in London, the burning question on everyone's lips was whether the media was guilty of murdering Diana. Earl Spencer's emotional outburst had stoked the fires and brought the question to the forefront of the nation's thoughts.

Many people wholly agreed with the words and the sentiment of Earl Spencer's condemnation of the tabloid Press and many believed that the media was guilty of her murder. Over the years, the public had grown irritated, then appalled and finally angered at the pictures of *paparazzi* chasing and hounding the Princess as she went about her daily routine. Her life had become so unbearable, thanks to the greedy, pernicious photographers, that she could not step outside her home without being harassed.

'Are you happy now, you Press scum?' screamed a motorist as he drove past a knot of photographers recording the scenes outside Buckingham Palace on that first day.

The fact that French police arrested seven French photographers at the scene within minutes of the crash went some way to assuage the feelings of many who felt that, either directly or indirectly, the photographers were responsible for her death, especially when they were later charged with manslaughter, along with the lesser charge of failing to help victims of an accident. Both charges carry a maximum sentence on conviction of five years' imprisonment and a fine of Ff500,000 (£52,000). Later, police would arrest three more photographers.

The great majority of the British public had become increasingly revolted by the antics of the *paparazzi*. And the public had not been fooled by the protestations of innocence on the part of the British tabloid editors who claimed they that they had never invaded Diana's privacy themselves, but who happily agreed to pay tens of thousands of pounds to a freelance *paparazzo* who offered them exclusive pictures of the Princess. And, of course, the proprietors were also aware of exactly what was going on, for none of the editors had the authority to spend £100,000 on a photograph without first clearing it with the proprietor.

Some have suggested that the general public, those who buy the tabloid newspapers, must also take their share of the blame for without readers, hungry for the latest gossip about Diana's life or to see the latest photograph of her, there would be no muck-raking tabloid Press; without the public demand, there would have been no interest on the part of newspaper editors to print stories about her or publish pictures of her. But that argument goes some way to absolving the tabloids, the editors and the proprietors from blame, and vindicates their intrusive and insensitive attitude towards Diana.

At her death, the people showed the true spirit of the nation, despite the tabloids which had seemed keen in recent years to destroy the Princess they loved. By the end of that first week of mourning, 15 tons of flowers lay in the cellophane and patterned-paper wrappings before the gates of Kensington and Buckingham Palaces with heartrending messages of love attached to them. Among the flowers were favourite teddy bears, willingly given up, and children's coloured drawings, some of them with 1p and 2p pieces taped to them.

Tens of thousands queued patiently, often for the better part of a day and into the night — some for 12 hours — to write messages in the official books of condolence that they knew might never be read. At first, four condolence books had been laid out but, as the queues lengthened, a total of 30 books were required for those wishing to pay their personal respects to the Princess. Thousands of people kept all-night vigils in the royal parks and they burned candles throughout the night, replaced by ordinary people determined to make sure that the flame, her flame, would never be extinguished.

London became a still ocean of flowers, bowed heads, thoughtfulness and kindness. People talked more softly, walked more slowly and were noticeably more courteous, even to total strangers. They consoled each other as they drew nearer the banks of flowers, for at that moment of truth, many thousands were overcome with grief, the tears impossible to stem as they stood in their silence remembering the woman they had come to love, as though Diana had been a close friend, a sister or a daughter. They had read so much over the years about the details of her private life, they had argued about her so often, seen her pictures many hundreds of times and held such strong opinions about her — both for and against — that many had come to believe that they knew her extremely well. It felt to them that they were personally bereaved, and they were suffering all the symptoms of the sort of intense private grief that people usually experience only after the sudden and unexpected loss of somebody close to them. The fact that Diana was so young, so beautiful, so vulnerable and a mother inevitably heightened the grief.

As the days passed, the early anger of the nation, which had been aimed squarely at the tabloids and the photographers, moved gradually towards the 'reckless' and 'irresponsible' driver of the Mercedes, and then more forcefully towards the Royal Family.

Thirty hours after the fatal crash, post mortem results were published revealing that Henri Paul, the driver of the Mercedes who died in the crash, had been found to have three times the legal limit of blood alcohol and had been driving at excessive speeds. Later investigation by the Paris police showed that Henri Paul had been drinking heavily for the entire week before the crash.

Police sources, who had studied film from video cameras situated at the entrance to the tunnel, showed that the chasing pack of photographers, on motorbikes and scooters, were between 100 and 200 yards behind the Mercedes when it crashed. In a bid to shift the blame away from their comrades facing prosecution, members of the *paparazzi* protested that it was 'scandalous, unimaginable, suicidal' for anyone to have permitted Henri Paul to drive the Princess of Wales having drunk so much alcohol that evening.

And that was not all. Ten days after the crash, the Paris prosecutor's office issued a statement saying that Henri Paul was not only, in the eyes of the law, heavily under the influence of drink when he began the short car journey, but also present in his blood were traces of fluoxetine and tiapride.

Although there was no verifiable record, no way of knowing the precise speed the Mercedes was being driven immediately prior to the crash — estimates varied from 80mph to 122mph — the fact remained that Paul was driving at an extremely dangerous speed for any city centre. When Paul's recklessness is added to the likely effect of the cocktail of drink and drugs in his system, it becomes all the more difficult to imagine him completing any journey, let alone one complicated by the aggressive attentions of chasing motorcyclists, without mishap.

As a result of the forensic evidence, the chasing photographers, the number of whom arrested finally totalled nine, plus one dispatch rider, claimed that Paul, not the *paparazzi*, were to blame for the tragedy. The Al Fayed family, however, continued to claim that photographers swarmed around the Mercedes in the final stages of the pursuit. The chasing *paparazzi* claimed that they were 600 yards behind the Mercedes when it crashed.

Even if they had not contributed directly to the accident, the photographers stood accused of insensitive and possibly disruptive conduct at its immediate aftermath. Several took photographs at the scene and a policeman was quoted as saying that they pushed him out of the way in an effort to obtain better pictures. And, worse than that, all the photographers present at the crash site that night, including their dispatch riders, stood accused of failing to report the accident to the emergency services although they all carried mobile phones. Police analysed their mobile phone records and not one called for police, ambulance or the fire services.

A lawyer for the Al Fayed family commented, 'French case law states that it is enough to prove that the chasing photographers had a role in what happened. The drunkenness or otherwise of the driver does not change matters.'

But the mood of the nation was turning from what had happened in Paris during that fateful night to the events back home. Understandably, the public were angry and outraged at the chasing photographers who had so blighted Diana's life for so many years, and they were stunned by the revelations that the Mercedes driver was not only drunk but also under the influence of drugs when he drove the car away from the Ritz.

Those tens of thousands of people who flocked to London throughout that first week of mourning were also becoming frustrated and annoyed with the behaviour of the Royal Family and the Queen in particular. They were showing increasing impatience and indignation at the Sovereign not travelling down from her holiday home, Balmoral, to lead the nation's mourning for the Princess they had loved. By remaining at Balmoral, 800 miles from those grieving and desolate in their sorrow, many believed that the Queen and Prince Philip were deliberately snubbing Diana in death as they believed in their hearts that Diana had been snubbed by the Royals in life.

And they didn't like it.

Many believed that their sovereign, the nation's monarch, should have left Balmoral and joined them in London, showing that they cared and shared the nation's feelings of sadness and loss. But there had been virtual silence from Balmoral. The nation had only seen a two-line statement from the Royal Family saying they were 'deeply shocked and distressed' by the news, and the only time they had been seen was in television news pictures of the family attending church, as usual, on the Sunday morning of the crash. Otherwise, the public had seen and heard nothing of their Queen.

The mood on the streets of London, particularly around Buckingham Palace where the mourners gathered to grieve, turned from open criticism of the Queen to a more ugly, defiant attitude towards the monarchy. Forty-eight hours after Diana's death, there was anger on the streets and the public's unease was directed squarely at the Queen. The newspapers took up the sentiment of the people and the front pages of Britain's tabloids left the Royal Family and their advisers in no doubt that their policy of private, family grief was one which the nation did not appreciate.

YOUR PEOPLE ARE SUFFERING, SPEAK TO US, MA'AM screamed the *Daily Mirror*; SHOW US YOU CARE, the *Daily Express* urged and the *Sun* demanded, WHERE IS OUR QUEEN?

It was at that point that advisers to the Queen and to Prime Minister Tony Blair realised that they had to act, and quickly, to stem the growing tide of criticism. Unbelievably, the Queen, Prince Philip and Prince Charles, as well as their advisers, had totally failed to appreciate the mood of their nation. Throughout Diana's years with the family and throughout her marriage, the Royals had not fully appreciated the extraordinary love and affection the people felt towards Diana, and that, since her divorce, the great majority of people had become even more protective and caring towards her. They believed in their hearts that the Royals had never cared for Diana as a family should, and had not protected her from the incessant hounding of the *paparazzi* or the constant intrusion of the tabloid Press.

Desperate to put forward the Royal Family's viewpoint, royal aides were keen to point out that Balmoral is a family home whereas the London Palaces were places of work with accommodation attached. One said, 'Put yourself in their shoes, losing someone. You want to be at home. And Balmoral is home.'

The argument, however, was disingenuous at best and cynical at worst. Throughout Diana's marriage, she had spent very little time with the Queen and Prince Philip, not seeing them for weeks and months at a time except on royal occasions when she was duty bound to be 'on parade', whether it was meeting a Head of State or attending Ascot races. Rarely would Diana eat with the Queen and Prince Philip or take tea with them, though she did on occasions. Diana was never close to the Queen or to Prince Philip and she never believed that they felt close to her.

In an effort to quash suggestions that the Royal Family had shown insufficient public grief over the death of Diana, Tony Blair said, 'The Royal Family are trying to make all the practical arrangements for the funeral, at the same time as comforting the two boys. They share our grief very much and we should respect that.'

A Downing Street spokesman dismissed criticism of the Royal Family as 'unfair', pointing out that the family should be allowed to grieve in private like any other family.

Prince Charles's Press Secretary, Sandra Henney, took the unusual step of appearing on television to appeal for understanding. 'All the Royal Family, especially the Prince of Wales, Prince William and Prince Harry, are taking strength from the overwhelming support of the public, who are sharing their tremendous sense of loss and grief. They are deeply touched and enormously grateful.'

It is true that Prince Charles was spending all his time with William and Harry, talking to them and comforting them whenever they were tearful and miserable. When they felt strong enough, he would go for walks with them and they went fishing together on one occasion, but their hearts weren't really in the sport and they returned to the castle. They spent time watching television and reading books and they ate most of their meals together with Charles, the Queen and Prince Philip.

But the vast majority of the nation were not placated by the statements from both the Palace and Downing Street. And some Members of Parliament took up the cry. Angela Smith, MP for Basildon, Essex, commented, 'A little bit of emotion from the Royal Family would not be amiss. The whole country is embroiled; they expected some emotion from the Royal Family.'

Gerry Bermingham, MP for St Helens South, said that 'something needs to be said'.

Particular concern was expressed over the fact that no flag flew over Buckingham Palace during those early days following Diana's death. That confused some people, outraged others. They could see the Union Flag flying at half-mast across London and the rest of the country on almost every building with a flagstaff. However, what the public did not realise was the fact that the only flag ever to fly above Buckingham Palace is the Royal Standard, and it is raised only when the Sovereign is in residence. It is never flown at half-mast, even when the monarch dies, because of the principle that 'the king is dead, long live the king' — in effect, the sovereign never dies.

However, despite the reasons and the excuses, the protocol and the tradition, 24 hours later everything changed. The general public demanded action and the monarchy finally bowed to their wishes.

Five days after Diana's death, the Royal Family responded publicly. They were urged to do so not only by the thousands of mourners queuing night and day to sign the books of condolence but also by the screaming headlines of the tabloid papers lying on the table in the room where the Royals take breakfast at Balmoral. At that moment, the Queen realised that she could no longer remain in the confines of Balmoral, hidden from the grieving nation.

Thursday, 4 September was cold and misty at Balmoral Castle, the peace and quiet only disturbed by the birds and the occasional sound of horses braying. It ended with a somewhat perfunctory walkabout by the Queen and Prince Philip to see the flowers outside the gates, placed there by people from the nearby villages. The Duke of York went on an 'impromptu' walkabout along The Mall in London and Prince Edward arrived to sign the book of condolence, the first Windsor to do so. All these events were, however, captured by the television cameras. Something was finally happening.

More importantly, orders were also given to the most senior Buckingham Palace advisers to show their faces and tell the nation what had been going on behind the scenes. Never before had such an array of the most senior officials been ordered to parade in front of the television cameras in order to, effectively, explain themselves and their plans for the funeral of the people's Princess.

Under the stained-glass dome of the Central

Conference Centre of Church House in London, next to Westminster Abbey, the senior palace officials held a Press conference. In the middle of the row of four men and one woman was Geoffrey Crawford, the Queen's Press Secretary. To his left, wearing a similar black tie and dark suit, sat Lieutenant-Colonel Malcolm Ross, the Comptroller of the Lord Chamberlain's office. Next to them were Penny Russell-Smith, the Deputy Press Secretary, Dickie Arbiter, Director of Media Affairs and the Very Reverend Wesley Carr, Dean of Westminster Abbey.

Ross spoke first. 'Perhaps if I could just preface the following with this — in putting together this funeral plan we have not followed precedent. We have broken with convention for this unique day for this unique person. We have followed primarily the wishes of the Spencer family.'

Finally, the admission of error had been made. After a week defending decisions not to fly flags at half-mast, defending protocol and tradition, and after nearly a week of almost total silence from the Royal Family, it was admitted that the entire House of Windsor and their advisers had sorely misjudged the mood of the people.

The balance was to be addressed. The Queen would give an address to the nation on television; the Union Flag would fly at half-mast above Buckingham Palace; the Queen would travel to London earlier than planned and Elton John, a longtime friend of Diana's, would sing at Westminster Abbey.

In fact, the battle to change the minds of the Queen, Prince Philip, the Queen Mother and all their most senior advisers had been fought for three days. The old guard, led by the Queen, Prince Philip and the Queen Mother, were against affording Diana a state funeral because she was no longer a member of the Royal Family; they were against treating her with the pomp and ceremony that she would have been due as the wife of Prince Charles; and they were against a full-blown funeral which would have been attended, like a state funeral, with all the Heads of State from Europe, the Commonwealth and the United States.

Ever since his arrival back in Britain with Diana's body, Charles had been urging his mother to show that the family cared for Diana. The week of official mourning declared by the Queen was in danger of becoming a week of severe embarrassment for the monarchy. In death, Charles explained time and again, Diana appeared to be exposing the Royal Family's detachment, which she had always complained about in her life.

Prince Charles, aided by Earl Spencer who had returned from South Africa, and his sisters Sarah and Jane, took the decision to thrash out the funeral Diana would have wanted. They all knew that she would not have been happy with the ceremonial display of a state funeral, but they also knew that she would have wanted those people involved with whom she had forged relationships and friendships, and those who understood her role in helping the 120 or so charities and good causes.

It was that nucleus of four who decided that Diana should have a 'unique funeral for a unique person'. And they won the day. Prince Charles also talked to both William and Harry about the funeral arrangements and they wholeheartedly agreed. They, too, wanted something special for their mother.

Also supporting the proposals were Robin Janvrin, the Queen's Deputy Private Secretary, and Stephen Lamport, Prince Charles's Private Secretary. Together, they persuaded the Queen to issue a statement, unprecedented in the circumstances, concerning the family's attitude to Diana's appalling death in a desperate bid to show the nation that the family had a heart.

But the Queen, like her father George VI before her, was far more comfortable with protocol and tradition, always asking on such occasions what had been done before, and unwilling to introduce new, untried practices. The lessons are in history. After the 1966 Aberfan disaster, she was criticised, even in those more deferential times, for taking six days to decide to visit the scene. More recently at Dunblane, she misjudged the mood when, the day after the massacre, she gave an address to the Royal Armouries in Leeds.

A Press release was issued: 'The Royal Family have been hurt by suggestions that they are indifferent to the country's sorrow at the tragic death of the Princess of Wales. The Princess was a much-loved national figure, but she was also a mother whose sons miss her deeply. Prince William and Prince Harry themselves want to be with their father and grandparents at this time in the quiet haven of Balmoral. As their grandmother, the Queen is helping the Princes to come to terms with their loss, as they prepare themselves for the public ordeal of mourning their mother with the nation on Saturday.'

Once more, the general public was not particularly impressed. This time, it could be interpreted that the Queen was using the two Princes as an excuse, suggesting that it was their demands that were keeping her and Prince Philip in Scotland and, by implication, away from the crowds that were besieging the three royal Palaces in London. In reality, the Royal Family had inadvertently become locked into a 'no-win' situation, by adhering as strictly as they could to the old royal favourites — protocol and tradition.

The neat decision to make Diana's funeral 'a unique funeral for a unique person' permitted, at a stroke, flexibility in the guest list, the Order of Service and the funeral procession.

Yet the whole point about protocol is that it lays down fixed rules in advance which are then rigidly adhered to, as its defenders put it, to avoid insult or lack of respect. The rules, of course, are also designed to buttress the established order. Royal protocol is monitored by the Lord Chamberlain, currently the Earl of Airlie, with the assistance of his deputy, Lieutenant-Colonel Malcolm Ross. Its rules are implemented by courtiers, many of them serving or former armed forces officers or diplomats, professionally trained to stick rigidly to the rule book, however inflexible or out-of-date.

Protocol comes in tablets of stone, for every occasion. The rules are, by definition, imposed, normally from on high. But during that first week of mourning for Diana, the nation showed that they did not want protocol to be imposed upon the mourning or the funeral arrangements of the people's Princess. They demanded that protocol be brushed aside for Diana because, to her, formality was anathema. And finally, the Queen, the most conservative of monarchs, caved in. It was a legacy Diana would have loved.

As a result of the people's demands to overthrow protocol, and backed by the tabloid Press, the monarchy was forced to acquiesce. Old protocol reserved state funerals for top-rank monarchs or winners of wars; Diana was neither, so she was awarded a lower-rank funeral. New protocol would not permit that. The people loved her. She was royalty's superstar, the people's Princess. So new protocol demanded a unique funeral for her and one was arranged. Old protocol said that the flag should fly over the Palace only when the monarch is there, and never at half-mast. New protocol decreed that the nation was in mourning and some symbolism should mirror that. Old protocol said the funeral procession was a matter for the Palace; new protocol said that the people's Princess should be seen by all those who wanted to see her cortége. Old protocol said a monarch was not required to offer a public tribute to the deceased; new protocol said she would be publicly harangued in the Press until she did. Old protocol made no provision for a pop star to sing at such a funeral; new protocol invited Elton John.

What occurred in Britain that week was unprecedented. Protocol, hated by Princess Diana, was turned on its head. No longer was protocol to be dictated solely by those detached individuals whose job it was to uphold tradition, but instead by the people, the subjects who shop in the supermarkets, go to football matches, drink in pubs, play bingo and the National Lottery and are addicted to TV soaps. For once, the ordinary people of Britain had made their voices felt and they changed the status of protocol for ever.

Handing over the details of the funeral

arrangements to Prince Charles and the Spencer family meant that the British people would be presented with a funeral that they felt would be appropriate for someone of Diana's character and personality. Charles appreciated that restricting the funeral procession to less than a mile from St James's Palace to the Abbey would never be long enough to accommodate the hundreds of thousands, if not millions, of people who were expected to attend. So he demanded, and was granted permission, to double the length of the procession, the coffin starting its final journey from her home, Kensington Palace, and to go past St James's to Westminster Abbey. He organised giant television screens to be erected in Hyde Park, through which the cortége would pass, so that thousands could watch the proceedings live. Police predicted that six million people might flock into London to watch the funeral. Charles feared that there was a potential danger of children being crushed unless sufficient space was provided where people could see the cortége and then view the rest of the procession and the service live on television.

Finally, on the evening before Diana's funeral, the Queen bowed to her people.

In the most remarkable and personal message of her 46-year-long reign, the Queen set the tone for the country's day of mourning when she called on the nation 'to show the whole world the British nation united in grief and respect for Diana, Princess of Wales'.

Making her first unscheduled, live broadcast for 38 years, the Queen spoke, as ever, with composure but also with visible emotion as she reflected on the life and death of the Princess two hours before the coffin was moved from St James's Palace to her home at Kensington Palace in preparation for the two-mile journey to Westminster Abbey.

In what amounted to an opening plea for understanding, the Queen began by saying, 'Since last Sunday's dreadful news, we have seen, throughout Britain and around the world, an overwhelming expression of sadness at Diana's death.

'We have all been trying in our different ways to cope. It is not easy to express a sense of loss, since the initial shock is often succeeded by a mixture of other feelings — disbelief, incomprehension, anger — and concern for those who remain.

'We have all felt those emotions in these last few days. So what I say to you now, as your Queen and as a grandmother, I say from my heart. First, I want to pay tribute to Diana myself. She was an exceptional and gifted human being. In good times and bad, she never lost her capacity to smile and laugh, to inspire others with her warmth and kindness. I admired and respected her — for her energy and commitment to others, and especially for her devotion to her two boys.

'This week at Balmoral we have all been trying to help William and Harry come to terms with the devastating loss that they and the rest of us have suffered. No one who knew Diana will ever forget her. Millions of others who never even met her, but felt they knew her, will remember her. I, for one, believe there are lessons to be drawn from her life and from the extraordinary and moving reaction to her death. I share in your determination to cherish her memory.'

She went on, 'Our thoughts are also with Diana's

family and the families of those who died with her. I know that they, too, have drawn strength from what has happened since last weekend, as they seek to heal their sorrow and then to face the future without a loved one.'

The Queen, accompanied by Prince Philip, had flown to London and together they inspected the ocean of flowers outside the gates of both Buckingham Palace and nearby St James's, stopping to read some of the messages on cards taped to the bouquets and bunches of flowers.

But by far the most heart-rending moments in a week charged with emotion took place hours before the Queen's television broadcast when Prince William and Prince Harry moved among mourners outside Kensington Palace, the home they had shared with their mother. All week, concern for the boys' feelings and the way they were coping with the grief had been in the minds of millions. The boys had only been seen, briefly, through the windows of the car that took them and Prince Charles to church on the morning their mother died.

With a maturity that Diana would have been proud of in both young Princes, William, just 15, and Harry, nearly 13, spoke a few words to mourners and accepted bunches of flowers handed to them by those standing near the gates of the Palace. To everyone, the boys just kept repeating, 'Thank you, thank you'. At first, the boys seemed taken aback by the sheer volume of floral tributes in front of the black-and-gold iron gates. Throughout their brief appearance, accompanied by Prince Charles, they displayed dignity beyond their years and a composure that was beyond many of the tearful adults meeting them. Over and over, as they spoke or listened to well-wishers, the Princes offered their gratitude for the shared sense of loss. Unforced applause punctuated the subdued nature of the occasion as the family group passed through a side-gate to inspect flowers attached to the ornate fence. Charles pointedly drew his sons' attention to various parts of the extraordinary display. At times, both boys seemed close to tears, touched by the genuine feelings of grief and sadness of those who had queued for up to eight hours to sign the books of condolence at Kensington Palace.

Mourners cried out 'We love you' and 'God bless you' and the boys repeatedly thanked everyone they met as they patiently shook outstretched hands. Immediately before returning to the royal car, Prince Charles and the boys were given large white lilies, the traditional symbol of death.

As the boys drove away, they passed hundreds of people who had decided to camp out for the night along the route the cortége would take the next day and, whenever the onlookers saw the royal car passing with William and Harry and their father inside, they cheered and applauded.

# CHAPTER THIRTEEN

## FAREWELL

When they awoke in the doorways and on the hard pavements, on the grassy banks and in the parks, the cool, early-morning mist causing them to shiver, they were quiet. These were the people who braved the cold of the September night because of their determination to get a first-class view of the Princess's cortége that day. And after they awoke and shook the damp night air from their clothes, they stood almost in silence, not wishing to disturb the peace that had settled over London in expectation of a day of tears.

Shortly after dawn, those who had kept vigil were joined by hundreds of thousands who had left their homes in the early hours to secure a good position from which to watch Diana's final journey. There was no formality about the crowd; they did not come because Diana was a great person, or because they respected her for her station in life, a Princess who had been married to the heir to the throne. They came because she had managed, in 16 short years, to make them love and admire her for her good deeds, her warmth, her compassion and her informality.

Black ties and dark suits were for the courtiers and the guests. The people came in the clothes they would usually wear at weekends, not because they had no respect for Diana but because, in her life, she had dressed like them on so many occasions; in shorts, a sweat shirt, a baseball cap and trainers. It was one of the reasons they loved her, showing a healthy disregard for the formality and the pomp and ceremony of royal protocol.

More than a million people thronged the streets of London to pay their last respects while an estimated 2.5 billion — half the world's population — followed her funeral on television and radio.

Prince William and Prince Harry woke early, and after breakfast, watched on television the start of what would be the most heart-wrenching day of their young lives. No decision had been taken as to whether they would walk behind their mother's coffin with Prince Charles and Earl Spencer. Their grandfather, Prince Philip, had said that he wanted to walk behind the coffin to represent the older generation of Royals and Prince Charles had agreed to his request, out of respect to his mother and his grandmother.

After their meeting with the mourners the previous day, Prince William had told his father that he wanted to walk with him behind the gun-carriage and Prince Harry had said that if William was to walk, then he would also. Charles advised them to wait until the morning before making the final decision. Their father did not want to expose them to too much grief and sorrow which might become too much for them. He knew from experience that neither William nor Harry would want to break down in tears as they walked along the route, their private distress exposed for half the world to see.

When Prince Charles asked his sons how they felt at around 8.30am, they both said that they wished to accompany him along the route to Westminster Abbey. And both assured their father that they felt quite capable of undertaking the ordeal which they understood would be something they had never experienced before.

'I want to do it for Mummy,' said Harry.

Everyone who lined the route that day hoped that William and Harry would have the composure and the maturity to cope with the situation. All eyes were on the young Princes as they made their way, their heads bowed for most of the time, from St James's along The Mall, through Horse Guards Parade and down Whitehall towards the Abbey. Along some of the mile-long walk, the boys, walking either side of their uncle, Earl Spencer, joined hands with him. At one stage, at Horse Guards Parade, Earl Spencer put his arm protectively around young Harry, comforting him for a moment or two.

There were no fanfares, no military bands and no clattering cavalry to be heard that day, only the solitary tenor bell ringing out every minute, the traditional sign of a nation in mourning. Many cast their minds back to the noise and acclaim, the cavalry, the cheers, the coaches and the fanfares that had roused London 16 years before at her spectacular wedding. Now there was nothing but silence, which hung in the bright sun of this Saturday in September like a shroud above the sombre city.

The body of Diana left her home at 9.08am in bright autumnal sunshine. Her coffin, draped in the Royal Standard, was topped with three wreaths, two of white lilies from Earl Spencer and Prince William, the third of white roses from Prince Harry with a card bearing the single word 'Mummy'.

It was drawn on an antique gun-carriage by six black horses and nine members of the King's Troop, Royal Horse Artillery, and flanked by a bearer-party of 12 Welsh Guardsmen of the Prince of Wales's Company. Preceded and followed by mounted police, the cortége first passed a sombre line of Kensington Palace staff and then turned down the private road of Palace Avenue.

Here, the first members of the general public who had come to say 'goodbye' cheered the cortége with cries of 'God bless you' and 'We love you'. As the procession turned into Kensington High Street, a shower of white flowers was thrown at the coffin, and for the first time the sound of weeping could be heard from the 20-deep crowds who had gathered near the Princess's home.

Many hugged each other and wept openly as the cortége passed; others gripped tissues and handkerchiefs and stood holding them to their faces, alternatively wiping away their tears and choking back the emotion. And after the cortége had passed, many remained motionless, unable to speak, seeking comfort in each other and staring dazed into the distance as their eyes followed the gun-carriage until it was out of sight. There had been other state funerals, there had been other royal funerals, but never before had there been a funeral charged with such emotion, dejection, and heartache. Even the police officers who lined the route seemed moved by the occasion.

As the gun-carriage passed slowly through the Wellington Arch and down Constitution Hill towards Buckingham Palace, the Queen and three generations of Royals — all dressed in black — walked out to the gates of the Palace and stood waiting for the coffin to pass. At that moment, the royal mourners, including the Princess Royal, Prince Edward, Princess Margaret, the Duke of Kent and the Duke and Duchess of York with their two daughters, looked frail and vulnerable as they stood in silence. And when the Queen bowed her head in respect and deference as Diana's coffin passed within a few feet of her, the crowd cheered, as though in this moment of sadness and mourning they forgave her rigid adherence to royal protocol.

As the procession headed up The Mall towards Horse Guards Parade, a lone piper standing on the verge played 'Abide with Me'. And minutes later, the crowds and those millions watching on TV across the world caught the first glimpse of the young Princes as they waited for the cortége with Prince Charles, Earl Spencer and Prince Philip. Earl Spencer made the sign of the cross as the coffin passed by, before all five stepped out to follow the cortége on the last mile of its journey to the Abbey. Behind them stood 500 people of all ages, those members of Diana's various charities who had all been invited to walk behind the cortége. They were dressed not in customary dark suits and black ties, but in their uniforms with their bright sashes and T-shirts, the same uniforms they would have worn when Diana came to visit them.

Leading in wheelchairs were those from Disabled Sport England and Debra, a research charity into a genetic skin disorder. Other charities included the Great Ormond Street Hospital, the Leprosy Mission, London Symphony Orchestra, the Red Cross, Barnados and Relate.

As the Queen and the rest of the Royal Family left by car from the Palace to make their way to Westminster Abbey, the Royal Standard was lowered and the Union Flag was raised and then lowered to half-mast. As the crowd saw the Union Flag lowered, a cheer went up, acknowledging the fact the Queen had bowed to the people's wishes.

At the Abbey, the coffin was lifted from the gun-carriage by eight bare-headed Guardsmen. As Big Ben struck 11.00am, the coffin was carried slowly into the Abbey through the Great West Door, preceded by the Dean of Westminster, the Very Reverend Dr Wesley Carr. Nine minutes later it was laid on a blue-draped catafalque below the altar.

From that moment, a world in mourning focussed its grief on the ancient towers of Westminster Abbey as the great and the good, friends and family and hundreds of charity workers gathered for a solemn and moving service for Diana. Two thousand people, whose lives were most directly touched by the Princess, filled the vast church for the final farewell to a woman who combined the roles of Princess and ordinary mother.

Then came the family mourners, led by Diana's mother, Frances Shand Kydd, her eyes shining beneath her black-brimmed hat, a crucifix sparkling at her breast. She was followed, as protocol dictated, by the Royal Family — Princess Margaret first, then the Princess Royal, elegantly veiled, poised and purposeful; and the Duke and Duchess of York's two daughters, Beatrice and Eugenie, clasping each other's hands. The Queen looked to either side as she walked through the nave and, behind her, Prince Edward walked closely by the side of his grandmother, the Queen Mother, who leaned on her walking stick.

The 2,000 guests at the Abbey reflected the wide range of Diana's interests. Of course, in reality, it was a state funeral in all but name for someone who was royal in all but name, but the vast majority of those gathered in the Abbey for the most poignant service in its 1,000 year history were really just friends.

Among the congregation was one representative from each of the 120 charities the Princess wholeheartedly backed during her lifetime.

In addition to the members of the Royal Family and the Spencers were politicians, the US President's wife, Hillary Clinton, and the French President's wife, Madame Chirac. British politicians included Baroness Thatcher and her husband Denis; Prime Minister Tony Blair and his wife, Cherie; Foreign Secretary Robin Cook and Deputy Prime Minister John Prescott; Opposition leader William Hague and his fiancée Ffion Jenkins; Liberal Democrat leader Paddy Ashdown and his wife, Jane; and Lord and Lady Steel. Other notable guests included Henry Kissinger, Lord Callaghan and Lord Deedes, Sir Robin Butler, and Sir Edward Heath.

Among Diana's friends were Imran Khan and his wife Jemima, Richard Branson and Lady Annabel Goldsmith, as well as those from the world of fashion including Karl Lagerfeld, Donatella and Santo Versace, Jasper Conran, Victor Edelstein, John Galliano, Bruce Oldfield, Zandra Rhodes, Valentino,

Catherine Walker and David and Elizabeth Emmanuel.

From the world of entertainment there were Sir Richard Attenborough, Tom Cruise and his wife Nicole Kidman, Stephen Spielberg, Tom Hanks, Sting and Trudi Styler, Sir Cliff Richard, Anita Dobson and Diana Ross, George Michael, Tom Conti, Michael Barrymore, Shirley Bassey, Brian May, Chris de Burgh, Wayne Sleep, Esther Rantzen and Ruby Wax. And perhaps one of Diana's favourites, the opera singer Luciano Pavarotti.

Some of her friends from her younger days and those she held dear were also present including Lavinia Baring, Susan Barantes, Carolyn Bartholomew, Anne Beckwith-Smith, Lady Bowker, Lucia Flecha de Lima, James Gilbey, Michael Gibbins, Anna Harvey, Kate Menzies, Rosa Monckton, Vivienne Parry, Laura Lonsdale, Victoria Mendham, Diana Lindsay, Ruth Rudge, Angela Serota, Suzie Townsend and Caroline Twiston-Davies.

Only once during the entire service did Prince William and Prince Harry show their emotions, as the strains of Elton John's rewritten tribute 'Candle in the Wind' echoed around the ancient Abbey. The Prince of Wales, too, seemly deeply affected by the song's opening line.

The funeral service, relayed by loudspeakers to the throngs of people outside, and watched on the giant TV screens in Hyde Park, left people both inside and outside the Abbey in tears as a week of national grief culminated in a simple 64-minute service that combined ancient and modern in what was billed as a fitting tribute to the life of the Princess.

The Dean of Westminster read The Bidding.

'We are gathered here in Westminster Abbey to give thanks for the life of Diana, Princess of Wales, to commend her soul to almighty God, and to seek His comfort for all who mourn ... In her life, Diana profoundly influenced this nation and the world ... She kept company with Kings and Queens, with Princes and Presidents, but we especially remember her humane concerns and how she met individuals and made them feel significant ... let us re-dedicate to God the work of those many charities that she supported; let us commit ourselves anew to caring for others.'

This was followed by the hymn by Gustav Holst, 'I Vow to Thee, My Country', and Sarah McCorquodale, Diana's elder sister, gave a reading:

'If I should die and leave you here awhile,
Be not like others, sore undone, who keep
Long vigils by the silent dust, and weep.
For my sake — turn again to life and smile,
Nerving thy heart and trembling hand to do
Something to comfort other hearts than thine.
Complete those dear unfinished tasks of mine
And I, perchance, may therein comfort you.'

The BBC singers, with the soprano Lynne Dawson,

sang 'Libera Me, Domine' from Verdi's Requiem, followed by a reading from Diana's other sister, Jane Fellowes:

> 'Time is too slow for those who wait,
> Too swift for those who fear,
> Too long for those who grieve,
> Too short for those who rejoice,
> But for those who love, time is eternity.'

The hymn, 'The King of Love My Shepherd Is', was sung by the whole congregation and then the Prime Minister, Tony Blair, read from Corinthians 1.

Perhaps the most enduring memory of the entire funeral was when Elton John walked to the grand piano that had been specially brought to the Abbey to sing his famous song 'Candle in the Wind'. When he launched into the first line 'Goodbye, England's rose ...' both William and Harry looked down and both pressed their lips together as if fighting back the tears.

As Elton John sang the final verse, many in the congregation and thousands outside standing silent in the sunshine, burst into tears.

> 'Goodbye, England's rose,
> from a country lost without your soul,
> who'll miss the wings of your compassion
> more than you'll ever know ...'

Later, Elton John would admit that the reason he sang most of the song with his eyes closed was because of the tears that he could not stop. At one stage, he wondered if he could continue, so emotional had he felt singing that song for Diana.

Within minutes of listening to Elton's heartfelt rendition, Earl Spencer strode into the pulpit to deliver one of the most remarkable tributes ever heard at a funeral, let alone a royal funeral of someone so loved by the nation. He pulled no punches.

'I stand before you today, the representative of a family in grief, in a country in mourning before a world in shock. We are all united not only in our desire to pay our respects to Diana but rather in our need to do so. For such was her extraordinary appeal that the tens of millions of people taking part in this service all over the world via television and radio who never actually met her, feel that they, too, lost someone close to them in the early hours of Sunday morning. It is a more remarkable tribute to Diana than I can ever hope to offer her today.

'Diana was the very essence of compassion, of duty, of style, of beauty. All over the world she was a symbol of selfless humanity. All over the world, a standard-bearer for the rights of the truly downtrodden, a very British girl who transcended nationality. Someone with a natural nobility who was classless and who proved in the last year that she needed no royal title to continue to generate her particular brand of magic.

'Today is our chance to say "thank you" for the way you brightened our lives, even though God granted you but half a life. We will all feel cheated always that you were taken from us so young and yet we must learn to be grateful that you came along at all. Only now that you are gone do we truly appreciate what we are now without, and we want you to know that life without you is very, very difficult.

'We have all despaired at our loss and only the

strength of the message you gave us through your years of giving has afforded us the strength to move forward. There is a temptation to rush to canonise your memory; there is no need to do so. You stand tall enough as a human being of unique qualities not to be seen as a saint. Indeed, to sanctify your memory would be to miss out on the very core of your being, your wonderfully mischievous sense of humour with a laugh that bent you double.

'Your joy for life transmitted wherever you took your smile and the sparkle in those unforgettable eyes. Your boundless energy which you could barely contain.

'But your greatest gift was your intuition and it was a gift you used wisely. This is what underpinned all your other wonderful attributes, and if we look to analyse what it was about you that had such a wide appeal, we find it in your distinctive feel for what was really important in all our lives.

'Without your God-given sensitivity we would be immersed in greater ignorance at the anguish of AIDS and HIV sufferers, the plight of the homeless, the isolation of lepers, the random destruction of landmines. Diana explained to me once that it was her innermost feelings of suffering that made it possible for her to connect with her constituency of the rejected.

'And here we come to another truth about her. For all the status, the glamour, the applause, Diana remained thoughout a very insecure person at heart, almost childlike in her desire to do good for others so she could release herself from deep feelings of unworthiness of which her eating disorders were merely a symptom. The world sensed this part of her character and cherished her for her vulnerability whilst admiring her for her honesty.

'The last time I saw Diana was on 1 July, her birthday in London, when typically she was not taking time to celebrate her special day with friends but was guest of honour at a charity fundraising evening. She sparkled, of course, but I would rather cherish the days I spent with her in March when she came to visit me and my children in our home in South Africa. I am proud of the fact that, apart from when she was on display meeting President Mandela, we managed to contrive to stop the ever-present *paparazzi* from getting a single picture of her — that meant a lot to her. These are days I will always treasure. It was as if we had been transported back to our childhood when we spent such an enormous amount of time together — the two youngest of the family.

'Fundamentally she had not changed at all from the big sister who mothered me as a baby, fought with me at school and endured those long train journeys between our parents' homes with me at weekends. It is a tribute to her level-headedness and strength that, despite the most bizarre life imaginable after her childhood, she remained intact, true to herself.

'There is no doubt that she was looking for a new direction in her life. She talked endlessly of getting away from England, mainly because of the treatment that she received at the hands of the newspapers. I don't think she ever understood why her genuinely good intentions were sneered at by the media, why there appeared to be a permanent quest on their behalf to bring her down. It is baffling. My own and only explanation is that genuine goodness is threatening to those at the opposite end of the moral spectrum. It is a point to remember that, of all the ironies about Diana, perhaps the greatest was this — a girl given the name of the ancient goddess of hunting was, in the end, the most hunted person of the modern age.

'She would want us today to pledge ourselves to protecting her beloved boys William and Harry from a similar fate and I do this here, Diana, on your behalf. We will not allow them to suffer the anguish that used regularly to drive you to tearful despair. And beyond that, on behalf of your mother and sisters, I pledge that we, your blood family, will do all we can to continue the imaginative and loving way in which you were steering these two exceptional young men, so that their souls are not simply immersed by duty and tradition but can sing openly as you planned.

'We fully respect the heritage into which they have been born and will always respect and encourage them in their royal role, but we, like you, recognise the need for them to experience as many different aspects of life as possible to arm them spiritually and emotionally for the years ahead. I know you would have expected nothing less from us.

'William and Harry, we all care desperately for you today. We are all chewed up with the sadness at the loss of a woman who was not even our mother. How great your suffering is, we cannot even imagine.

'I would like to end by thanking God for the small mercies He has shown us at this dreadful time. For taking Diana at her most beautiful and radiant and when she had joy in her private life. Above all, we give thanks for the life of a woman I am so proud to be able to call my sister; the unique, the complex, the extraordinary and irreplaceable Diana, whose beauty, both internal and external, will never be extinguished from our minds.'

During the last three paragraphs of his speech, Earl Spencer's voice kept breaking with emotion and he had to struggle to complete the tribute, some words sticking in his throat as he fought to stop the tears that were welling in his eyes. But, somehow, he managed to complete the five-minute speech which he had written himself only the day before the funeral.

His words were listened to in total silence except for three distinct occasions when the people on the streets and in the parks reacted with emotion and enthusiasm, lending support to Earl Spencer's tribute which they wholeheartedly endorsed. The first applause, which could just be heard in Westminster Abbey, occurred when Earl Spencer spoke of Diana having no need of a royal title to generate her brand of magic. One can only speculate as to the effect of those words on the senior members of the Royal Family seated nearby.

The second, louder round of applause came when Earl Spencer castigated the newspapers for trying to bring down Diana. That sentiment was cheered along Whitehall, down The Mall and in Hyde Park, where tens of thousands had gathered to watch the service on the giant screens. But the loudest, most fervent applause occurred near the end when Earl Spencer vowed to protect Diana's sons, William and Harry. It seemed at that moment that a million people joined in the clapping and cheering, endorsing his every word. So great and so spontaneous was the feeling that Earl Spencer had hit exactly the right nerve, that unbelievably, and without precedent, those members of Diana's charities inside the Abbey began to clap, and then to cheer his words. The applause went on and on until everyone had to join in — prelates and peers, Presidents and Prime Ministers and even members of the Royal Family.

No one ever applauds at funerals of this magnitude, and perhaps they never will again. But this occasion was unique. The demand for new procedures and attitudes prevailed, and the sound of it had reached and penetrated the cloistered confines of Westminster Abbey and the whole congregation found it impossible to ignore the desire to applaud.

By delivering his speech, Earl Spencer ignored convention and tradition, as Diana would have loved, and instead of knitting wounds he deliberately acknowledged them. It was a courageous act for the speech showed on the one hand a desire to look after the children, but on the other hand forced them to become victims of a public tug of war.

To some, Earl Spencer had gone too far for, they argued, if he had had a genuine concern for the Princes he would not have issued such damning words. It was a brutal speech but nonetheless brilliant, speaking his mind to the world when the targets of his attack — the Royal Family — were sitting opposite, unable to escape his criticism. The people who lined the streets outside, who had come to say farewell, loved it.

The remainder of the funeral service seemed an anti-climax as it followed on the strong words from Earl Spencer, but the vast crowds outside remained quiet when listening to the final hymn 'Alleluia. May Flights of Angels Sing Thee to Thy Rest ...' by John Taverner and there was silence across the entire nation when the cortége carrying Diana's body halted at the West Door of the Abbey and the half-muffled bells rang out. No shop tills rang that morning, no supermarkets opened their doors and the business life of the country was put on hold. Even the sporting fixtures which so dominate Britain's Saturday afternoons were postponed, permitting time for the nation to mourn.

Indeed, electricity use fell so dramatically across the entire country during Diana's funeral that National Grid chiefs declared that the country was doing nothing during those hours except watching their TV sets. On Remembrance Sunday in November, electricity use usually declines by 500 megawatts; during the funeral service, it dropped by 6,500 megawatts.

But there still remained a chance for millions of people to say their last farewell to Diana as the hearse carried her body from Westminster Abbey back to her family home in Northamptonshire. The route led her away from the ceremonial Britain of abbeys and palaces to a rather more prosaic landscape of shops and suburbs and takeaway joints that are north London. It was not Diana's own territory but that of the people who came to love her. As she was driven north, they came out in their thousands to see her cortége and weep one last tear.

In the north London suburbs, the tribute of those who lined the streets was more spontaneous and less regimented than the grand events in central London. There were no barriers along the sides of the road, no phalanxes of uniformed police, and no one was restrained by security precautions. The crowds, though, were large, in some cases larger than in some of the famous West End vantage points. They spilled out into the road, leaving only a narrow channel for the cortége to pass through.

Throughout the journey, flowers, tens of thousands of them, were thrown gently in the path of the procession by onlookers, young, old and middle-aged, and they began to garland the car in a haphazard splash of colour as the hearse wound through the suburban streets. Soon, the flowers were piled so high on the driver's windscreen that the wipers could no longer remove the deluge of beautiful blooms which obscured his view.

At its start, Diana's final journey passed many significant landmarks as it moved along Whitehall, down The Mall towards Buckingham Palace, and then up Park Lane to Marble Arch, along a stilled and quiet Oxford Street where no shop had opened, and then turned left and headed north up Gloucester Place. In its wake, the cortége left a trail of flowers, brightening the grey surfaces of the roads.

Amid the concrete desert of Staples Corner, where the cortége joined the M1, the crowds were massive, at least 1,000 people stood on the flyovers and pavements. At the roadside, another home-made sign surrounded by flowers said, 'Farewell and God Bless. From all the kids of London.'

As the hearse headed up the wide, open expanses of the deserted motorway, people seemed to come from nowhere, sitting on the grassy embankments and some standing on the edge of the motorway, determined to say 'goodbye'. The bridges over the motorway were packed with people.

It was after the cortége had passed that the tears flowed. They came as the flowers bounced off the hearse and people realised in that instant that they would never again see the wonderful smiling face of the Princess they loved. People sat on the verges, hugged each other and cried, many sobbed, unable to control the emotion that engulfed them. While most cried, others broke into spontaneous applause as the three-vehicle motorcade with police out-riders swept by at 45mph towards Diana's final resting place.

After the cortége had left the motorway, it slowed once more to permit the 250,000 people who had gathered along that part of the route to Althorp House to say their goodbyes. Once more, the tens of thousands had waited for an hour or more to applaud and throw yet more flowers, the most personal way they could offer their own farewells. On the last leg to Althorp House, along windy, narrow, country lanes and through tiny villages, it was the turn of the local people to cheer, applaud and throw their flowers as the cars slowed to weave through the lines of mourners. By the time the cortége reached the wrought-iron gates of Althorp House, it was more than an hour late, leaving in its wake thousands of people weeping quietly and hugging each other in their despair.

Waiting on the island in the middle of the oval lake in the grounds of Althorp House were Prince Charles, Prince William and Prince Harry, along with Earl Spencer, Diana's sisters Sarah and Jane and Frances Shand Kydd. They had all arrived earlier by train for the private family burial which the Spencer family had requested. The vicar from the local church and six pallbearers accompanied the coffin from the hearse to the burial site and the two young Princes watched as they stood just a few feet from the edge of the grave into which they saw the coffin being slowly placed.

As always, prayers were said and holy water sprinkled on the coffin. Otherwise, all was silent and still on the tree-covered island, Diana's final resting place. After ten minutes, the service was over and, with their father, Earl Spencer, and the rest of the family, the boys walked back to Althorp House for tea and sandwiches.

After tea, William and Harry drove with Prince Charles to Gloucestershire where they stayed for a few days until they felt confident about returning to their respective boarding schools, William to Eton to continue studying for his 'O'-level exams, and Harry to Ludgrove for his final year before he, too, joins his elder brother at Eton. Also staying with them at Highgrove was Tiggy Legge-Bourke, the young woman who was hired by Charles in 1992 to help look after the boys.

Later that day, Earl Spencer was contacted by Buckingham Palace and an offer was made, which could only have come from the Queen and Prince Charles, to restore the royal title of 'Her Royal Highness' to Diana. Sir Robert Fellowes, the Queen's Private Secretary and principal adviser, and husband of Diana's sister, Jane, made the offer which the Palace believed was a powerful symbolic gesture to her memory. Ironically, the Princess wanted to keep the title 'HRH' at the time of her divorce in 1996, but this was refused on the grounds that she was no longer a member of the Royal Family.

Many saw the removal of the title as an unnecessary, even petty, decision by the Royal household after the divorce. There was also a strong view held by some constitutionalists that the mother of the future King should have remained Her Royal Highness. But by refusing Diana's request to keep the title, it meant that henceforth Diana, Princess of Wales, would always be a little distanced from the Royal Family proper. That, of course, was what was intended.

In the event Lord Spencer told Sir Robert that he was sure his sister would not have wanted the title reconferred upon her after death. A Palace statement confirming the offer and refusal was immediately issued against the background of gathering Press and public calls for such an initiative. 'The Spencer family's very firm view was that the Princess herself would not have wished for any change to the style and title by which she was known at the time of her death. The Spencer family itself also did not wish for it to be changed.'

The offer did, however, reveal the eventual willingness of the Royal Family to respond to the public will.

In the tranquil peace and the sunshine the following morning, Earl Spencer returned once more to his sister's grave on the tiny circular island, only 20 yards wide, which is planted with oak, birch, beech and lime trees. Althorp estate workers spent the morning collecting the flowers that had been left at the gates of Diana's ancestral home and ferrying them across the ornamental lake by rowing boat. Staff, aided by Lord Spencer, removed the wrappings and laid the thousands of flowers in the leafy glade surrounding Diana's grave. The flowers have never been removed, even when they wilted and died, but left to become the organic sustenance for more flowers in the years to come.

Diana's death had caused a storm that would not rest with her body in that Northampton grave by the lake. Within 24 hours, Prime Minister Tony Blair spoke of Diana's legacy.

'I think the monarchy changes and adapts the whole time from generation to generation,' he told BBC television, 'and Prince Charles's generation is not the same as his mother's and William and Harry are very much children of today, with today's attitudes. So there's a continual process of change. William and Harry will be brought up differently, too.'

He went on, 'I believe the Princess's legacy should be a more compassionate Britain. I think, as we look at it now, what we say is — let there be some good that comes out of this.

'The people want some good to emerge from this. They want something that allows them to take forward that sense of unity. She had that gift of human sympathy that was so real to people. People want to be taken forward. They want to say, "How do we keep that spirit alive in our country?" '

# CHAPTER FOURTEEN

# QUESTIONS THAT WILL NOT DIE

One year after the death of Diana, the argument still rages — was she murdered or was the fatal crash in Paris a genuine accident?

Not only in pubs, clubs and bingo halls across Britain, but also in Buckingham Palace and in the Houses of Parliament, the possibility that Diana was murdered by MI6 agents has been discussed, debated and dissected in the year since the crash. And today, there are as many people who believe this conspiracy theory as there were only days after the appalling crash that killed her. And yet there is a strong body of opinion that Diana's death was a genuine accident, the result of a car being driven far too fast by a man who had been drinking heavily. What does seem to be extraordinary, however, is that there are very few people supporting either contention who are prepared to change their minds.

There is no doubt whatsoever that there were many people — in the Royal Family, in Buckingham Palace, in the Establishment, in Parliament — who believed Diana to be a loose cannon, a serious and potential threat to the monarchy, a woman who had not only brought the House of Windsor into disrepute but, by her behaviour, threatened to undermine the nation's need for a monarchy. Furthermore, there were many in Establishment circles who believed that the future of the House of Windsor was in grave danger the longer Diana continued to steal the limelight and lead her own very public life.

Diana's love affair with the British people — and many other people from across the world — began even before her marriage. In reality, however, it was the traumatic news of the break-up of that marriage, unfolding month by month, that caused an extraordinary ground swell of sympathy and support for her. It was not only stories of her unhappy marriage, her faithless husband, her anorexia and her problems with the Royal Family that caused people everywhere to feel for her, but women understood the nightmare life she was living; she was a young woman, unloved by her husband and his family, trying to help others by devoting her life to charity work. Of course, ever since her engagement to Prince Charles in February 1981, Diana had won the hearts of countless people with her warmth, gentleness, shyness and, more importantly, her instinctive understanding of other people's problems. But it was when her own problems became fully known that the nation flocked to her defence, supporting her in her hour of need. They didn't see Diana as a loose cannon or a threat to the monarchy, but as an honourable young woman who had been treated disgracefully.

And cynics everywhere knew that, as far as the Royal Family was concerned, Diana had carried out her life's work for the House of Windsor. In her own words, Diana used to say that she had supplied 'an heir and a spare' following the births of William and Harry. Now, in her heart, she knew she was superfluous and, since her divorce in December 1994, she believed she had been deliberately made to feel expendable. Diana believed that those who lived and worked in Buckingham Palace realised that Wills and Harry were no longer babies; they spent most of the year away at boarding school and, therefore, there was no longer such a need for a close relationship between a stubborn mother, with her hostile views of the Royal Family, and her beloved sons. She sensed that the fact that there was an extraordinarily strong bond between her and her children didn't seem to matter a jot.

In her last two years, Diana had captured the nation's attention to such an extent that all other members of the Royal Family, including the Queen, felt almost redundant. And Prince Charles had received such a pounding in the Press that he felt unwanted, expendable even. People didn't bother to turn out when the Royals went about their duties, attending functions, opening factories, going on walkabouts, meeting the people. But every time Diana was to make an appearance people turned out in their hundreds to cheer her on. And it was the same for the national press. Virtually every time Diana stepped out of Kensington Palace there would be reporters and photographers, as well as the paparazzi following her every move, tormenting and chasing her for no apparent reason.

And then, of course, there was Dodi. Not only was Dodi a rich playboy but also a Moslem. He also had a well-known father, Mohamed Al Fayed, the owner of Harrods, whom many Establishment figures believed to be an embarrassment. Some politicians believed that Mohamed Al Fayed was a man who would stop at little to ingratiate himself with the Royal Family and that to have Diana, Princess of Wales, as his daughter-in-law would be the pinnacle of social acceptance the world over. But that thought left some people extremely nervous that the upbringing of the two young princes would, to a certain extent, be undertaken by the Al Fayed family. The Establishment, the Diplomatic Corps, the faceless courtiers who advise the Queen, could not tolerate the idea that the future King of England should be brought up by a middle-class Egyptian family, ardent Moslems, whose main claim to fame was that they owned Harrods.

The courtiers imagined the day, not far distant, when Prince William would ascend the throne and his mother, married to Dodi Al Fayed, would then be in a position to advise him. They knew that Diana had become increasingly disenchanted with members of the Royal Family, and she dismissed most of the courtiers with derision and a wave of the hand. They knew that Diana had rebelled against the system, had stubbornly refused to heed advice, and wanted to persuade her sons that her attitude to Royal protocol and tradition was the right one to follow. One day, Prince William would be King and Defender of the Faith, the Protestant. Church of England bishops as well as Establishment figures could envisage a scenario whereby William would try to reconcile the two faiths, and they were convinced that this would be bad news for

Christianity in Britain in general and the Protestant faith in particular.

Those same courtiers also feared what effect such a marriage would have on Prince William. They understood that Diana and Dodi would, in all probability, set up home in California so that he could be at the heart of Hollywood. That would mean Prince William and Prince Harry would spend holidays there, and be influenced by the Californian lifestyle. More than likely, such an experience would affect their young, vulnerable minds, giving them a different and jaundiced view of their mother country. It was known that Diana had no intention of remaining in Britain, mainly beacuse of the disgraceful antics of the tabloid press and the ever-present paparazzi. Wherever Diana chose to live it would affect the view Wills and Harry had of the Royal Family, and so the very essence of the monarchy itself. All this spelt danger and alarm.

And there was also the future of the existing Royal Family. Already Diana had sidelined them. Prince Charles had complained in the early years of their marriage that he had become all but superfluous, because everywhere they went people only wanted to see Diana; they had lost all interest in him, the Prince of Wales, the future King of England. It would not be forgotten in Buckingham Palace that when Prince Charles went on an official three-day state visit to Germany after their separation, only one photographer and reporter accompanied him. Weeks later Diana went on a visit to the Far East and 400 photographers and reporters followed in her wake. Nothing could have revealed the extent to which Diana had become the one and only member of the

Royal Family that interested the press, TV, the nation and people across the world; and nothing could have so embarrassed and concerned everyone in Buckingham Palace, from the Queen down to the lowliest courtier. Diana had all but reduced the Royal Family to a sideshow, while she stole the limelight whenever she appeared. Even when Diana wasn't making the news, the only stories in which the papers were interested involved her, never the Queen, Prince Philip, Prince Charles or any other members of the family; all this despite the great charity work they were carrying out quietly and efficiently without fuss and virtually without recognition.

It could not continue.

But the problem remained, and the difficulties posed by Diana's increasing popularity caused many headaches inside the Palace. It had been hoped that by forcing Diana to accept the separation and divorce from Prince Charles, it might cast her into the wilderness so that she would lose her star appeal. Hopefully the newspapers and magazines would turn their attention to Charles and the rest of the Royal Family. Diana had never wanted a divorce from Charles but had grudgingly accepted the deal of a good pay-off, the right to live forever in Kensington Palace and the promise that she would always have equal rights to see and care for Wills and Harry. In the protracted legal arguments that continued for months the Royal Family, with the blessing of the Queen, gradually gave in to Diana's terms. In fact, they had no choice. The house of Windsor desperately wanted to be rid of Diana and, in the end, and against their better judgement, gave in to each and every one of her demands. She was even permitted to keep the title of Diana, Princess of Wales, which, originally, the Royal Family emphatically opposed. They did not want Diana cavorting around the world in her self-appointed title of Royal Ambassador, grabbing the headlines and the TV news bulletins while the rest of the house of Windsor were all but ignored by the media.

Within months of the divorce it became apparent that, far from being pushed into the background, Diana was being thrust even more into the limelight. The nation had taken Diana's side in the divorce and now they wanted to hear everything about her life, and particularly about any man that might attract her. And Camilla Parker Bowles, Charles' mistress and close friend, inadvertently helped generate the nation's concern for Diana. Many saw Camilla as the woman who had stolen Charles from Diana, and the women of Britain naturally and understandably took Diana's side. They wanted Diana to be happy in the same way as they wanted to be happy in a loving relationship with a trustworthy man. Nothing else really mattered.

And Diana's involvement with the International Red Cross and the International Campaign to Ban Landmines catapulted her to the status of an international superstar. She was photographed in Angola and Bosnia, talking to children wounded by landmines, touring deadly landmine areas, and across the world these pictures were seen in every home with a TV set. Here was Diana, Princess of Wales, not only cuddling and caring for children injured by landmines but, by doing so, taking on the major governments of the world including the United States, Britain, Russia and France. In each and every country the cry of 'Ban the Landmines' grew in its intensity and politicians realised that they had to accept the treaty banning landmines or risk the wrath of their nation. Though Diana did not live to see the treaty being accepted, signed and implemented, her close involvement in such an international political decision caused alarm bells everywhere to ring loud and clear. This stunning young mother's capacity for championing causes which affected the ordinary people of the world created a dangerous precedent. No one knew what cause Diana might take up next, but politicians in the most powerful nations knew full well that if she did take up a cause there was every probability that she would achieve her objective. By the summer of 1997 Diana had become a political time bomb.

It seems improbable, outrageous, even monstrous to suggest that anyone living or working in Buckingham Palace would consider arranging for the removal of Diana so that she could never again cause trouble in her inimitable, innocent, caring manner. The Royal Family had tried to remove her from attracting media attention by demanding her divorce from Charles. Two years later that scheme had evidently failed.

It is fair to say, and widely recognised in political and Establishment circles, that the house of Windsor will stop at nothing if they consider that their position is being challenged or, indeed, is under threat. It was accepted that Diana's continued popularity and escalating involvement in political affairs had relegated the house of Windsor in the eyes of the world to also-rans whose sell-by date had passed. As the new millennium approached, the house of

Windsor could be seen rapidly back-pedalling in a desperate attempt to regain popularity with the people and so ensure that the monarchy would continue and flourish. But the opinion polls showed the most popular Royal to be Diana (although, officially, she was no longer a Royal, for her title 'Her Royal Highness' had been removed).

There was no denying that the Royal Family and the Establishment wanted Diana removed from public life. If she had met and married an Englishman and happily retired to the country, set up home, perhaps even had another family, and enjoyed a quiet life away from the spotlight, given up the great majority of her charity work and become a detached member of society, everyone would have wished her well. It seemed to them, however, that Diana was hellbent on causing trouble, on upstaging the Windsors, on making them eat humble pie. Diana felt there had been a conspiracy against her for years; she had no wish to go quietly and, by God, she would not do so.

Time and again, Diana had told friends, and sometimes only acquaintances, 'They [the Windsors] want to be rid of me. If I retired to the country and kept mum they would be happy. Well, because of what they have put me through I have no intention of doing so.'

Both British and French security services have given me precise details of how Diana could have been killed in the circumstances in which she did in fact die. Indeed, both government services emphasised the fact that Diana's death bore all the hallmarks of an 'executive order' killing (i.e. a killing ordered by a highly-placed government minister through a senior member of a security agency). In

Britain such matters are handed over either to MI6, Britain's secret intelligence agency, or the SAS. In France such matters are dealt with by the DGSE (Direction Générale pour la Securité de l'Etat), part of the DST, the French secret intelligence agency.

The first worrying sign was the very fact that Diana was killed outside Britain and, therefore, outside the jurisdiction of the British courts. And, in France, such matters are easily controlled by the State, the facts covered up, press investigation hindered, secrecy maintained. Even more helpful in such a situation is the fact that France has a cumbersome, old-fashioned way of investigating suspicious deaths and possible murders. It seems incredible that at the time of the new millennium the French authorities are still investigating deaths in virtually the same way as they did in the 19th century. The French talk in terms of an investigation lasting years, when in Britain the same investigation would take only months. The French system generates massive amounts of paperwork and, even today, the French police make scant use of computer technology.

In the French system, an examining magistrate is put in charge of a murder investigation, not a police officer. Every step the police want to take has firstly to be approved by the magistrate. This makes detective work slow, if not irrelevant, because detectives are not permitted to undertake any line of enquiry themselves without permission. There is total secrecy about murders, manslaughters or suspicious deaths. Neither the Magistrate nor the police are permitted by law to reveal anything whatsoever to the press or the public. It may seem unbelievable outside France but, despite overwhelming demands from the media, no press conferences are permitted, no details of the death can be made known, no inquests are held, no public inquiries ordered. In effect, the reasons and the circumstances surrounding the death of Princess Diana, her lover Dodi and the driver Henri Paul have been kept secret, hidden from legitimate investigation by the Press.

What has been proved beyond any doubt are the circumstances surrounding her death. It is accepted that Diana and Dodi, and their bodyguard, Trevor Rees-Jones, were being driven in the Mercedes by a Ritz security chief Henri Paul, 41, which careered out of control in the tunnel below the Pont de l'Alma, part of the expressway along the bank of the River Seine. We also know that a number of paparazzi photographers were witnesses to the crash, although they were some three to four hundred yards or more behind the speeding Mercedes on their motorbikes. They did not, however, get a good, close look at the crash because at the entrance to the tunnel is a curve and a dip which partially obstructed their view. There were also other paparazzi photographers giving chase, but they were so far behind the Mercedes that they saw nothing of the actual crash.

However, there are three points of great importance which have never been solved. One concerns the white Fiat Uno. There is now no doubt that the Mercedes did collide with a Fiat Uno car either immediately before entering the tunnel or as the Mercedes was speeding through the tunnel. Experts from the Fiat Motor Company of Italy have confirmed that the white paint found on the Mercedes was of the type used on that particular Fiat car. They also confirmed that the remains of a rear light found in the road near the wrecked Mercedes was indeed part of a Fiat Uno's rear lamp. Four paparazzi who were following on motorbikes also confirmed that they saw a small white saloon car driving away from the wrecked Mercedes as they entered the tunnel. Furthermore, the French police confirmed on December 31, 1997, that two previously undisclosed witnesses had corroborated the theory that a Fiat Uno was involved in the crash. The witnesses, identified as François, a financial director, and Valerie, said that seconds after the the accident they saw a white Fiat Uno zigzagging out of the tunnel. It was making a loud noise as if the exhaust pipe had been damaged. There can be no doubt that a white Fiat Uno was involved in the crash. And yet it has never been traced.

Examining magistrates Herve Stephan and Marie-Christine Devidal were informed in November 1997 that a white Uno had been involved, the French police were ordered to trace the vehicle and the driver. However, only one such vehicle and its owner were ever traced by the police and, after being interviewed and the driver's story checked, he was eliminated from police enquiries. It does seem extraordinary to senior British police officers that the Uno was never found. However, officers attached to Britain's intelligence services were not in the least surprised the vehicle was never traced or the owner interviewed.

Paparazzi photographers also informed police in interviews that they believed the Fiat Uno was probably hired, borrowed or used by other photographers because immediately prior to the crash they saw what they assumed to be the flash of a camera inside the tunnel. It was just after midnight; even inside a lit tunnel, a photographer would need to use a flash to make sure he caught the images of Diana and Dodi in the back of the car. However, all police enquiries among French photographic agencies, Italian and French paparazzi photographers and other freelance photographers failed to find anyone who owned a white Fiat Uno. They also failed to find any photograph taken at the time in the tunnel.

However, British intelligence officers now believe that the flash seen that night could well have been a high-powered light from a 'Home Defensive Flash Light', an AL-22 used by people afraid of burglars breaking into their homes at night. The AL-22 blinds someone by a beam that's 110,000 lumens strong. This blinding burst of light causes disorientation of the victim. Anyone firing an AL-22 from a distance of less than twenty yards totally blinds the victim for five to ten minutes. If fired at closer range the victim can be blinded for fifteen to twenty minutes. The AL-22 can be purchased over the counter from specialist shops. More importantly, this powerful weapon, only twelve inches long and weighing under two pounds, is also used by special forces the world over when they need to 'blind' a suspect. Such a flashlight would have been perfect to 'blind' Henri Paul who, under the influence of alcohol and driving at excessive speed, would have been unable to control the Mercedes or bring it to a halt quick enough before crashing into one or other of the concrete pillars.

And what of the aftermath of the crash? The Mercedes crashed at approx 12.24am French time in the early morning of Sunday, 31 August. One minute later a French doctor, Frederic Mailliez, on his way home from a party, enters the tunnel, sees the wrecked Mercedes and runs to the scene. At 12.26 Mailliez calls the emergency services which arrive at 12.40am. Mailliez informs the paramedics at the scene that Diana complained of incredible pain in her chest before she collapsed unconscious. And yet, after extricating Diana from the car and putting her in an ambulance, Diana does not arrive at the Pitie Salpetrière Hospital until 2.05am — one hour and forty-one minutes after the crash.

Across the world, leading heart surgeons have debated the death of Princess Diana. Most have reached the conclusion that if the French paramedics and ambulance crews had taken Diana to hospital immediately, enabling a stand-by emergency team to start working on her one hour sooner, there is every likelihood that her life would have been saved. Heart surgeons in Britain, in particular, are convinced that had the accident occurred in Britain, heart surgeons would have saved her life. And yet, inexplicably, those doctors and medics at the scene knowing she was suffering great chest pain, took one hour and forty-one minutes to get her to hospital. What the British heart surgeons want to know is why the decision was taken to travel so slowly to hospital when speed was necessary, and urgent treatment essential. Who ordered the ambulance to drive at ten kilometres per hour, therefore wasting valuable time? Who ordered the ambulance to take Diana to the Pitie Salpetrière Hospital rather than the Val de Grace military hospital, an automatic choice for VIPs because it has a trauma team on stand-by around the clock? There have never been any answers to these questions. They demand answers.

And yet, despite so much evidence to the contrary, the majority of people believe that the crash that killed Diana was a genuine road accident. Their argument runs like this: no security service ordered to carry out the murder of Diana could have reacted so swiftly to the succession of changes in plans that Diana and Dodi made that day. As that Saturday dawned Diana and Dodi, sharing the *Jonikal*'s master bedroom, awoke, intending to fly directly back to London; instead, they changed their minds and decided to share a last night together in Paris. Because of the pantomime of having to dodge the paparazzi they finally decided to eat at the Ritz and, only after midnight, made the decision to swap cars and leave by the hotel's rear exit. And, the argument continues, the driver Henri Paul was drunk, allegedly three times over the French limit. Then he drove too fast and lost control. Crash. Road accidents happen every day, especially when the drivers are drunk.

To suggest for one moment that events moved so fast that a trained squad from MI6, or a four-man squad from the SAS could not have changed plans and made the hit is laughable. They are trained to carry out precisely that type of operation, at speed. All that was needed in Paris was someone watching the Ritz hotel, a couple of mobile telephones, fast cars and the easiest of targets.

And Diana could not have been an easier target that night. There was virtually no security. No one protected Diana during that Saturday save for one man, Trevor Rees-Jones. From the moment Diana entered the outskirts of Paris from Le Bourget Airport at approximately 3.00pm there were no police cars, no police outriders, no covert protection, no security, save for one lone ex-British paratrooper. No one watched over Diana that day. It is extraordinary that the French authorities offered Diana police protection after her unexpected arrival in Paris but, according to Paris police authorities, this offer was turned down. In France, a High Protection Police Security service is available to VIPs, like Diana, but it has to be officially requested. Apparently no such request was made this day. She was undoubtedly one of the world's most famous people, a Princess, someone who should have been given round-the-clock police protection. In Britain a visiting princess of her fame would automatically have been given a high level of police security whether she wanted it or not. Once again, by their inaction and lack of initiative, the French police had made it so easy for a crack squad to take out Diana. And yet no one has asked why Diana was given no protection that day. No one has raised the matter in Parliament; no questions were asked of the Prime Minister Tony Blair or the Foreign Secretary Robin Cook. And no questions were aimed at the French authorities either.

As a result, Diana's protection and safety throughout her stay in Paris was left in the hands of one young man, Trevor Rees-Jones, a former paratrooper, and employee of Mohamed Al Fayed. Police authorities in Britain understand that no single person can ever satisfactorily guard a VIP in today's world. No president or prime minister, and no senior member of the Royal Family, ever puts their personal safety in the hands of a single bodyguard when they are in such public places as that in which Diana found herself during her few hours in Paris.

And there are also the claims and counter-claims

surrounding the blood samples taken from the body of Henri Paul, who was asked by Dodi to drive them across Paris, but whose main role at the Ritz was to act as Head of Security. Blood samples were taken from the body of Henri Paul at the scene of the crash before he was extricated from the wreckage. According to the French police, these blood samples revealed that Henri Paul was three times over the French limit for drink-driving, equivalent to twice the British limit. The French authorities maintained that Henri Paul had drunk the equivalent of eight whiskies that night. And yet, the only hard evidence proposed so far was that Henri Paul was seen drinking two pastis in the Bar Vendone in the Ritz a couple of hours before Diana and Dodi emerged from their suite in the hotel. Despite the fact that more than 100 journalists descended on Paris in the aftermath of Diana's death, not one has been able to establish that Henri Paul had another drink in any bar or club that evening.

Several people saw him that evening, including a barman next to his flat in the Rue des Petits Champs and the owner of a lesbian club, the Champmesle, in the Rue Chabanais. Both denied that Henri Paul had had a drink.

The blood sample also revealed that Henri Paul had taken Prozac, the anti-depressant, which some doctors suggested was used cover up Henri Paul's severe drink problem. And yet only two days before the crash, Henri Paul, a keen pilot, underwent a full pilot's licence medical examination. He passed with flying colours and his blood sample did not indicate that he was a heavy drinker. His responses were fast, too, especially for a 41-year-old man, suggesting that he may not have been as heavy a drinker as the authorities claimed.

And perhaps the greatest mystery is why on earth Henri Paul's blood sample contained 20.7 per cent carboxyhaemoglobin saturation. This means that 20.7 per cent of the iron-carrying pigment in his blood had combined with carbon monoxide to form carboxyhaemoglobin. But what is confusing forensic medical experts is how Henri Paul came to have such a high carbon monoxide level. He certainly could not have received such a dose in the immediate aftermath of the crash because he died almost instantly from a broken neck and the body does not not absorb carbon monoxide after death.

The usual sources of carbon monoxide poisoning are from faulty gas fires, open fires, vehicle exhausts and heavy smoking. A cab driver in London would show a level of 5 per cent; a 40-a-day smoker, a level of 10 per cent; and a smoker of big fat cigars, perhaps 20 per cent. The same level would usually be found in someone in a car with the engine running and a hose poking through the window connected to the exhaust pipe. A fatal dose is about 50 per cent. The physical symptoms of 20 per cent levels understandably vary from person to person. In some, a 20 per cent level would make them feel tired and lethargic; in others, it would give a very nasty headache. The 20 per cent level is usually found in victims of fire who have suffered from weak heart conditions. But the question that has never been answered is this — where did Henri Paul acquire such high concentrations of blood gases? He must have been contaminated from somewhere, but the crash occurred at the end of August, so there would have been no fires burning in his apartment in Paris during the previous weeks.

It has been suggested that Henri Paul could have been attempting to commit suicide at some time during that fateful day but there is no evidence to support this theory. In any case, he was looking remarkably relaxed and happy, smiling and chatting with other Ritz employees in the videos taken by the Ritz security cameras that evening. All this evidence suggests that the French doctors who conducted the autopsy had collected incorrect data when they tested his blood or else they tested the wrong blood. The implications of this are far-reaching. If it was not Henri Paul's blood that was tested, then it means we do not know if he was drunk or had been taking anti-depressants. And if the wrong blood sample was tested, was it a genuine mistake or did someone else, an unknown party, switch the samples?

In June 1998, the examining magistrates held a day-long investigation behind closed doors, interviewing and taking evidence from anyone who was associated with the crash, including the paparazzi photographers who were chasing the Mercedes at the time. Every aspect of the tragic accident, including medical and forensic evidence, was considered but no conclusion was reached. The French authorities hope to issue their report on the facts of the crash and Diana's death towards the end of 1998.

And yet, one year after the tragic accident, there are people in Buckingham Palace and St James's Palace, the House of Lords and the Commons, the Diplomatic service and a host of highly-placed Civil Servants who believe that Diana was the victim of a conspiracy to kill her. But, in the time honoured way, no one is prepared to speak out openly, even to offer their opinion, because they know such questions would be to no avail. Diana is dead, and nothing will change what happened, whether her death was an accident of fate or a carefully planned operation to kill her. There is, apparently, no point in raising contentious issues, causing embarrassment or challenging the received wisdom that her death was an unfortunate accident. But to many ardent monarchists, to many who believe that everything must be done to preserve the house of Windsor, the death of Diana removed, once and for all, someone who had challenged the Royal Family so successfully that she had usurped their position. Diana has gone, but the debate over her death is not finally over.